OVERCOMING YOUR PARENTS' DIVORCE

5 Steps To A Happy Relationship

OVERCOMING YOUR PARENTS' DIVORCE

5 Steps To A Happy Relationship

by
Elisabeth Joy LaMotte, MSW, LICSW, AAMFT

New Horizon Press
Far Hills, NJ

New Horizon Press
P.O. Box 669
Far Hills, NJ 07931

Elisabeth Joy LaMotte, MSW, LICSW, AAMFT
Overcoming Your Parents' Divorce:
5 Steps To A Happy Relationship

Cover design: Robert Aulicino
Interior design: Susan Sanderson

Library of Congress Control Number: 2007939910

ISBN 13: 978-0-88282-329-4
ISBN 10: 0-88282-329-9
New Horizon Press

Manufactured in the U.S.A.

2012   2011   2010   2009   2008   /   5   4   3   2   1

"Those who cannot remember the past
are condemned to repeat it."

George Santayana

AUTHOR'S NOTE

This book is based on the results of a survey of adults with divorced parents, my counseling work with clients and my own experience growing up with divorced parents. All names have been changed and recognizable characteristics disguised except for those of contributing experts. This book is not intended to replace any necessary therapy with mental health professionals.

viii

DEDICATION

For Russ, Charlotte Rose and Amelia,
with all of my heart

ENDORSEMENTS

"Finally, a therapist brave enough to declare what so many 'children of divorce' understand intuitively: a healthy RESPECT for marriage's commitment can be a welcome legacy of divorce. LaMotte's book is highly readable relationship self-help from a woman who knows firsthand, from her life and fifteen years counseling others, the joys of longterm love and mutual commitment."
—Leslie Morgan Steiner, editor of *Mommy Wars* and daily work/family columnist for washingtonpost.com

"Elisabeth LaMotte's book, *Overcoming Your Parents' Divorce*, is a welcome breath of fresh air for those who believe that the divorce of their parents has turned them into 'damaged goods' that will keep them from ever having a fulfilling adult relationship. Unflinchingly citing her own experience as well as those of others, LaMotte acknowledges that while divorce is a tragedy for children that may drive their own fear of commitment, it can also be a wake-up call that interrupts the cycle of the past and leads to better choices and happier lives. This is a must-read for children of divorce and their families."
—Gloria Hochman, co-author with Edward Beal, M.D. of *Adult Children of Divorce*, co-author with Patty Duke of *A Brilliant Madness: Living with Manic-Depressive Illness*

ACKNOWLEDGMENTS

First and foremost, I want to thank my family. Mother, thank you for being my inspiration, my mentor and my loyal friend. Thank you for all of the ways that you encouraged me in all aspects of my life and helped me to write this book. Stan, thank you for your strength, your constancy and your understated and unending kindness. Dad, thank you for your reliable presence, for your unwavering calm, for clipping every relevant article to show me you care, and for never giving up. Susan, thank you for sharing your engaging energy, enthusiasm and creativity. Thank you, Kathy and Ken, for your encouragement and your honest support. Thank you to all of my siblings and their spouses for being there with me every step of the way. You are my silver lining.

Connie Thompson, your tremendous help at the very beginning, your precious time, your smart critiques and your elegant encouragement gave me the confidence and motivation to pursue this project. Leslie Steiner, your invaluable ideas, proposal edits and enthusiasm inspired me to keep trying. Dr. Joan Dunphy, your vision for this book, your talent and your psychological depth improved everything. You are a gifted editor. JoAnne Thomas, your positive personality and your smiling voice are a joy. Russ, you sometimes know me better than I know myself. Your clear mind and generous heart inform this book and enrich my life. You are my best critic and my best friend. Without all of you, this book would not be.

Thank you Nancy Jacobson for caring about this book and for caring about your friends the way that you do. Thank you Laurel Wingate for telling me, years ago, that "of course" I could write a book, and then helping me along. Thank you Ashley Allen for "stressing for me" so that I didn't have to stress as much myself. Thank you Kinney Zilesne for understanding my ideas for this book within minutes and improving it as easily as you did, in your gifted way. Thank you Howard Yoon for your time and experience and for helping me to find "a hook". Thank you Gay Coiffi, Penny Wilson, Judy Bishop, Kathleen Jenkins, Katie Brown, Anne Davis, Melissa Scala and Virginia Shore for your early enthusiasm and support. Thank you to Ron Hart and everyone at New Horizon Press for your time and your talent. There are so many dear friends—Emily Ball, Deborah Block, Elizabeth Brass, Kathyanne Cohen, Matthew Kogan, Jo-Ann Marshall, Jennifer Heller, Nancy Braveman, Sandy Harris, Nicole Bagley, Missy Walker, Stephanie Lilley, Jill White, Ana Maria Roche, Dahlia Neiss, Dr. Susan Ascher, Dr. David Miller, Dr. Stuart Wolfe and many others—who supported me through this process, and I am very grateful.

Finally, thank you to my current and former clients and to the survey participants. You inspired me to write this book and it has been a privilege working with you. A special, tremendous thank you to those of you who were generous enough to share your stories in the pages that follow. Your journey will help others, just as you have helped yourselves.

TABLE OF CONTENTS

introduction

■

Many experts will tell you that children of divorce are doomed to be unlucky in love. I feel these experts are wrong, and this book will explain why.

As millions of children of the 1970s divorce boom come of age, academic researchers and the media have increasingly focused on the long-term impact of divorce on children. Current research on adults with divorced parents has produced some noteworthy books that shed light on the tremendous long-term difficulties of growing up with divorced parents. These books point out that children of divorce frequently enter adulthood with tremendous trepidation about relationships and fear of long-term commitment.

Finally, the ramifications of divorce are being studied with serious attention to the long-term impact on children.

Unfortunately, I believe these books and the studies on which they are based interpret their findings through a negative lens. They assume that because adults with divorced parents tend to fear commitment, the parents have basically destroyed their children's chances to achieve and enjoy happy marriages. They argue that, unless a couple is struggling with substance abuse or physical abuse, unhappily married adults should probably take the sacrificial high road and stay together for the sake of their children.

This over-simplified interpretation illustrates how adults with divorced parents are bombarded with negative messages from researchers and the media about their compromised potential for emotional happiness and relationship fulfillment. Adults who grew up in a divorced household hear, all too often, that the way they were raised has turned them into damaged goods. Unfortunately, the leading books about divorce portray the delayed marriage and delayed parenthood of adult children of divorce as a completely negative consequence of divorce. Oddly, they do so while simultaneously giving examples of the happy marriages that many of these children of divorce eventually manage to achieve! The current literature on divorce overlooks the likelihood that children of divorce can actually <u>benefit</u> by delaying marriage and parenthood and by making their milestone life choices once they are more emotionally mature than their parents were when they were married.

The pages that follow will reveal this dynamic–adults with divorced parents struggling with dating and fearing commitment, but eventually achieving great relationships–and explore it in detail. Readers will gain valuable insights and positive affirmation that their fear of commitment is, in fact, healthy and can function as a gateway to great fulfillment and relationship success.

While a number of books about divorce shed light on the difficulties of growing up with divorced parents, none offer concrete strategies for overcoming these difficulties. My goal is to offer adults with divorced parents hope about the unanticipated silver lining of growing up in a divorced family. This book outlines five critical steps toward understanding how a parental divorce can help readers achieve healthy relationships. These steps are rooted in the underlying message of the book: that the fear of commitment, which so many Generation X and Generation Y singles confront, can be a dividend in disguise.

Overcoming Your Parents' Divorce is geared towards young, single adults with divorced parents, but the Five Step Guide can also be helpful for anyone struggling with commitment in their adult romantic relationships.

The Five Step Guide is based on my experience as both a child of divorce and a psychotherapist working with many adults whose parents divorced. My parents separated when I was seven and my younger sister was four. Pain associated with their divorce shaped much of my childhood and still plays a complicated role as an adult. Their divorce, however, was a necessary one, and I am convinced that my sister and I, as well as our parents, are much better off than we ever could have been had our parents stayed together. By building happier lives for themselves—lives that better suited their very different priorities and goals—my parents taught me by example to find fulfillment and happiness in my adult life. Their divorce also broke a cycle of disappointment and unhappiness flowing from their own parents' unhappy marriages. Without our difficult journey through divorce, I question what my own adult choices might have brought. I fear that I would have ended up in a marriage very much like that of my parents', and that I would have continued a legacy of discontent and unhappiness that my parents had the courage to break.

During my fifteen years practicing social work and psychotherapy, I have been continually struck by how many adults with divorced parents build happy and rewarding marriages. Yes, their early adulthood is frequently a time when they fear commitment and choose substandard partners or reject available partners or do both. However, for so many of these adults, these difficulties are temporary. Fortunately for some of these adults, their struggles are followed by phenomenal relationship success.

Recently, Gina, a forty-something, happily married client with divorced parents, described the impact of her folks' divorce with great insight:

> My parents' split was like a dreadful shot in the arm; a shot of reality that forced me into premature adulthood. It's not how anyone would want to grow up. But my parents became different people when they broke up. I swear, it was as if they were each living in a cloud and then they both broke out and woke up! Without that awful shot, well, I would have been raised in a cloud and there's no way that I would be who I am today.

Adults with divorced parents will frequently discuss their struggles with dating. One of my clients, Carl, a thirty-three-year-old with divorced parents, admitted:

I know I don't take the women I date as seriously as I should. I'm always late, and I head for the hills as soon as I realize that someone is really interested. I just don't want to end up like my parents. Married at eighteen, parents at nineteen, and at each other's throats until they divorced. I'm twenty-eight and I haven't had a relationship last longer than six months, tops.

One could interpret Carl's unavailability as a scar from his parents' divorce; this interpretation would be accurate but incomplete. As it turned out, once he took the time to fully explore the meaning of his parents' divorce for him and the upside of his delaying commitment, Carl was able to treat women differently. In his mid-thirties, he achieved a very happy marriage.

I believe when divorce researchers make blanket statements and conclude that, unless physical violence or substance abuse is present, couples should stay together for their children, they overlook the tremendous complexities that make each family different. Such generalizations disregard the potential long-term damage that could result from raising children in a household with parents who are constantly fighting or totally disengaged and disconnected.

Each person, each family, each marriage and each divorce is complicated and unique. Yes, divorce is a major problem in our society. In spite of this, many children of divorce have the potential to be better off in their marriages than their parents. Children of divorce are more likely to enter young adulthood with their eyes open, and such awareness holds the potential for great relationship success. Of course, coming from a divorced family does not guarantee a happy marriage. But there is a compelling phenomenon of children from divorced families building fulfilling life-long partnerships. Yes, divorce is a terrible, tragic life event that never goes away. No, it does not have to mean a lifetime of doom and gloom for its children. Yes, in many cases divorce is the worst possible marital outcome for a family to bear. Unless one considers the alternative.

In my own life, I remember the pain of learning about my parents' plans to divorce as if it were yesterday.

It was a Saturday morning and I was watching cartoons. I was seven years old and my younger sister, Kathyanne, was four. The morning started out just like any other regular old Saturday. Climbing out of bed somewhere around six, I draped my pink satin blanket over my shoulders. I pretended that I was a cartoon character and that the blanket was my trusty cape. As usual, I flew fearlessly forward, down three flights of dark wooden stairs, gently tracing the banister winding down to our living room and its television.

Each Saturday was appealingly similar to the one before. I was too young to understand the definition of a ritual, but I did understand that my weekly cartoon marathon brought me a great deal of comfort and pleasure. Kathyanne joined me each Saturday by the television, routinely awakening an hour or so after me. Into this private, perfect morning, the familiar sounds of a new parental fight began to intrude once again. Kathyanne and I were both well accustomed to our parents' screaming matches. The high volume of anger in their voices filtered through our home and still filters through my heart. I can't recall much of the substance of this fight, or any of their fights. I do recall the process, my intense agitation building as this ordinary Saturday morning evolved into something quite different. And something quite terrifying. The screaming and door slamming persisted for hours. And when it finally stopped, they didn't come down from their bedroom to deliver their usual explanation that everything was okay.

"Grown-ups sometimes need to yell a little," they delicately explained. "But then we always work things out. There's no need in the world to worry." When this yelling finally settled, Kathyanne and I listened intently to a frightening blend of our cartoons and a toxic silence coming from upstairs. My nosiness and worry got the better of me, and I knew that someone needed to get up to their room and find out what was going on. Kathyanne alternated her glance from the cartoon character on the screen to me and then back to the television. It went without saying—something planted in the dichotomy of little versus big sisterhood governed that Kathyanne would stay with the television, and I would venture upward to find out what was happening with our silent parents.

Clutching my baby blanket cape like a shield from the unknown, I studied my pale feet as I hiked upstairs. Our babysitter, Norma, had painted my toenails hot pink earlier that week. I was not permitted to polish my fingernails, shave my legs or wear make-up of any kind until officially entering my teens. But colorfully polished toenails were an exception—a treasured caveat to this family rule. (I still enjoy the look of painted toenails, though over time I have graduated to deeper, darker, wine-colored shades. Once in a while, when I look down at my painted adult toes, I flash back to my childhood fear and contemplation as I climbed the stairs that morning.) Two flights to their floor and then down the bookcase-lined hallway towards their bedroom. Still silence. I hesitated for a second and then knocked.

"You get it."

"No you get it." They debated angrily with a numb familiarity that results from too much debating. My tear-drenched mother answered the door and glanced towards me with pink swollen eyes that looked exhausted.

"You tell her."

"No, I really think you should tell her." I looked at my father who was sitting on his bed with the empty expression of a lost child. I couldn't speak, I could barely stand. In spite of my parents' routine battles, from my perspective, they stood larger than life. Now, out of nowhere, my perfect parents were before me and, for a split, twisted moment, they were the children and I was the parent. They looked to me with ashamed expressions, as if they had something horrible to reveal, like they had earned a school suspension or broken a piece of priceless china they were forbidden to touch.

"Your father and I are getting a divorce," my mother trembled as she spoke. "Daddy needs to live somewhere else. We can't stay together anymore. I wish we could…believe me, Honey…but we just can't." I lost my balance and fell back against their bedroom wall. The words pierced through me like arrows, knocking me over like nothing my seven-year-old spirit had ever known. My mother's revolting words left me knotted, terrified and floating fast in a downward direction. Like I was falling back down the stairs I'd just climbed, straight through the oval in the center of the spiraling banister. I suddenly felt as dizzy as if I'd spun around for ten minutes straight on the swivel chair. Their bedroom began to blur and I wished I had stayed in the living room with Kathyanne. Why was I so nosy? I know I was crying, but I don't know how long I stayed with my parents, or if they said anything further. I only recall turning from the wall behind me, clutching that ratty blanket in a defeated march down the hall and then descending the stairs alone.

Divorce. I pretty much knew, in theory, what that meant. But, at the time, I thought about orphans. I knew I wouldn't be an orphan if my parents divorced, but I also knew that the loneliness an orphan must experience mirrored a loneliness I suddenly found in myself. Something had flipped over inside my mind, and everything seemed strange and different. I'd been split apart and altered into someone else. Out of nowhere, I'd gained abrupt insight into the cruel ways of the world. All I knew, my entire world, revolved around my mother, my father, my sister, our home and our family. In spite of their frequent fights, I had never

ever considered the possibility of anything different. How could my world fall apart so suddenly? Looking down the stairs, spinning in tears and panic, I remember caring about one thing: I didn't want my sweet and still innocent sister to feel this kind of sadness. And I didn't have a clue about how to protect her. I sat down with Kathyanne and the television, crying and disheveled. The rubber-band holding my messy ponytail was decorated with pink plastic flowers and had fallen from its proper place at the tip of my neck to the middle of my back, loosely clutching an assortment of tangles.

Kathyanne glanced toward me. Her round, baby-doll face was a fuller yet basically identical version of my own. Her four-year-old eyes communicated a quiet, reserved concern. I shook my head and contorted my face into an exhausted expression that begged her not to ask.

"It's nothing," my dramatic tone paralleled my bizarre demeanor. She'll know soon enough, I thought, I just want her to enjoy the cartoons. I don't want to be the one to ruin them for her. *I imagined Kathyanne's cartoon watching as if she were participating in some kind of a last hoorah, final moments of a clear calm state of mind that should be carefully savored without interference. I don't know how long we sat there without speaking before my father came downstairs and walked into the room. Alone. I noticed a stream of tears falling peacefully down his dimpled face. His tears seemed somehow shy. These flat, transparent, quiet tears were new to me. I had never seen him cry and his timid tears washed years off his already boyish features. He sat next to me carefully, wrapping his arm around me with a strange new caution, as if he feared that the exchange upstairs had turned me into a porcelain doll.*

"Please don't worry Lizzy, everything's going to be just fine, there isn't going to be any divorce. Nothing like that. We didn't mean it," he whispered quietly, turning away from Kathyanne. Perhaps he shared my unspoken yet obvious need to protect her. "It's okay, come on now, don't cry. I'm not going to live anywhere but at home with you girls and your mother where I belong." I wanted to please him, and keep him from leaving, so I listened and plugged my tears as fast as I could. Amidst my relief, and my stomachache from holding in tears, I felt especially pleased and proud that I'd successfully contained my feelings with Kathyanne. My suddenly wise and weathered self quietly raised up from the inside out to pat myself on the back and offer a hushed congratulations.

My parents managed to stick together for a couple more unsettling months before finally separating on Halloween, 1975. Then, my parents divorced. Many times, my sister and I felt like odd accessories during our parents' active dating lives. Eventually, they both re-married, and Kathyanne and I inherited a stepfather, stepbrother and stepsister, and, later, a stepmother and two more stepbrothers. I watched my mother struggle with paralyzing grief in the wake of my father's absence. I became close to one of my mother's boyfriends whom she did not marry and whom I missed for quite a while after their break-up. When I grew up and started dating, I felt confused and out of place with respect to my peers from intact families. Meeting guys was always easy, but existing in a relationship felt almost impossible.

Like so many adults with divorced parents, I fumbled through years of disappointment and pain in the dating department. But (like many survivors of their parents' divorce) the painful searching, self-doubt and dearth of romantic mishaps was followed by meeting and falling in love with Russ, my husband of nine years. By the time we met, I had given myself a chance to work through the ways my parents' divorce was affecting my choices and my relationships. I was ready to work on my personal fear of commitment. It didn't come naturally, but, for the first time, I tried to simply be myself. I tried to get used to being respected and loved, not just in the personal, social or emotional sense, but as a professional. Russ was the first guy to take a genuine interest in my work. More accurately, he was the first guy to express an interest while I, in turn, was able to respond in a positive way. Before we met, I was more drawn to relationships where my career as a social worker (and eventually a psychotherapist) was a non-issue.

In my twenties, when I met someone who asked intelligent questions about social work, I dropped him into the "available" category and pushed him away. Having worked as a social worker and psychotherapist for fifteen years, I have watched many of my clients with divorced parents do precisely the same thing. They choose relationships where the romantic interest is unavailable in some way, or they choose available partners and then push them away.

One way to summarize these common relationship patterns is to term it "fear of commitment." Fear of commitment is often more complicated than a conscious reluctance to take a healthy relationship to the next level. Many times, it involves a pattern of choosing flawed relationships and trying, at times desperately, to save them. If one succeeds in prolonging the relationship, then one remains in a flawed situation where intimacy is impossible. In this mode, the unconscious goal is achieved, as genuine commitment does not occur. If one fails (as is usually inevitable), the break-up can be interpreted as evidence of personal flaws or defects, thus perpetuating an illusion that one simply is not cut out for an intimate, satisfying relationship. So, again, commitment is out of the picture. People who follow this pattern may tell themselves (and others) that they <u>embrace</u> commitment, and that they try hard to make their relationships work. However, trying to save a relationship with an unsuitable partner is not a form of embracing commitment—it is a form of <u>avoiding</u> intimacy.

The common counterpart of this dynamic of choosing flawed relationships is a profound discomfort with choosing a partner who is genuinely available. An available partner would be open to an increasingly committed relationship over time, and this can seem terrifying to someone who simply is not used to it. It took years before I felt ready to be with someone who genuinely cared about what I thought, how I felt and what I did. But, like some other adults with divorced parents, I married (later rather than sooner) and have a happy and fulfilling marriage.

Dating Russ felt genuinely different than dating other guys. Reflecting on what was so different, I'm struck by the energetic interest Russ took in my career. And by the way I allowed him to do so. When Russ and I discussed my work, I felt encouraged and accepted and was surprised by his innate psychological sense. His kind, thoughtful questions and comments remind me of a quotation from Jill Ker Conway's *The Road to Coorain*:

> It was intoxicating not to have to set a watch on my tongue, to be actually found more interesting because of my mind. In his company I enjoyed the experience a [professional] woman needs most if she has lived in a world set on undermining female intelligence: I was loved for what I was rather than the lesser mind I pretended to be.

My mother and my father clashed on so many levels. Ironically, one way to understand how truly unsuited they were for one another is to understand their professions. He is a lawyer. She is a social worker. My father's reserved and intelligent analysis persistently clashed with my mother's principles and passions. They fought constantly and I have no memories involving any form of professional support for one another. No sense of a shared vision. He's a Republican, she's a Democrat, and they saw the world through different lenses. This major disconnect with regard to a life view is what stands out when I reflect on their relationship. If there was a time when they saw eye-to-eye and could converse passionately about shared values, or even contradictory ones, it took place before I had the capacity for memory and is lost as an aspect of their lives that neither parent has ever shared with me.

I was raised with the unspoken sense that a lawyer and a social worker could never make it work—that what lies at the core of a social worker would forever clash with a lawyerly counterpart. Yet I married a lawyer. I have trouble picturing my parents having the kind of conversation that would allow my mother to feel loved and understood by my father in the way I feel so very loved and accepted by Russ: accepted and embraced for who I am, personally and professionally, rather than for who I may (at times in my past) have pretended to be. I know Russ respects what I do and is always interested in and supportive of my career. I love what I do and this priority is fully respected.

Perhaps, if my parents had stayed together, I would have dated more naturally and made fewer short-term mistakes. I could have developed more enthusiasm and confidence about relationships and I wouldn't have hurt like I did, early on. I am convinced that if my parents had continued forward in a false and unworkable life, I would have been much more likely to marry younger and more easily, as they did. However, I probably would have chosen a relationship that sparkled on the surface, like my parents' marriage, but would never bring true intimacy and lasting happiness. Without their divorce, I can easily picture myself making unconscious decisions reflecting how their anguish remained alive, yet unacknowledged; how our lives seemed picture perfect from the outside, while masking torment from within. I fear I would have made choices that looked good on paper but would have shredded into bits just as my parents' had, before our young and terrified eyes. Without their divorce, I strongly doubt I would have waited long enough to work on myself, learn to enjoy being on my own, and to eventually find Russ and the joy of our peaceful and happy relationship.

Gaps in Existing Literature

I have been dissatisfied with the treatment of divorce in recent high-profile books. Judith Wallerstein's influential book, *The Unexpected Legacy of Divorce* (Hyperion, 2000), makes groundbreaking, astute observations about the way children of divorce tend to struggle in their young adult relationships, including how they hesitate to commit and how they link their hesitation to their childhood history of divorce. I feel the overall message of Wallerstein's book is that unless a couple is dealing with physical violence or severe substance abuse, the optimal solution is for parents to take a sacrificial high road and stay together for the sake of the children.

In *Between Two Worlds* (Crown Publishers, 2005), Elizabeth Marquardt (a happily married adult with divorced parents) observes how children of divorce are forced to make sense of the two distinct and potentially contradictory spheres of their divorced parents' lives, and how this struggle negatively affects their inner emotional world. Like Wallerstein, Marquardt emphasizes that parents must pay better attention to the potential devastation that divorce entails.

Obviously, these studies are relevant and long overdue. At the same time, they lack a nuanced depiction of the complicated dynamics that make each family and each marriage so different. They do not adequately reflect the many divorces that are necessary even if physical violence or substance abuse is not present. And they fail to genuinely address the lasting negative psychological impact that can result when parents stay together unhappily for the sake of their children.

More important, while both authors identify the obstacles that adult children of divorce contend with, such as fear of commitment and other emotional struggles, they fail to recognize that these struggles can be valuable. Marquardt fails to relate her own happy marriage to her past struggles, giving readers the impression that her successful partnership is due to her unique virtue rather than being a product, at least in part, to the trauma she experienced as a child.

Within the great pain and struggle that young adult survivors of divorce face, there exists the potential for healing and growth. The larger dynamic of pain as an opportunity for growth is a common theme in the field of psychotherapy, but it has not been adequately explored in the context of adults whose parents divorced. What the literature about divorce has largely failed to articulate is that children of divorced parents may, because of their struggles, be in a position to have it better than their parents with respect to their adult relationships. By overlooking this potential, I feel Wallerstein and Marquardt provide precisely what adult children of divorce do not need: another reason to feel like damaged goods.

In my opinion, both Wallerstein and Marquardt are also extremely focused on the *parents who divorced*: what the parents did wrong, what the parents could and should do differently, and how the parents have slighted their children. The chapters that follow re-frame this discussion to focus less on the shortcomings of the adults who divorced and more on the strengths and potential of *their children*. Rather than emphasizing the supposed source of their problems, this book emphasizes the possibility for healing and growth that their struggles may offer. It explores how their pain, if properly understood and addressed, may enable them to experience relationships on a deeper level than their parents, thus leading to happier and more fulfilling marriages.

Other books have presented more positive messages about the long-term impact of divorce: E. Mavis Hetherington's *For Better or For Worse: Divorce Reconsidered* (W. W. Norton and Company, 2002) and Constance Ahrons' *We're Still Family: What Grown Children Have to Say About Their Parents' Divorce* (HarperCollins Publishers, 2004) both point out the many ways that adult survivors of their parents' divorce fare quite well, and their perspectives regarding the long-term consequences of divorce are far less fatalistic. But these more positive books are geared toward parents considering whether to divorce, not toward adult survivors of their parents' divorce. I feel they tend to gloss over the tremendous emotional difficulties that plague so many children of divorce, and they do not adequately acknowledge how these difficulties carry over into adulthood. As a result, in my opinion, these books do not fully speak to adults with divorced parents.

Two noteworthy memoir-based books use anecdotal material to depict how divorce affects children during their adulthood. These books, Stephanie Staal's *The Love They Lost* (Dell Publishing, 2000) and Ava Chin's *Split: Stories from a Generation Raised on Divorce* (Contemporary Books, 2002), use interviews, essays and true stories to paint a textured, realistic portrait of divorce, and detail how divorce leaves a lasting, painful legacy. Interestingly, both Staal and Chin touch on the dividend of divorce. Stall refers in her conclusion to the way "…we can use our ingrown caution about love to make careful choices in our partners…" Similarly, Chin writes in her introductory overview about how "lessons in the fragility of relationships help them to better appreciate the ones that work." While these books clearly acknowledge that children of divorce often grow up to achieve great success in their adult relationships, this dividend is mentioned only briefly, as a surprising and hopeful footnote, and is not given adequate exploration. Instead, these two books focus primarily on the pain and challenges associated with growing up in a divorced household and how these challenges have long-term consequences.

A Review of Relevant Psychological Theories

In order to get the most out of the Five Step Guide, it will be helpful for you to briefly review some relevant psychological theory, so as to familiarize yourself with some of the language and concepts that frame this book. This framework will provide a clearer understanding about why the painful struggles faced by adults with divorced parents can also yield an important dividend.

When an adult with divorced parents successfully builds a rewarding and fulfilling marriage, he or she is often breaking out of a long-standing, intergenerational family cycle of unhappy marriages. Breaking these cycles is no easy feat. Why is it so hard to break family patterns? To answer this question, it is useful to consider the teachings of key theorists and psychologists.

With so many different schools of philosophy and psychology, a striking similarity among a number of them is an emphasis on how individuals are highly likely to repeat the past. Adults will frequently shy away from examining childhood pain, and ironically end up repeating the very things they promised themselves they would never relive.

Freud coined the term "repetition compulsion" to describe an unconscious desire to repeat the parts of one's past that are most painful with a fantasy attached to this repetition that you will somehow master the unresolved anguish of your past. According to this Freudian theory, you rarely succeed in fixing the pain of the past. Instead, you compel yourself to stay stuck reliving the unresolved conflicts that have burdened you all along.

The more modern school of "systems theory" emphasizes that whatever a person experiences during childhood becomes comfortable, even if it is not healthy. The "family system" resists change and seeks to maintain its equilibrium through "homeostasis", regardless of whether or not the repeated dynamics of the system are positive ones. In other words, if you grow up in a household where your parents are completely disconnected, rarely speak with one another, and sleep in separate bedrooms, this level of disengagement becomes very familiar, and thus remains comfortable. As a result, you are more likely to choose a marriage that mirrors the spousal isolation you observed while growing up. If you grow up in a home where your parents share compatible values, communicate in kind and productive ways, and genuinely love, respect and support one another, then this happy marriage you observe will feel comfortable. You are therefore more likely to make choices in your adult life that will lead to a similar marital dynamic. Your parents' healthy, happy relationship is what you see, and what you know, so in your adulthood it comes to represent what you are comfortable with and most likely to find.

Repeating the past is obviously very appealing if your past involved a happy, healthy, stable environment. Repeating the past if you grew up observing the constant tension, animosity, anxiety and depression that can accompany a dysfunctional marriage, however, becomes far more problematic.

Reflecting on this relevant psychological theory lays the groundwork for explaining how divorce, as awful as it is, becomes a painful but powerful wake up call that can interrupt the process by which individuals are likely to repeat the past. Divorce is so traumatic that it often forces reflection on the past. It does so in spite of the common underlying tendency to shy away from the past, brush it off and eventually repeat it.

Why might divorce cause some children who live through it to break these patterns rather than repeat them? This is a complicated question that is difficult to answer with certainty. Unlike with many other traumatic events, such as emotional, physical, sexual or substance abuse, the very act of divorcing announces the acknowledgement of a mistake. With other forms of abuse, the family dysfunction is more easily covered up and denied. But the very public logistical shifts that a divorce entails make it essentially impossible to deny the problem.

It is psychologically appropriate that children view their parents as perfect, or near perfect. This helps them to feel safe and secure. Perhaps children who suffer the consequences of divorce are forced into a heightened awareness that even their perfect parents can make a mistake. Awareness of one's parents' flaws and susceptibility to mistakes can be extremely unsettling. But maybe the difficulty of denying that a divorce is happening causes children who lived through the ramifications of their parents' mistakes to be more cautious about making their own mistakes. Many adults with divorced parents seem determined—even programmed—to break historical patterns and struggle toward charting a healthier, happier course.

Clearly, adult survivors of childhood divorce display increased levels of fear of commitment. But fear of commitment can be a good thing–a dividend in disguise–as long as you learn to identify it, figure out what it means and address it. Fear of commitment gives us time to know ourselves before making tremendous life decisions with long-term implications. Had I not been afraid, I could have made terrible mistakes far outweighing the temporary pain or disappointment associated with my serial breakups. Describing fear of commitment as a silver lining for the otherwise turbulent clouds of divorce is probably a reach. But it is an unanticipated and unlikely upside to an otherwise dreadful event—a consequence of divorce that hurts and makes dating harder, but carries with it great potential to lead children of divorce to make better choices and build happier lives.

This book outlines five critical steps towards understanding how having divorced parents can help you achieve a healthy relationship. Please keep in mind that this book focuses on mature adult relationships that occur once you are out of college and more settled in your adult life. This book is not intended to encourage you to marry every person you date. It is simply a guide to overcoming the ways that your parents' divorce may be affecting your adult relationships. It is also a guide for examining how you operate in relationships. It is a guide for exploring what relationship patterns are working for you, and what patterns are not serving you well in your adult life.

Despite common fears, be reassured that many adults with divorced parents have happy and fulfilling relationships and marriages. The Five Step Guide draws on their experience to prepare other adults with divorced parents to achieve that fulfillment. These steps are rooted in the underlying message of the book: that fear of commitment can be a dividend in disguise because it can enable adult survivors of their parents' divorce to eventually achieve what their parents missed out on—a happy, healthy, first and only marriage.

The vignettes recounted in this book are based on my personal and professional experience. The book also reviews the results of my recent survey of adults with divorced parents (ages twenty-two through sixty-nine). The vignettes and the survey results paint a detailed picture of divorce and its lasting psychological toll. At the same time, my story and those of my clients and research subjects come together to explain how, in spite of great pain and disappointment, divorce can generate a surprising and unexpected dividend.

the survey

■

Before you begin the Five Step Guide for overcoming your parents' divorce, take the time to complete the following survey. These are the same questions posed to the survey subjects discussed throughout the book. Answering the questions may bring up some strong and difficult feelings—this is part of beginning the healing process. If you are unsettled or upset by the questions and your answers, please make sure to discuss them with someone you trust. As you read the book and complete the tips and suggestions that conclude each chapter, you may find that the answers to some of your survey questions will change. Feel free to go back and edit your answers. As you complete the Five Step Guide, compare your survey answers to those of the survey subjects, and make note of any differences, similarities or insights that arise through your comparison.

1. First name:

2. Age:

3. Ethnicity:

4. Your age when your parents separated:

5. Your age when your parents divorced:

6. Place of birth:

7. What is your understanding of why your parents divorced?

8.   How did your parents' divorce affect you as a child?

9.   How does your parents' divorce affect you in adulthood?

10.   How has having divorced parents affected your adult romantic
      relationships?

11.   What did you learn about marriage from your parents?

12. What did you learn about marriage from your grandparents?

13. Did either of your parents re-marry? (If no, please skip to question 14)

13a. If yes, which parent? (If both parents re-married, please answer questions 13a, 13b and 13c with information about your mother first, and then your father)

13b. Is your re-married parent still married?

13c. How would you describe your parent's second marriage?

14. Are you currently married? (If no, please skip to question 15)

14a. If yes, at what age did you marry?

14b. Would you describe your marriage as happy or unhappy? Why?

15. If you are not married, are you currently in a relationship? (If no, please skip to question 16)

15a. If you are currently in a relationship, would you describe this relationship as happy or unhappy? Why?

15b. Do you view your current relationship as serious and long-term? Or do you view it as temporary? Why?

16. Have you ever divorced? (If no, please skip to question 17)

16a. If yes, how old were you when you married?

16b. How old were you when you divorced?

16c. What is your perspective about why you married and why you later divorced?

17. How would you describe your dating history?

18. If you are not currently in a relationship, do you think that you avoid commitment?

18a. If you avoid commitment, please describe the ways in which you avoid commitment.

18b. Do you reject available partners?

18c. Do you choose unsuitable partners? Are they abusive or unavailable?

19.   If you are not currently single, was there ever a period when you feared
      or avoided commitment?

19a. If yes, please describe the ways in which you avoided commitment.

19b. Did you reject available partners?

19c. Did you choose unsuitable partners? Were they abusive or unavailable?

Step One: Re-write Your Story

Step One is a two-part process of re-writing the narrative of your family history from a new, adult perspective. This process involves:

- re-evaluating your parents' marriage
- learning more about your grandparents and their marriages

Step One is more time consuming than most of the subsequent steps, and can be surprisingly difficult. We all, on some level, are most comfortable viewing our parents and our history from a child-like perspective. That perspective colors our sense of history and our understanding of the past. However, by Re-writing Your Story, you can begin the process of overcoming pain from the past and recognizing the underlying dividends of your parents' divorce.

Remember, it is not necessarily appealing to re-visit the past. You may ask: *Why spend time thinking about my parents' marriage? They have been divorced for years and their marriage was a disaster—why go down that unsettling road?* However, if you are struggling in your adult relationships, facing your past may be necessary in order to develop a more mature understanding about why your parents divorced, how your parents' childhood influenced their adult choices, and how your story relates to your current relationship struggles.

Note: in order to take Step One and all of the subsequent steps, you will need to get a journal. Your journal will function as your personal narrative and guide through the process of overcoming your parents' divorce.

chapter one

■

CONSIDER YOUR PARENTS' MARRIAGE FROM AN ADULT PERSPECTIVE

■

Step One begins by you re-writing the story of your parents' marriage. In order to grow from your parents' mistakes and avoid repeating them, it is essential to re-visit and re-think, from an adult perspective, the reasons that your parents divorced. This is a common first step that I take with my clients, even if they have not initiated therapy to focus on their past.

Rachel, a twenty-six-year-old graphic artist, expressed reservations as we talked about remembering her past and reflecting on her parents' marriage:

> I can picture a lot of things. My parents' separate bedrooms and how I was embarrassed to have friends over because I worried that my friends would figure out that my parents didn't sleep together. I can picture the times I heard them fight, late into the night. I used to hide in the closet with my markers and draw in the dark! It makes me feel literally sick, and scared. That time is just too painful and I don't want to go back there.

In Rachel's case, we went slowly, as it was important to respect her reservations about remembering the traumatic period leading up to her parents' separation.

Dana, who is thirty-seven years old, had parents who separated when she was only nine months old. Her pain was evident as she explained the reasons for her parents' divorce:

> My mother simply says she did not want to be a wife/mother anymore. She was very young when she married and, truth be told, she wanted to enjoy her life.

She proceeded to explain her adult perspective on marriage and relationships:

> I never believed marriage was a good thing or something that would add happiness to my life. I knew if I did it would be forever so I sort of envisioned myself making the best of the situation. I also believe I dated men that were horrible for me so there was no real fear of losing a good thing. Dating inappropriate men always gave me the easy out.

In spite of a prolonged period of choosing flawed relationships, Dana married happily at thirty-two:

> My marriage is very happy. We are very much in love and very kind to one another. I think our marriage works because we both share similar goals and ideals when it comes to marriage/family.

Dana's difficult but ultimately successful path toward a happy marriage has much in common with Madeline, a young hairdresser I had worked with.

Madeline began therapy when the salon where she worked was sold to a larger company and her management changed. She initiated our sessions because she felt agitated by her new supervisor. She began going into detail about her angry feelings toward her new, young and less experienced female manager, and her grief about missing her older, more experienced, more attentive, male boss. I asked Madeline if she had ever felt this way before. The situation seemed extremely charged, as many management changes can be, and it is always important to look for what many therapists refer to as the "parallel process"—meaning, the ways in which a situation at the office may mirror a charged dynamic from one's family history or current family structure. Madeline soon discovered that the dynamic at the salon was bringing up painful memories about her parents' separation and her father's exit from her daily life.

"I thought I was here to figure out how to get along with Margot. It's not easy having a young, inexperienced, incompetent boss. And please don't get me wrong, I am still here to deal with that and I need to work it out. I need to stop hurting so much about the loss of Harry—he was the greatest and I don't want to be this sad about his leaving. But, since you are pushing this 'explore your past' business. I mean, since you mentioned it—I hadn't thought of it, but I can definitely see how the drama at work is a lot like the drama with my parents."

"How so?" I queried. Madeline's hair was always pulled up in a meticulous bun. Her pale make-up was polished and professional. Today, a bright green chiffon scarf framed her hairline and complimented her soft features. She was short and muscular yet petite, and she wore her all white salon uniform with authority and style.

"Well, my father was a lot older than my mother and, just like Margot, my mother often seemed like she didn't know what the hell she was doing. She just had this constant nervous energy." Madeline went on to describe how her parents met when her mother was only nineteen and her father was thirty-five. They married shortly after they met and they separated when Madeline was five years old. "When my dad left, he didn't even say goodbye and I saw him MAYBE every six months. I felt totally abandoned and I blamed my mom. Seemed to me she drove him away and ruined our lives."

"How did she drive him away?" I asked softly.

"Well," Madeline raised her feet on the sofa and curled herself into a ball. She rested her chin between her knees as she continued. "She gave him an ultimatum. Said he needed to get a job or he was out. She'd been constantly on his case to get a job. He had a job, if playing in a band that doesn't get much paid work counts as a job. My mom even set fire to one of his guitars and burned it in our yard! She finally told him if he didn't get a job by Christmas, he was out. So on Christmas Eve, off he went."

"If your father wasn't working, was he doing most of the childcare? I mean, did his work with the band allow him to take care of you?" I asked, feeling this was an important question to address. If her father was Madeline's primary caregiver, this could make his exit

even more traumatic, and I did not want to overlook the value her father might bring to his family by staying home while Madeline was young.

"No, come to think about it, he didn't even do housework. He was the fun one. Silly and fun but not exactly what you would call 'hands on'. My grandmother watched me most of the time until I started school. Then, my mother would take me to school in the mornings, and my father would pick me up and take me to my grandmother's house after school. Then, my mom came and got me after her second shift."

"Second shift?"

"Yeah. She waited tables—lunch and dinner—so I barely saw her. I usually fell asleep at my grandmother's and barely remember my mom picking me up and taking me home." *I noticed Madeline's silent reflection as she contemplated her mother's motivation for wanting her father to work. She sat silently and sighed.*

I encouraged Madeline to discuss with her mother the reasons she married. And the reasons she divorced. Madeline had previously explained that while she and her mother had a tense and sometimes rocky relationship, they could always talk. Since Madeline agreed that her mother would be open to discussing the past, I encouraged her to initiate a dialogue.

Soon I received a telephone message from Madeline asking if we could meet earlier than our next scheduled appointment.

"I know I am seeing you on Friday, but I was wondering if we could meet sooner. I really want to tell you about my talk with my mom." *Her voice sounded excited and engaged, and I was pleased that I could schedule a Tuesday morning appointment. Madeline arrived early and seemed to fly into my office, bursting with psychotherapeutic energy.*

"Good morning." *I greeted her as she walked in, white uniform neatly pressed, bun up, make-up done. Madeline was ready to go. She was fiddling with her fingers in a constant motion that made me wonder, for a second, if she was having the urge to cut someone's hair while we talked.*

"Morning. Well, you know I get a little annoyed with all of this focus on the past, but you were right to have me talk to my mom. I can't believe it. All of these years, I never asked my mother about her marriage. I missed my dad, and I resented how overwhelmed she sometimes seemed after he left. But our talk really gave me a whole new picture."

"Really, what did you learn?" *I don't even know why I interrupted to ask this* question, as Madeline was clearly about to tell me.

"I never realized that my mom's whole reason for marrying my dad was to get out of her house and away from her own parents' miserable world. My mother never shared with me how stressful it was, with her parents always fighting and being broke. Neither of them had a steady income. When my mom met my dad, he was an assistant manager at a large store and she thought he would provide some stability. Of course, she barely took any time to get to know him, or she would have realized that the job at the store was clearly not one he would keep. She imagined him moving up some ladder of success. And that ladder was truly imaginary. My dad was at the store for less than a year. My mom never dreamed she would end up with two six hour shifts on her feet while my dad practiced with his band for their monthly gig at a local bar. I hate to say it, but I'm lucky that my grandfather died just after I was born. Had he been alive, he would have been in the picture and I would have been in the picture and I would have been exposed to all of the problems between my grandparents. It's so sad and ironic, my mom made all this effort to get out of the house. Then my grandfather died, the house settled down, and my mother had her own set of problems."

What seemed especially interesting about Madeline's response to her conversation with her mother was that she'd certainly known all along that her mother worked two shifts while her father practiced guitar and left most of the childcare to her grandmother. But Madeline was describing her past in a very different way, through a different lens. She was re-telling her story and considering her parents' marriage from an adult perspective.

"How did it make you feel to talk to your mom and learn about her reasoning for marrying and divorcing your father?" I queried.

"It's heartbreaking, but it is also just plain strange. A strange relief. Hearing her talk a little bit about her own past, and how she's always had to work so hard. My mom wanted to protect me and she never said a bad word about my father. I appreciate that and know it made my life a lot easier. I mean, stuff like the guitar burning on the lawn. All of that stopped once she divorced. She was busy and stressed, but I guess she didn't have to resent my dad's lack of a contribution. I always knew, intellectually, that she was our bread-winner even though Dad was twice her age when they married. But I never pictured it from her side. I just pictured how much fun my dad was to play with and how much I missed *him when Mom pulled the plug. God, I never even thought about how he didn't bother to keep in touch, really, and rarely sent money. And I certainly didn't think about how it would drive me CRAZY to be married to someone who sat around and didn't work while I did the kinds of hours my mother did at the restaurant." Madeline paused, suddenly, and shook her petite head.*

"What is it? What are you thinking?" I asked as she lifted her feet in unison, hugging her knees and curling herself back into the same ball-shaped position from our last session.

"Well, it's funny — I can say this conversation helped me realize that, while my dad had a lot of fun, positive qualities, being married to a lazy, jobless guy would be awful. I can say I have a clearer picture of my mother's reasons for the divorce. But maybe I'm just a hypocrite."

I leaned forward. "How so? It sounds like your discussion with your mother just gives you a fuller picture of why your parents married. And why they divorced. In my experience that kind of clarity can be therapeutic. You are re-writing your story and doing so can free up a lot of productive energy. You may even find that having more understanding about your past, and more empathy for your mom, gives your more empathy for your current supervisor. That empathy may improve your working relationship and may also have positive benefits for your overall experience and work and your career."

"I can see that. But that's not what I'm getting at. I'm a hypocrite because I've been doing the same thing as my mom. I don't know if I've EVER dated a guy with a career or even a job. No, I choose the bad guys—the free spirits. I even have a name for my type. I call them 'the strugglers'. I see a problem, and I'm just dying to help them fix it."

As Madeline and I continued meeting, she worked hard to reconcile her past and re-tell her story. Her discussions with her mother helped her consider her parents' marriage from an adult perspective. By doing so, she was able to grow from her parents' mistakes. For example, she adjusted extremely well to her new management structure at the salon. Her new supervisor gave her a promotion and a raise. As her career improved, she began exploring the relationship between her parents' divorce and her tendency to avoid commitment by choosing unsuitable partners. By the time she ended therapy, she was able to choose differently and have a healthy relationship.

When reflecting on the importance of considering your parents' marriage from an adult perspective, I also remember my work with a client named Jeff who came into therapy because he was experiencing significant anxiety about his marital engagement.

"I just don't want to repeat my parents' mistakes. I love Barb more than I ever thought I could love anyone. But what if I screw it up?"

Jeff had a habit of twirling his pen while he spoke. He'd reach into his pocket, remove his sleek, black, expensive-looking pen and weave it through his fingers without effort or attention. Jeff was one of many idealistic, optimistic, energetic young people who have an interest in politics, move to Washington D.C. for college and then make Washington their home. He'd built a satisfying career as a Capitol Hill staffer who worked his way up to a senior position on a prestigious congressional committee. Khakis and a blue spread collar shirt were basically his uniform, and he explained that he had always derived great pleasure from his professional life. His romantic life had not always been so satisfying. Jeff admitted to a long-standing tendency to push a woman away if he thought she was the type of person with whom he could have a future. He dated often, and did not have any relationships that lasted longer than a few months.

Barb was a colleague and a friend of Jeff's for many years. Jeff explained his hesitancy to begin dating Barb and his fear of damaging their friendship.

"It's so different with her than with anyone else. She totally gets me in a soul mate kind of way. Being with her is—well — for the first time I don't have any interest in other women. And I know I only want to be with her. But I have this strong fear of screwing it up."

"Why do you think that is?"

"As I said, I don't want to repeat my parents' mistakes."

I asked Jeff to go into detail about what his parents' mistakes entailed. While he mentioned his mother's infidelity and his father's intense ambition and excessive business travel, he didn't have much he could tell me about their actual marriage. We spent many sessions talking about his childhood memories and the way Jeff, in his own words, "grew up too fast" when his father left. We also discussed many details about Jeff's life before Barb and his self-diagnosed "dating ADD". We also talked in detail about the many ways that he and Barb were well suited.

"*We always have so much to talk about, our careers overlap, our views are compatible, we're both Democrats, we want the same things, and I'm more attracted to her physically than I've been to anyone else.*" Jeff smiled whenever he mentioned Barb. In spite of his passionate feelings and obvious love for Barb, his anxiety about marriage and his fear of repeating his parents' mistakes persisted.

Jeff described a good relationship with each of his parents, and I encouraged him to talk with them and try to learn more about the reasons they married, and the reasons they divorced. He set aside time to visit each parent and talk. Upon returning from his visits, he was eager to discuss what he learned. He grabbed the pen without notice and began his signature twirling.

"*I always knew the basics—how my mother cheated and how my father was never around. But I'm glad that you encouraged me to go into more detail. Not that I discovered anything so shocking, but it helped to hear things from each of their perspectives. My father told me that he felt that my mother always resented him for not being as wealthy as their other friends. My parents fell into a crowd of people with significant wealth, but I never knew that my father felt inadequate compared to the families in their social circle.*"

"How would you say they fell into that crowd?"

"*Basically, my mother is impressed by money. She's so pretty and my father would do anything for her, in the material sense. She wanted a new wardrobe, she got one. She wanted to join a country club they couldn't afford, so we joined. And it's kind of as if the beautiful people simply flock to her. She's always surrounded herself with very wealthy, very glamorous friends. I never thought about it much. And my dad's so ambitious that I just assumed he was in on it too. I never realized how his drive was directly related to trying to please her and live up to her expectations. I think, even after they split up, he stayed driven in an 'I'll show you' kind of way. My father also said he thinks, looking back, that he resented my mother's beauty. How easily she maneuvered social situations. How easily she made friends. In retrospect, he says he thinks he pushed her away when he should have told her how he felt. She IS gorgeous, still, and she's not always so sensitive to how the world is different for us regular people. It helps to hear my father acknowledge that he pushed her away.*" Jeff paused and quickly scanned the room, as if hesitant to continue.

"Because..."

"*Because the truth is, he pushed us all away, and we paid a pretty big price for that. His admitting it doesn't make it okay, but it helps to hear him admit it.*"

"Did he mention that as well, how he pushed you away in the process?"

"Surprisingly, yes. It's the most we've ever talked about it. He didn't make excuses or make a big deal about it. He acknowledged how he pretty much disappeared there for a while there, and how he knows it wasn't okay. I mean, he didn't totally disappear. He provided financially, he took us for one or two weekends each month, but it felt like he gave up on us. And I used this as a chance to tell him as much."

"How did he respond to that?" Jeff's pen twirling slowed to an almost stop as his thin face opened with emotion.

"He apologized. It's not as if either of us are the types to sit around and discuss how we feel. We don't ever talk about this kind of stuff, but it helped to ask him about everything, to hear his side, and to hear that he's sorry. Seriously, it helped me see things a little bit differently. And it also helped to talk with my mother."

"How so?"

"Well, she was definitely more defensive. She didn't want to discuss her affair. She never has. All she said was that she was lonely all the time. She said she felt as if she was raising us alone. And that it was better to actually be on her own than to pretend to be with someone who wasn't there. When I was in high school, she married someone who fit in a bit better with her crowd. Not super wealthy, but wealthy enough, and more into her whole country club scene. It's not as if she's going to say that, but these discussions have helped me see how my stepfather, Tom, is just a better, easier fit. So I didn't get some big explanation or apology, but—I don't know—it helped to hear her say how lonely she felt in the marriage." Jeff returned the pen to his blue checked pocket without looking at it. He cracked his knuckles and gave a hesitant smile. *"Here's the funny part, hearing all this from her view, and from his, it brings both of them down to earth. I never realized the extent to which I idealize them both."*

"I think it's only natural, to idealize our parents. Until you marry, they are your most important people, psychologically speaking, and they can seem larger-than-life."

"That's what I mean. So if these larger-than-life entities can screw up like they did, how do I not do it? That's been my question. But you know what—my parents married when they were all of twenty-one. Straight out of college. Until now, I've been beating myself up for all my years of dating ADD and for being so far behind. By the time my dad was my age, he had two kids—ages eight and ten. But maybe being behind is a good thing. Maybe being behind—by that I mean marrying later, will help me NOT screw it

up. I mean, hearing about my mother's loneliness, and my father's resentment. And his never telling her, directly, how he felt. I don't know, it sounds kind of..." Jeff paused again, re-scanning the room and looking uncomfortable about what he wanted to say.

"Kind of what?"

"Kind of immature. I've always seen them as so big and all-knowing. My glamorous mother and my hard-working father. Suddenly, I see them a little bit more like who they were, twenty-nine-year-olds who were not exactly at their best. Their marriage and their approach to the problems in their relationship seems kind of immature. I feel weird saying it, but it helps."

"How so? Talk about how it helps." Jeff looked literally lighter as he straightened in his seat and retold the story of his parents' marriage from an adult perspective. The child in him had obviously been beating himself up, irrationally, for years.

"Well, I feel like Barb and I are in such a different place. We're already in our thirties. We both have divorced parents. We both know we don't want that. If I feel something about Barb, I tell her. I let her know. Not that I'm this bucket of feelings always expressing myself, but I can barely relate to some of the ways that my parents seemed to relate—or NOT relate—to one another. I'm relieved that I waited until now to get married. Talking with my parents, I see that I'm in a different place."

"You're in a different place," I replied. "And I also think you're saying that you have a different approach to your relationship. Maybe even a more mature approach."

"Yes. Not that I'm Mr. Maturity or anything. If I were, I wouldn't be stressed about getting married. But I'm less stressed now, realizing the differences and seeing their story from a different angle."

"You're less stressed now, can you say a little more about why?"

"Oddly, I'm starting to see my stress as a good thing. Shouldn't I be stressed? I mean I'm glad we didn't just jump into this. That's another thing that both of my parents mentioned. They met during their last month of college and got engaged right after graduation. Never, until now, did I consciously think about how little they knew each other when they got engaged. I'm glad I'm approaching this whole marriage thing with more thought."

"What you're saying makes so much sense. You've known Barb for years, and you've taken time to really get to know each other. And to fully reflect on this decision. If you weren't stressed, you could interpret your lack of anxiety as a sign that you were not *taking the whole endeavor as seriously."*

"That's right. And, believe me, growing up with divorced parents, I can promise you that I take this seriously. But, before I talked with my parents, I didn't realize the distinction. I mean, I didn't realize what a different place I'm in, going into the marriage. Making that realization is a definite relief."

Jeff and I continued to meet, and his anxiety about his approaching wedding day continued to lessen. When he left for Barb's hometown the morning of his rehearsal dinner, he said that he felt completely ready and excited about making a life-long commitment to Barb. Jeff ended therapy soon after his wedding, but he sent me birth announcements for each of his sons. From the proud notes scribbled in the margins of the announcements (presumably written by his signature pocket pen!) and from the family photos he enclosed, it seemed that he and Barb remained very, very happy.

Like Madeline, Jeff was able to reflect on his parents' marriage from a different angle. By doing so, he was able to see his parents from a more human perspective, and he gained confidence by realizing and acknowledging his own maturity. He grew to view his anxiety about commitment as evidence that he took the decision to marry very seriously, and this realization was freeing.

You, too, can consider your parents' marriage from an adult perspective. Think about whether or not each parent can handle an honest discussion about his or her marriage and divorce. If you trust that they will be able to tolerate an exchange about the suggestions listed, by all means, talk to them! If you cannot ask either or both parents about the past, speak with a relative or trusted family friend. By discussing these topics, you can start to re-write your story and re-frame the way you understand your past. By doing so, you will begin to understand how your parents' divorce can actually help you achieve a healthy relationship!

Tips and Suggestions:

- Ask each parent to share their version of how he or she met the other parent. Ask about the courtship and early years of the marriage. *If you are not comfortable asking each parent these questions, ask the parent with whom you feel most comfortable. If you cannot ask either parent, ask a relative or a trusted family friend.*

- Ask each parent what he or she loved most about the other. Ask them why they chose to marry.

- Ask each parent what he or she remembers as the marriage's greatest challenges.

- Ask each parent to share his or her version of why they divorced. *Remember, you are the best judge of whether or not your relationship with either or both parents can tolerate difficult questions.*

List the answers to these questions in your journal and compare the different answers you receive. Your comparison may help illuminate essential incompatibilities and reveal how your parents may see the world through very different lenses.

chapter two

■

LEARN MORE ABOUT YOUR GRANDPARENTS AND THEIR RELATIONSHIPS

■

Step One next turns to the process of understanding your grandparents' stories. Many of the parental relationship patterns and dynamics that you are examining can be further understood by learning more about your grandparents and their history. It's surprising how many people do not even know how their grandparents met! When asked what they learned about marriage from their grandparents, many of the subjects who were surveyed said that they learned "nothing". The high percentage of respondents who have not learned anything about marriage from their grandparents may be indicative of how, as the world continues to change and families continue to spread out, we then miss out on a valuable opportunity to learn from past generations.

The more you understand about your grandparents and their relationships, the more you will understand about your parents and your adult selves. If your grandparents are still living, talk to them! Learn more about their childhoods and their marriages. Their insights can give great insight into your parents' strengths, limitations and choices. As with your parents, you are the best judge of how much your grandparents can handle in terms of a frank discussion. However, when grandparents are willing to talk, and grandchildren are willing to initiate a dialogue, this can strengthen the relationship. And people are frequently surprised about how much new information they discover.

It can also be helpful to talk to your parents to learn more about your grandparents and their relationships. If an honest conversation with either or both parents is possible, talk with them about their perspectives on your grandparents and their relationships.

Gerry, a twenty-six-year-old attorney, told the story of her grandmother who came to live with her and her mother when her parents separated. She re-told her story by initiating a discussion with her grandmother that helped her forgive her parents' for divorcing. Her grandmother was forthcoming about her own desperately unhappy marriage, and how her children did not have a settled or healthy role model for relationships. As Gerry explained to me, "My grandparents' physically abusive marriage perfectly mirrored my parents' emotionally abusive marriage." This insight helped Gerry explore her own tendency to enter abusive relationships.

Her grandmother's honesty and insights did not justify the pain and sorrow that Gerry experienced because of her parents' separation and divorce. Gerry frequently felt as if no one other than her grandmother had time for her. And she struggled terribly, both in her childhood and her adult years. She explained how her parents' marriage affected her childhood and adolescent years:

> It had contributed to my insecurity, self-consciousness and anxiety growing up. My parents were incredibly self-involved and neglectful before and after the divorce. They were nervous and stressed out and continued to blame each other and disagree long after they both remarried. My siblings and I were constantly in the middle of their battles. Their divorce made my life more complicated and stressful— constantly moving between houses—and it forced me to see sides of my parents before I could properly understand things like their fragility or their sexuality. They asked far too much of me and it made me nervous and withdrawn.

Gerry's experience growing up with divorced parents was highly traumatic. However, it was clinically valuable for Gerry to ponder what life would have been like had her parents stayed in an abusive marriage that mirrored that of her grandparents'. Gerry wondered if she would have chosen a marriage that mirrored her parents' and grandparents' relationships. This hypothetical assumption helped Gerry overcome some of the pain associated with her parents' divorce. It was also extremely therapeutic for Gerry to realize how much her grandmother was a source of strength and constancy growing up. Her grandmother's honesty and insights about her own unhappy marriage helped create a broader context for Gerry's understanding of the past.

As Gerry's experience illustrates, learning more about your grandparents' marriages can shed light on why your parents married, and why they divorced. By contrast, reflecting on your grandparents' marriages can sometimes be an inspiration and source of hope. Phillipe, a thirty-three-year-old survey subject, described his own marriage of four years as "very happy. We are very different people and learn from each others' strengths and faults." When this subject was asked what he learned about marriage from his grandparents, he stated that his grandparents' marriages taught him that marriage "is a source of strength for the various phases of one's life." Brendt, another happily married survey subject whose parents' separated when he was six, explained that he learned a lot from his grandparents:

> On both sides of my family, my grandfather fell ill and my grandmother gladly looked after everything for years. So I learned about love and constancy.

Timothy, a thirty-four-year-old survey subject whose parents separated when he was sixteen, described his own marriage as "happy. I am lucky, my spouse is a grounded, capable person with very strong values. [She is] a gifted mother, and a loving spouse." He said the following about his grandparents:

> Both sets of my grandparents are remarkable and I use them as a model

for how I would like my life to be. Both sets went through a lot with each other and sacrificed, suffered, worked and loved. They placed marriage and their spouses at the top of their priorities, and they really reaped the rewards in all the years I have known them... [They have had a] very big influence on me.

Personally, I have found it very helpful to remember and reflect on all of my grandparents and their marriages. Re-visiting and re-processing information about my grandparents from an adult perspective has given me important information about my parents and what led them into their unsuccessful marriage. Acknowledging my grandparents' limitations and unhappy marriages helped put my parents' choices into perspective and painted a picture of the intergenerational cycle that their divorce helped me break.

One of my visits to my father's childhood home stands out in my memory as a symbolic window into the way my father grew up and how his childhood impacted his adult life.

My sister Kathyanne and I traveled to Harrisburg to celebrate and to attend a small luncheon for our father's mother, in celebration of her eightieth birthday. Kathyanne was in seventh grade and I was in tenth. We always enjoyed seeing our father, but never much cared for Harrisburg. Our grandmother's home was not exactly welcoming. A zero-tolerance "no trespassing" rule governed her kitchen, and her strict rules gave us the sense that unauthorized cookie-eaters risked being arrested, or at least yelled at and sentenced to a dinnerless evening in our Aunt Jane's bedroom. Never, ever, under any circumstances, could we be trusted to take anything out of the refrigerator or, heaven forbid, cook the French toast breakfast we so freely enjoyed preparing in our father's Philadelphia apartment. Only our father was old and wise enough to assume such responsibility, and I suspected that my father's graduation to kitchen clearance was a recent one. I wondered whether my grandfather had been allowed to use the kitchen when he was still alive. And I wondered if my grandmother had always been so rigid. The fact that I was old enough to drive a car and would soon be off to college was excluded as irrelevant evidence in my failed case for culinary privileges. In my grandmother's unwavering book, such liberties were strictly reserved for the over-thirty crowd who had paid their dues in the real world and were finally ready to handle a stove and its flame.

As we entered her wallpaper-ensconced home, our grandmother stood in the center of her formal entryway shaking her silver-topped head in obvious disappointment.

"It looks like you've gained some weight there," she mentioned immediately walking toward Kathyanne and granting her a restrained kiss. "And you, Elisabeth," she headed my way as she forged ahead with insult number two, "your father never had pimples like yours," she announced while examining my substandard skin. "I am sorry dear, but you did not inherit this acne or whatever they call it from our side of the family, I can promise you that."

According to our grandmother, our hair was never combed enough, our teeth were never straight enough and our clothing was a far cry from fashionable. She'd been shortchanged with sorry excuses for grandchildren. Her profound lack of enthusiasm with regard to our looks and our culinary competence led me to feel exceptionally self-conscious the minute I set foot in her stately and elegantly decorated suburban home. I became a peasant lost in a palace. I never knew what to wear or how to tame my trendy teenage hair. No matter what I wore, no matter how I toned down the layered hairstyle so popular among my classmates and so unpopular with my grandmother, I always felt frazzled and displaced.

After reading John Irving's A Prayer for Owen Meany, I became convinced that Irving must have met my grandmother while researching his novel. Mrs. Wheelwright was Mrs. Cohen's literary twin. Stately and strict. Fastidiously dressed for all occasions, and committed to perpetuating traditions such as perfectly polished silver and butlers. Her matter-of-fact demeanor covered up a curious kindness, a cautious compassion that lingered mysteriously, far beneath the surface, and difficult to pinpoint amidst her criticism.

Kathyanne and I slept in our Aunt Jane's bedroom, still decorated with pink flowered wallpaper and matching bedspreads. Like my father's room down the hall, my grandmother had frozen Jane's room in time. A series of pale, oil-painted, skinny ballet dancers pirouetted along Jane's walls, gracefully respecting the boundaries of the gold frames containing them. An assembly of pastel cashmere sweaters hung from the puffy pink hangers still lining her closets, their posture as confident as the dancers on the opposite wall. Surveying this perfectly preserved room, one would never guess that Aunt

Jane was now in her fifties, divorced, the mother of two grown children and the manager of an intense yet never discussed drinking problem. Sleeping in this room gave me the creeps. The ghost of Aunt Jane as a little girl haunted the air and filled it up with years of unanswered sadness and longing. During her childhood, she had been treated terribly. She was not the beautiful social butterfly my grandmother had hoped for and imagined. Far from it. Jane was chubby, awkward, bookish and shy.

Jane died in her fifties following a stroke and series of subsequent medical complications. I recently had lunch with my mother and one of her friends who, coincidentally, had been Jane's childhood bunkmate at overnight camp. She shared her memories of my aunt, laying out a vivid description of Jane during her young life as a camper.

"Jane was such a lonely child. Each year she took the bed at the corner of the bunk, and children were cruel to her. Just cruel. She was overweight, unathletic, and that didn't help at all." Aunt Jane's former bunkmate, now in her sixties, shook her head as she spoke. "But it's funny, she was always so neat. Meticulously clean, really. She was the first to make her bed each morning. Even when she was teased, and I mean bitterly teased, she'd hold herself with a tidy kind of dignity. I can't believe how we treated her."

I felt like an outcast each time I visited my grandmother. The recollection of Jane's bunkmate made me realize that my struggle was a drop in the ocean compared to Jane's. Still, I felt so close to my misunderstood aunt that I could smell her, the fastidious scent of clean, cool sheets tucked into perfect hospital corners, trying desperately to reflect composure in spite of her pain and her status as an outcast.

Jane could do no right. My handsome, athletic father, five years her junior could do no wrong. My father remembers how her academic aptitude was grossly ignored while her ability to overeat became a centerpiece of family focus. While Jane was blessed with high intelligence and a sweet demeanor, she was raised as if she were a total disappointment. And this cruel prophecy eventually fulfilled itself. The put-downs my grandmother distributed to her only daughter continued throughout Jane's childhood and adult life. One example sticks in my mind's eye: as a little girl, I once made the mistake of asking my grandmother for a second serving of her lemon meringue pie. She refused me instantly, pointing across the table to her overweight, middle-aged, divorcing daughter and reminding me that I didn't want to end up like my Aunt Jane, did I? Jane just stared into her plate. She showed no visible reaction to her mother's cruel words. No response other than her recoil into her food. I guess she'd grown far too accustomed to excessive insults.

Perhaps she'd adapted to a lifetime of perpetual put-downs by cutting off her conscious-ness and cutting into her rare roast beef when the conversations became too painful.

My quiet, slouching grandfather sat in silence, saying and doing nothing. I remember wishing he would speak up and do something to protect the honor of his defenseless daughter. An elegant, dark-skinned man who wore silky, rust-colored smoking jackets and slicked his hair back in perfectly greased strands, my grandfather never said much. Looking back, he seemed completely overpowered by my grandmother and unable to assert himself. Did my grandmother's words upset him as much as they upset me? Was there a time in their past when he would have told her to cut it out and leave Jane alone? Or did my grand-mother always shoot uncensored insults about in all directions with no one to reel her in?

Kathyanne and I awoke the morning of the birthday party, showered and began attempting to dress like young ladies who lunched. Kathyanne disappeared into the bathroom for what felt like an inconsiderate eternity. She finally emerged with her pale face looking panicked, as though she'd seen the ghost of Aunt Jane's past.

"Elisabeth," she walked towards me, a frightened tear clinging to each eye. "I'm not exactly sure, but I think I just got my period. I'm all bloody down there."

I was stunned. Kathyanne was barely twelve! I hadn't had the pleasure of my first period until I was fourteen! The last in the class, and most everybody knew it. Now it looked like Kathyanne would be the first. I remembered being in Burger King celebrating someone's fourteenth birthday with a group of friends when I first got my period. I hadn't realized how lucky I was that I could simply excuse myself, run home to our mother and figure out the basics.

How could Kathyanne begin womanhood now? So soon? Barely twelve years old! I knew I had to calm my agitation so that she didn't sense it and get too upset. I'm sure all she wanted was our mother who was two hours away in Philadelphia. By default, I was all the feminine comfort she'd have.

"Don't tell Daddy," she commanded. We looked at each other not quite sure what to do or say.

"Okay. We don't need to tell him if you don't want, I'll just run to the store after the party and get you what you need. We can't go now, so you'll have to fold some tissues in your underwear until I can get to the store. Is that okay?"

"I guess," she began to cry. Poor thing. She had turned twelve, bought her first brasserie, and started a new school all in one month. And now this. The last thing she

needed was her first period and the last place she needed to get it was here in Harrisburg. The last day she needed to get it was on her grandmother's eightieth birthday. She must have felt so scared, and I didn't know how to help her. I showed her how to fold the tissues in her panties as a temporary sanitary napkin and I promised to pick up something she would be more comfortable with as soon as lunch was over. Reluctantly, we waited for our father and grandmother to escort us, and we kept our solemn secret to ourselves.

An hour later, as we dined on cobb salads in the formal dining room at Maverick, my grandmother's favorite haunt, I noticed Kathyanne growing flushed. Our father sat between us, elegantly filling the role of the only male diner, as he sat quietly and observed our efforts to fit in with our grandmother's friends. Almost everyone at the table was wearing a hat coordinated with some form of pastel clothing. Kathyanne continuously glanced toward me with her baby doll face and big brown eyes that seemed to be shouting get me the hell out of here! I felt her sweating and growing more nauseated with each fork full of salad. I reluctantly realized that Kathyanne would not make it to dessert.

My father ordered some champagne and raised his glass to make a toast. Just then, Kathyanne abruptly placed her flushed face in her hands and began to cry. She wasn't making much noise, but her whole body was shaking. Her dark hair fell over her face and we could see her heavy sobbing through the movements in her hunched over back. My father and grandmother exchanged questioning glances and my father took Kathyanne's hand. In addition to my grandmother's confused eighty-year-old friends, people at neighboring tables were beginning to stare as my father led Kathyanne from the table. They headed for the door to the parking lot. My father faced forward as he walked, seeming oblivious to the attention from various diners.

Kathyanne held his hand and faced straight down, looking ashamed. My grandmother and I remained, as she surveyed me from head to toe. I knew there stood no chance in hell that shy, contained Kathyanne would tell my father the source of her sudden outburst and tears. As far as she was concerned, my father had never heard of a period and that was that.

"You know what's the matter, don't you?" My grandmother whispered, taking me totally by surprise. Her intuition amazed me, and I nodded yes while gazing into the leftover avocado I had been unknowingly smashing with my fork. My grandmother must have known that it was Kathyanne's menstrual period. But rather than ask, she suggested that I go find my father and sister and explain.

How did she know? From such a coldly composed and distant woman, her perception and warm direction were as shocking as they were soothing. She smiled softly and pointed me towards the door, her hesitant but genuine smile shooting out a love I rarely saw—love that was always there, resting quietly, disguised beneath the surface, covered up by too many layers of French tablecloths and expensive china. A love she seemed to hoard with a vengeance and dole out when you least expected it. Worst of all, a love she tragically withheld from her only daughter while granting it to my father in abundance. I did my best to receive her smile and return it.

I headed for the door and, oddly, I found myself wondering if my father knew about it when Aunt Jane first got her period. I entered the parking lot to find poor Kathyanne sitting on a concrete divider, refusing to look up from the ground. She was running her index finger back and forth on the dirty window of a random car. My father had delicately positioned himself across from her, leaning on an old maroon station wagon, holding her hand. He kept saying it was okay, she could tell him whatever was the matter, and everything would surely turn out okay. I noticed a faint smell of restaurant food as I joined them, Kathyanne looked up from the ground. My father turned to me with bushy eyebrows stuck in a questioning "V".Their confused faces looked exhausted and intense. Kathyanne's less full but equally distinct eyebrows mirrored our father's in their dramatic shape. Her defensive "V" protected crying eyes, protesting his questions.

Kathyanne knew that if she held onto her silence long enough, I would eventually show up and break it apart for her. And I did, like a firefighter finally arriving on the scene to shatter the window and pull the victims from the smoke into the safety. I couldn't bear seeing her sitting there so extremely scared and sinking with embarrassment. I wanted to protect and take care of her and make it all better. It felt like we were in the living room watching cartoons all over again. I was back looking down my stairs, spinning in tears and panic, caring about one thing. I didn't want my sweet and still innocent sister to feel this kind of sadness. And I didn't have a clue about how to protect her. I knew Kathyanne longed for a magical transport home to our mother who could explain to her what was happening and give her what she needed. I wished I could somehow carry her there, but, again, I couldn't.

"Tell him," she begged.

"Okay," I hesitated, and then said it, "Kathyannegotherperiod." The words flew from my mouth as I lost a long-standing language virginity. I never thought I could say such a thing in the presence of my father. Perhaps if our parents had stayed together, my mother

would have eased our adolescent tension by discussing menstruation and puberty openly at dinner or during family car rides. Maybe she would have said the word "period" in front of him, teaching me by example to mimic her and do the same. After all, I <u>do</u> remember sitting with them as a six-year-old, as my mother explained in a carefree voice how my father had used his sperm to fertilize her egg and that was how Kathyanne and I were made. In my memory, my father looked significantly embarrassed but willing to participate in the sperm and egg "where do I come from?" discussion. Maybe if we had grown up spending more day-to-day time with him, womanly hygiene wouldn't have become so painfully taboo. Sure, my father's girlfriend, Allison, was around; but as a retired but devoted hippie, Allison didn't explain sex, she merely displayed it. Without someone maturely easing the way, words like bra, period and sex were invisible from our father-daughter vocabularies. Perhaps they were equally invisible from our thoughts, since it seemed my father had not even considered this possibility. My grandmother seemed to know instantly, while it was nowhere near my father's radar screen of potential sources fueling Kathyanne's dilemma. Sharing this intimate milestone with his daughters, our naïve, well-intended father became a semi-stranger.

"Oh, yes." He paused. "I mean okay." He tried to appear comfortable and unfazed. "Let's go home and, uh, pick up what you need. Yeah, we'll uh, leave right now and take you home, what do you say?" Kathyanne nodded yes, she had returned her glance to the floor. My father asked me if my grandmother knew, and I said yes but I never mentioned her surprising perception. My father ran to quickly say goodbye while Kathyanne and I waited quietly in the parking lot. Then, we drove from the restaurant in a stiff silence with our young femininity overwhelming the car.

"Gee, you girls really will do just about anything to get out of a formal luncheon, won't you?" His attempt to slice the awkwardness with humor worked as we giggled and forgot our clumsy predicament for about ten seconds. I considered the curious coincidence of how I, too, got my first period while celebrating someone's birthday in a restaurant and decided to keep this fun fact to myself. The backdrop of tension quickly returned. Our shared embarrassment was watered down but absorbing. I felt almost as horrible for our father as I did for Kathyanne. His love and longing to put us at ease showed itself through his joke, his awkwardness and his desperately forced composure. He seemed torn between his guilt about Kathyanne's embarking upon pubescent womanhood in the presence of the wrong parent and his loving desire to have his daughters with him.

To be together, tripping and falling, rushing and racing, struggling to make up for lost, irretrievable time.

While these Harrisburg memories clearly reveal some of the many pains and malfunctions associated with having divorced parents, they also represent an opportunity to re-write some elements of my family history through considering how my grandparents' lopsided marriage and lopsided treatment of my father and Jane did not provide my father (or Jane) with a functioning model of a happy marriage. My father began attending over-night camp at age seven and boarding school by age twelve. In many ways, he raised himself. In addition, the imbalance of his parents' marriage and his mother's imbalanced treatment of him and his rejected sister did not prepare him for a balanced marriage or a balanced family life. I also wonder if he wanted to marry someone more emotional (like my mother) to make up for what he missed out on. Maybe he did, but he clearly was not suited for the level of emotional exchange my mother wanted.

My father is very much a thinker, and an issues discusser. He reads the *New York Times*, *Washington Post*, *Philadelphia Inquirer* and his local paper, the *Harrisburg Patriot*, on a daily basis. Handsome, curious, six foot two, and completely unable to throw away an unread newspaper, he lets unread news pile up for months with noble intentions of backtracking in his free time. When his wife, Susan, complains about the mess generated by piles and piles of unread pages, he replies without reserve, "That's no mess, that's history!" Tossing out an unread paper is almost as painful to my father as driving past an empty tennis court on a sunny day. A funny, charming, engaging yet somewhat distant man who can simultaneously talk on the phone, drink coffee, read the paper and drive his car. Cerebral, yes. Athletic, absolutely. Handsome, easily. Emotional, not exactly.

We have had countless wonderful talks about the news, history, politics and sports. However, opening up about our feelings or our sadness has been much harder. Open expressions of sadness or disappointment seem almost unthinkable if not for the few exceptions that stand out so sharp and solid. In spite of how much I love him, his reserve in the emotions arena keeps a clear distance between us, making him something of a mystery to me.

My mother is his virtual opposite. She'll sense my sadness before I do and has a gift for perceiving precisely what I, or others, are feeling. She knows just what to say to touch the root of what's really on my mind, and she always has. Her love for her children permeates her every action. As tough as our lives became, financially and emotionally, during the four years of my parents' separation and difficult journey towards divorce, she always tried to make things beautiful. When a piece of furniture disappeared due to my parents' ongoing debates about who would get what, my mother ran to auctions, thrift stores and generous friends, determined to replace each and every missing piece. Our bookshelves were never barren and she sold her engagement ring to finance the transformation of our filthy basement into a playroom. She filled this cherished mini village beneath our home with Atari and board games and all kinds of ideal distractions from the separation. On good days, we sang show tunes, held hands and danced through Philadelphia's city streets. We smuggled Butterscotch Krimpets and chocolate milk into the twilight cheap show at the movies. Who needed overpriced popcorn and oversized soda? On good days, we ate pancakes for dinner at my request and stayed up late in the evenings watching Bill Bixby, on the old television show, get angry and become *The Incredible Hulk*.

While my parents could not be more different, or less compatible, one thing they genuinely shared was the dysfunctional nature of their parents' relationships. Reflecting on my maternal grandparents and their relationship reveals a very different, but equally distant marriage.

My mother's mother, Charlotte, died of lung cancer when I was twenty-four years old. Just a few weeks before she died, my mother, Kathyanne and my step-father, Stan, went to Florida to say goodbye. As is a Jewish tradition, I told her that someday I would name a child in her memory. I was single at the time, and there was no chance of a baby Charlotte on the near horizon. Still, my grandmother said that my intention of someday giving her a namesake would help her go in peace. Cancer had taken her hair and her strength, but not her beauty, and she lay there in bed, smiling through her pain. She was seventy-five years old and, even with a merciless illness raging through her fragile bones, and a pink turban clenching her hairless head, she looked much younger. Her skin was soft beige and her big, brown, knowing eyes rested peacefully over firm and sculpted cherry tomato cheekbones. My mother says that when her mother was young and living in Baltimore, all the residents of their orthodox Jewish neighborhood agreed she was the most beautiful woman they had ever seen.

"That actress in Life is Beautiful, *Roberto Bennini's wife. That's just how she looked," my mother explained. "The whole time I was watching the movie, I could have been watching your Grandma. Like I was ten years old, and she was this young, breathtaking beauty all over again. I could sit and watch that movie all day."*

My grandmother and grandfather never once looked happy when they were together. My grandma's expression possessed a look of questioning sadness and regret. Her persistent beauty seemed compromised by her sad expression. As if she spent her life searching, in earnest, digging to discover something more in her husband and their marriage. Sifting through the layers and coming up empty. She was much more curious and compassionate than he, and she always looked lonely. She dreamed of the ballet and opera while he preferred comics and Bruce Lee and refused to see any movie that lacked his primary requirements: "blood and guts". You could almost hear her silent but constant desire to have someone to really talk to. It surfaced through the sound of the angry static of their air conditioning unit humming behind the strong and steady silence that hung between them.

My grandparents looked as glamorous and glowing as Hollywood royalty, yet they had nothing to say to each other. A photograph from their honeymoon hung in their apartment, a sepia memory of their physical perfection. They stood together on the Atlantic City boardwalk and they may as well have been standing on a movie set, taking a break between scenes. She in a slim floral dress and delicate wide-rimmed hat. He in loose beige pants and suspenders. His arm is wrapped around her neck in a telling clasp. Although they smiled gorgeously together, like living legends, he is practically choking her with his grasp. Her neck and head lean away as if to attempt an escape from his bondage, while their oxymoronic smiles project an image of glossy glamour and cinema quality love.

When my grandmother was in her late sixties, she found a job as a receptionist in a psychiatrist's office and the entire staff fell in love with her. When she became ill, they sent flowers and visited her frequently, telling our family that their office would never be the same without her. I used to love to call her up when she was working, just to hear her answer the phone, speaking like a song, with full character and competence.

"May I speak with Charlotte Sherman?" I requested.

"This is she," I can still hear her gently say.

Her immediate talent and enjoyment of her work seemed bittersweet. On the one hand, what a gift, seeing her so involved and invested. This was her first real job, and she couldn't wait to get there each morning. At the same time, how heartbreaking to witness and realize her unmet potential. Like so many women of her time, college was way out of the question. And seeing her work highlighted how much a career would have meant to her. And how brilliantly she would have succeeded in whatever she chose.

My sad, gorgeous grandmother hung onto life as long as she could, two years longer than the doctors predicted. But early in the morning of my mother's April 10th birthday, she let go.

"I guess your birthday is ruined," my mother's sister Marla said as they spoke on the telephone, the afternoon of their mother's death. I was sitting with my mother as she took a deep breath and sighed.

"Actually no, Marla, I'm not going to look at it that way," she spoke slowly between her tears. "I'm just not. I'm going to look at it that Mother loved me so much, she hung on so that I could have one more birthday with a mom." My mother's response says everything about who she is, and how she has approached her life. Determined to make lemonade from life's lemons, to give love to others and to feel love in return. Having her mother die on her birthday was a terrible shock, of course. But she was determined to understand it as a sign of the deep connection she and her mother always shared.

When Russ and I became engaged in September of 1998, we knew we wanted a brief engagement. Once we decided to marry, we wanted to do so as soon as possible. I anticipated that the planning and navigation of my parents would be stressful and complicated, and Russ knew enough about my parents' history to agree. We just wanted it over and done. As we looked into the logistics, we discovered that most of the summer '99 dates at local Philadelphia facilities were taken, so we decided to marry in the spring. However, various possible wedding dates were complicated by the Passover holiday. Jewish law states certain dates around this holiday when a couple should not marry, and April 10th was one of two possible dates that would work. My mother and I decided that it was a sign that my grandma was smiling somewhere and determined to be a part of the day. When we were married on April 10th, 1999, I could feel my grandmother Charlotte smiling through the candlelight of our celebration. I sensed her bittersweet spirit as we paused in her memory, as we danced the Horah and I married the most kind, gentle and brilliant man I have ever met. My best friend, my heart and my soul. My sky and my ocean, my sunshine and my moonlight. Always and forever, Russ.

Through the pain and sadness of re-visiting my maternal grandparents' history, I realize how my mother unknowingly followed in some of her mother's psychological footsteps and made many similar mistakes. My grandmother wasn't ever genuinely happy in her marriage, and longed for a more complete and fulfilling life. Her adulthood was full of missed opportunities, both in her marriage and in terms of her non-existent career. As if that clasp so clear in the sepia photograph held on for too long, too tight and strangled all of her potential. If only she had been born at a different time, with different choices. Once in a while, when talking with my mother, my grandmother could open up and share more about her hopes, dreams and longings. My mother could hear and accept these feelings in a way that my grandfather and my Aunt Marla could never tolerate. My grandparents visited maybe once each year. My grandfather rarely left the guest room, while my grandmother and mother sat in the living room and talked. Though she never possessed enough emotional ease to say it, my mother's professional success and her successful marriage to my stepfather, Stan, clearly brought my grandmother unprecedented happiness and pride.

Remembering and understanding my grandparents' mutually unhappy marriages puts my parents' illogical choice of one another into better psychological perspective. They were raised in different but equally disconnected households where their parents gave the outward impression that all was well. Growing up, my parents were spared the painful shock of reality brought on by a divorce. However, they entered adulthood lacking insight about their parents' unfulfilling, dysfunctional relationships. They both, unconsciously and unintentionally, repeated their parents' mistakes. In addition to my parents, each of their siblings also divorced and their equally unhappy marriages can be seen as further evidence of the inter-generational legacy of unhappiness that dysfunctional marriages can produce.

Learning more about your grandparents and their relationships can be one of the most rewarding parts of the Five Step Guide. Your grandparents are a fascinating well of information. Many grandparents are retired, older and wiser. All these factors can facilitate relaxed, reflective and interesting conversations. It is important to remember, however, that you are the best judge of whether or not your grandparents can tolerate a discussion of the topics listed below. With any grandparent who is capable of doing so, make it a priority to talk to him or her. By following some tips and suggestions, you may be surprised by what you learn!

Tips and Suggestions:

- Set aside time to talk with each living grandparent about his or her history and marriage. Ask each grandparent about meeting his or her spouse and what each remembers most from the early courtship. Ask either grandparent what they loved most about his or her spouse and what is viewed as the greatest challenges of the marriage.

- Ask each living grandparent to discuss any information he or she feels comfortable sharing about raising your parents. Ask them how they would describe your parent's childhood. What was wonderful about that period in their life? And what was most difficult? *If possible, make time to visit with each grandparent and ask these questions in person rather than talking on the telephone.*

- Ask each parent to tell you more about their parents' marriages. How would they describe the marriage? Did their parents seem happy? How were they compatible? How were they not compatible? What did your parents learn about marriage from their parents? *If your grandparents did not marry, these same questions are still relevant; ask about their relationships rather than about their marriage.*

Spend at least an hour writing about what you learn from these conversations. Put into written words what surprises you the most, and anything you learned that you didn't already know.

Step Two: Face the Mirror

The second critical step in the journey we are taking together requires you to Face the Mirror. This necessitates frank and heartfelt reflection about how your parents' divorce affected you in your childhood, and how it continues to affect you in adulthood. This step may seem straightforward: many adults with divorced parents can describe, in detail, how their parents' divorce rocked their emotional world. In order to understand how your parents' divorce can help you achieve a happy relationship, however, you must step beyond the obvious. It is not enough to intellectually acknowledge how some of your adult struggles are related to a childhood history of growing up in a divorced household. Instead, you must Face the Mirror and take full ownership of the tremendous extent to which this history can and has weighed you down and led to specific self-destructive behavior that does not work for you in your adult life.

The first part of Step Two, rethinking your childhood experiences and behavior, builds on what you learned during Step One about your past. By reflecting on your childhood, you build a bridge from your past to your present. It is obviously difficult to reflect on how your childhood was shaped by your parents' divorce. However, now that you have re-told your parents' stories from a psychologically mature perspective, you are in a better position to reflect on the past. Taking stock of how divorce shaped your childhood will put you in a clearer position to complete Step Two. You will take a difficult but honest look in the mirror and pinpoint how your parents' divorce affects you as an adult.

By completing Step Two and facing the ways your parents' divorce negatively influence the way you operate as an adult, you are preparing yourself to make the changes that will be necessary in order to have the happiest possible life.

54

■

chapter three

RE-THINK YOUR
CHILDHOOD
EXPERIENCES
AND BEHAVIOR

■

Begin Step Two by remembering and re-thinking childhood experiences and behavior. It can hurt terribly to recall certain aspects of childhood that relate to having divorced parents, but engaging with these memories is an important piece of the healing process.

I have worked for over fifteen years with adults whose parents divorced. In meeting with my clients, I have learned there are a number of common ways that a separation impacts a childhood. Many adults describe how they "grew up too fast" or how they went through a period of rebellion.

Elaine, a twenty-seven-year-old survey subject shares the following heartfelt description of how her parents' divorce affected her as a child:

> As the only girl, my mother often shared her emotional/financial stress with me as a young child, so I often bore the brunt of how much it sucked for her to be a divorcee. We often fought about how much she communicated with me about their divorce. She often used me as a sound board to vent, cry, etc., even when I was very young (four or so). When I was in college, one of my older brothers

casually mentioned that our mother never said anything bad about our father (which is quite the opposite of the experience I had growing up). I suppose she didn't want to burden the boys with her emotional problems. With few friends/girlfriends, she often turned to me. Now I see it as something that makes my mother and me closer, but at the time I didn't appreciate it.

Sadly, this subject's reflections symbolize the difficulties faced by many children who are overstimulated with too much information and can be forced to grow up too fast. (Interestingly, it is also an example of how children in the same family can experience the same divorce in very different ways.)

The most common childhood symptom that these clients remember is their development of increased separation anxiety. Separation anxiety is also commonly described as "fear of abandonment." A child experiencing separation anxiety is frightened by any scenario that involves her parent separating from her or exiting a physical space that they occupy together. She becomes terrified that the parent will leave and disappear or not return.

According to child development experts, separation anxiety is a normal developmental process that typically surfaces for the first time at about eight months of age. This is the period of life when infants first discover that they and their mother are two separate beings. Until this point, most infants do not fear being apart from their mothers, because they assume that the mother is an extension of themselves. Like an arm, sometimes you see it, sometimes you don't. By eight months of age, infants have developed the cognitive ability to figure out that they are not physically attached to their mother at all times. As a result, they become scared when they observe their mothers' exit. Separation anxiety tends to wax and wane throughout any normal childhood. For example, many children will experience separation anxiety when starting a new school. Young children may cry each day when a parent drops them off. When the child gets used to the new environment, the anxiety usually subsides. Experiencing a parental separation will frequently cause fears of separation to resurface, sometimes in dramatic ways. Three survey subjects' responses to the question of how divorce affects one's childhood demonstrate the prevalence of severe separation anxiety among children with divorced parents:

> Dana states: I had a real fear of abandonment as a child and felt very little security.

> Gayle recalls: [The divorce] made me cling to things I could control—grades, performance/achievement in school. I was more precocious as a child—entertaining, leading my friends, perhaps as compensation for the uncertainty...I also experienced a short period of anxiety of [when] being physically separated from either parent...if one of them needed to step out of the house for a moment, I thought that I was going to be left behind.

> Carole remembers: I had somewhat low self-esteem, cried a lot, was very sensitive and had a strong fear of abandonment. For example, I didn't want my mom to leave when she dropped me off at school...However, playing sports as a child helped to boost my confidence and inner strength, and without that influence in my life, I wonder how strong a person I would be today.

Is it any wonder that children who fear separation from their parents because of the trauma of their parents' divorce grow up to fear commitment? The most psychologically important people in a child's life are his parents. If your closest, most psychologically important relationships are disrupted by a parental separation, you must therefore learn to adjust to the unpleasantness of being physically separated from one of your parents, all (or most) of the time. The trauma of adjusting to this separation causes anxiety about your most significant relationships. So, when you grow up and prepare to find a committed partner, such fears can linger and taint your sense of security. The traumatic separations from the past can make it harder to feel safe enough to harbor close, important, committed adult relationships. It makes strong psychological sense that so many adults with divorced parents fear separation as children, and then grow up longing to protect themselves from this fear by avoiding it in some conscious or unconscious way. The logical relationship between fearing abandonment and fearing commitment can help illuminate how childhood experiences are relevant to adult struggles.

Many of the people with whom I have worked and surveyed reflect fears of abandonment. Robert, one of my clients, especially suffers from this fear.

Robert was in the second year of his medical residency when he suddenly experienced a full-blown first panic attack. The experience completely caught him off guard and was so frightening and out of character that he decided to seek counseling. During our first meeting, he described the terrifying sensation of a racing heart, a pained stomach and a total inability to move.

"I've never understood what people meant about panic attacks; it's paralyzing and I can't afford to be paralyzed."

"Do you have any sense of what precipitated the attack?" I asked.

"No, not really, medical school and my internship were very high pressure, especially the internship. I've always excelled in high pressure situations, and nothing like this has ever happened."

"Well, has anything changed?"

"No, not at the hospital. It's the same fast pace I'm used to; that's why I chose the medical field. I actually like the pressure."

"Has anything changed away from the hospital?" I responded.

"Only that my girlfriend, Susan, is traveling. That's a change."

Robert and Susan had been living together for over a year, and Robert described a happy, settled relationship. They met while Robert was in medical school and Susan was in graduate school for international relations at the same university. Robert was tall and thin with an unwaveringly serious expression. He seemed surprised as he pondered a possible relationship between Susan's travel and his unprecedented panic.

"I guess it could be related. I had sent her an email when I got home from the hospital. I hadn't heard from her when I went to bed, and I still didn't hear from her that next morning. I left at 6:00 A.M. for the hospital. Of course, by lunch I had an email

from Susan explaining that she had no service while traveling, but my panic attack happened in the morning, before I heard from her."

Since Robert was in such a demanding career, and described a long-standing pattern of enjoying a high-stress work setting, we talked about what not hearing from Susan brought up for him. I asked him if there was another time when he had experienced anxiety. Robert explained that his parents separated when he was nine, and he recalled a period of intense separation anxiety.

"I was always the kind of kid who loved school. I'd run in each day, ready to go. And when my dad moved out, it was like someone flipped my switch. It was a nightmare. Here I was, this nine-year-old, tall, tough kid, crying like a baby every morning at the bus. My mother had to literally carry me on. She was barely taller than I was, with my backpack over her shoulder, picking me up and wrestling me onto the bus. For the first few weeks after my dad left, she drove me to school so that the other kids wouldn't see me cry. But then she said she had to stop being late for work, and when I wouldn't get on the bus, she full-on carried me."

Robert became increasingly emotional, shaking his head and holding back tears. He scratched his heavy stubble with the back of his hand and explained how his crying fits lasted for weeks. He couldn't recall when they stopped; he could, however, clearly connect his tears and anxiety to his parents' separation.

"My dad was definitely my hero, took me to baseball games, catch, little league. I was all about baseball and he was right there with me. The first time he ever missed a game was the week he moved out. And he only missed that and a few other games, but that's when my switch flipped. Not when he moved out. It was when he didn't show up for my game."

I encouraged Robert to explore more about the background of his parents' divorce and how it affected his childhood. I was convinced that re-thinking his childhood experiences would help him better understand and manage his concern about the panic attack. Robert explained how his parents fought constantly before their separation and how he and his younger sister were sometimes caught in the middle of their fights.

"My mother once told me to get all of my dad's clothing and help her throw it out the window. And I did it! She seemed crazed and I felt like I had to listen. I remember wishing that she would just pack up her own stuff and leave. But I'll say this, she totally calmed down after he left. Then I became the stressed one! But my mom chilled out, and *stopped yelling so much. And my dad did everything to stay in our lives. Other than missing a few games while he was getting settled, he was always there for us 1000 percent. I figured out from a pretty young age that they would not be together forever, and I also figured out pretty quickly that they were better off apart. I understood that more than I should have—I was only nine, after all. Regardless of what I knew or understood, I continued to have this terrible fear of losing them. It was most obvious on the bus, but, for a while, if either of them left a room without telling me, I worried that they would leave me and I would lose it."*

"You say your mother chilled out after your father left," I said quietly. "And you describe her efforts to first drive you to school, and then to carry you onto the bus. How would you say she handled your fear of separating?"

"That's a good question. I wish she had kept driving me to school, but I can see, now, that she had to get to work herself. And, you know..." Robert paused and took a deep, extended breath, "I actually hadn't remembered this until now, but she also used to write me notes. In my backpack and my lunch box, telling me she loved me and was proud of me. And making these weird little drawings of kids playing baseball. Wow, I totally forgot about that."

"What does the memory mean to you?" I queried.

"A lot, actually. She was never like that when she was with my father. She really did try to help me. And my fits passed with time. My dad, too, he started coaching the little league team and I loved that. And he'd take me and Helen, my sister, out to this great pizza place every Saturday night. I have to say that my parents were both really there for us. I know it's not like that for everyone whose parents split up, and I'm grateful for that."

Robert began his next appointment with an announcement: "Just so you know, I get what you were doing last time. You never said that my panic attack was related to my history in terms of how I reacted when my dad moved out because you wanted me to figure that out myself." We both smiled a bit as he continued. There was levity in Robert's tone as if he had finally solved a medical mystery, made the correct diagnosis, and was thrilled by his clinical competence. "Susan was traveling for the first time since we've moved in together, and when I didn't hear from her, I got scared again, in the same way. It was like I became that same scared little kid who didn't want to leave my mom and get on the bus, who didn't want to play baseball if my dad missed the game. I think getting close with Susan is bringing up insecurities from the past. I don't want to push her away, but, since the panic attack, I've clearly pulled back."

"I think you're right."

"I know Susan is there for me, just like my parents were, but something about not hearing from her, just that once, brought it all back. It's amazing how making that simple connection helped me. But why didn't you just tell me?"

"Why do you think?"

"I don't know. I'm a doctor for heaven's sake. In my profession, we give our patients a direct diagnosis. But if I had to guess, I'd hypothesize that it means more if I figure it out for myself? What do you think?"

"I think maybe you should consider switching to a residency in psychiatry, you really seem to understand how this works!" I exclaimed with a smile.

We both laughed, briefly, before continuing the serious work of exploring more details about Robert's childhood history. I encouraged him to explore as many memories as he could about his reaction to his parents' divorce. He also eventually discussed his feelings about these memories with each parent. During the course of therapy, Robert did not experience another panic attack. He and Susan became engaged and married soon after his residency. They seem very, very happy.

By re-thinking his childhood experiences and behavior, Robert was able to work though difficult feelings about the past, and better understand his current fears and experiences. Understanding his history of separation anxiety helped him address his current panic over the very same issue—separation. He could also see how, as an adult, his fear of separation was closely related to his fear of becoming more intimate with Susan and growing more committed to the relationship. His difficult, vulnerable period following his parents' separation is similar to that of many other children of divorce, and his related adult symptoms demonstrate how the ramifications of divorce can continue to linger, beneath the surface, even for those who function very well in their adult lives.

Reflecting on Robert's childhood experiences recalls some of my own difficulties adjusting to my parents' divorce. Like Robert, I also feared abandonment as the next vignette reveals. And like Robert, I also responded to my parents' separation with another common symptom among children of divorce: rebellion. One of the toughest, most memorable periods of my parents' separation occurred when my sister and I were taken out of our summer day camp in Philadelphia and sent to stay with my mother's sister and her husband. As the following vignette points out, this difficult period is also when my rebelliousness reached its most obnoxious peak.

During the two years following my parents' separation, the perpetual disagreements between them built up and multiplied. By the time I was nine, the fighting reached its bitterest point. My mother decided she needed to send my sister and I out of town. We told her we would be very happy going to Camp Arrowhead in the Philadelphia suburbs. We were just starting to make new friends, and I was finally learning how to swim. We told her that we did not want to leave. We asked if we could please just stay with her. To our tremendous disappointment, she told us that we had seen and heard enough fighting and she was going to resolve this mess and get the "divorce papers signed, sealed and delivered, for once and for all." Why she needed us out of town to achieve this, I couldn't understand. I only knew that I wasn't happy about it.

We flew to Florida against our wishes to stay with her sister and brother-in-law, our Aunt Marla Sue and Uncle Fred. Kathyanne and I spent the following month and a half testing their tolerance and driving our unsuspecting aunt and uncle to the outer limits of their patience. I guess we had been under a lot of pressure at home. Also, Marla and Fred had no children of their own and were probably profoundly unprepared for the chaos we delivered to their peaceful, palm tree-shaded lives. Maybe any six and nine-year-old girls would have taxed their patience beyond its threshold, though I'll never know for sure. I do know that our eventual return to Philadelphia must have been one of the happiest days of their lives.

Their home was summer white on the outside and the inside reminded me of one big flower pot. I had never seen so many shades of orange. Orange sherbet sofas, charcoal orange tile floors, lion's mane rugs, and a pumpkin pie powder room. A trumpet-sized seashell adorned each side of their dense wooden front door, and the smell of thick wet sand implied that they lived close to the ocean, although this was not the case. I pretended that I was sent to Florida on assignment to work at Disney World. I prepared myself to play SnowWhite in the nightly parade and spent plenty of time rehearsing with my imaginary dwarfs.

In spite of my efforts to live within the castle walls of my fantasies about the Magic Kingdom, I arrived in Hollywood, Florida angry, lonely and ready to rage. Even our Uncle Fred's finest efforts to cheer us up enjoyed a limited and fleeting impact. Kathyanne and I had always enjoyed him. He threw us in the air and chased us around. His smiles unfolded easily and often, and he called me his princess. Best of all, he let me climb up his legs while I held each of his hands. I always leaned away from him and walked upwards, from his shins to his knees to his thighs, flipping myself over again and again. He called me "the human windmill" and let me go around and around until I became dizzy.

He taught us how to use all of the antique cash registers and piggy banks he and Aunt Marla collected as their hobby. I soon learned how to operate the shiny brass register displayed on the living room mantel that was way bigger than any of the others, and even bigger than their television. I spent hours inventing bills and prices and calculating imaginary transactions, trying to forget about all we were missing back at Camp Arrowhead, but wanting, deep down, to get out of this tropical holding pattern and go home. Poor Kathyanne soon grew bored with her role as the paying customer and made every effort to pull me away and find a new mode of entertainment.

To adjust to our abrupt arrival, our aunt and uncle took turns staying home from work to watch us. One afternoon when I was feeling particularly temperamental, I forced Kathyanne to play Monopoly, Parcheesi, Stratego and every board game under the steaming Florida sun. I beat her over and over, again and again. Our three-and-a-half-year age difference gave me an unsporting advantage. She didn't stand a chance. On this particular afternoon, I did not let her win every once in a while as my mother taught me I should. I knew better, but showed no mercy. I bought the "Boardwalk" from her (I already owned "Park Place") for thirty of those white one dollar bills and convinced her that was a great deal. She bought "Baltic Ave." from me and I charged her just four of those nifty yellow hundreds. No mercy. I was lonely for home, and I wanted my mother.

The brutal fact that we had been, to a strange extent, exiled, did not consciously cross my mind. Instead, I escalated my bad mood into bad behavior, and didn't care whom I pissed off. As much as my sister begged me to come play outside, I told her she had to *stay and keep playing the stupid board games. Finally, she began to cry and ran straight out the front door. I knew she wouldn't dare go far without me, so I shut the door with careless confidence and locked her out. I figured that was about the most obnoxious thing to do, so, without hesitating, I turned the swirly porcelain lock shaped like a sideways letter "s" and began walking the other way.*

"Let me in!" She quickly began to cry. "Please, Elisabeth, let me in…I'll play with you, whatever games you want, I promise." My merciless meanness was frightening. I had slowly but surely evolved into a miniature monster, and it wasn't pretty.

"You'll have to break in if you want to play with me," I declared. After a few minutes, her cries began to soften me a bit, so I added a new twist to the tension. "I know," I shouted out to her, "I'll unlock the door, but you'll still have to fight your way in okay? Let's see if you can do it, okay? It'll be fun!"

"Okay." Her tearful voice perked up a notch or two. We both began coming around to each other as we inevitably did after any period of drama and bickering. I unlocked the door but held the antique knob tightly between my pale, skinny hands.

"See if you can get in!" I shouted with excitement.

"I'm gonna," Kathyanne returned my enthusiasm and began to crack a laugh as we struggled. "You're gonna let me in!" The wooden door of their stately, terracotta, well-manicured home swayed slightly, as we continued our tug of war amidst genuine laughter. We were mutually thrilled to discover a new form of entertainment.

Earlier that summer, a friend from Camp Arrowhead had nicknamed Kathyanne "Down and Out" while granting me the title of "Long and Lean." Kathyanne's down and outness carried significant physical strength. I knew she'd soon make her way in, as her smaller yet solid frame carried more raw power than my own. Age was losing to determination as she began to wedge her way towards victory in our tug of war. At last, the win she so deserved was just around the corner. Then suddenly, without warning, the delicate and detailed doorknob broke free from the door and fell with Kathyanne straight and fast to the ground.

Kathyanne rose from the pavement quickly, brushed herself off and laughed for a moment until she turned and noticed the doorknob to her right. Kathyanne appeared just fine. The doorknob, on the other hand, had shattered into various antique pieces of screws and chips and painted porcelain, dirtying their doormat and disabling their door. We laughed awkwardly, looking around the living room, wondering what would happen next. *We knew that the shattered doorknob and lock-less door meant trouble. We also knew we were at a distinct, strategic advantage. As luck would have it, Aunt Marla was at her office, and our more forgiving, child-friendly Uncle Fred would be the one to receive the news about our destructive new form of fun. We called him down, and pointed towards the once elegant knob, now a victim of youthful frolic and ruin. We did our best to project our most innocent looks as we apologized.*

He looked less than thrilled, but managed to crack a smile as he told us we had just better try to get it fixed before Aunt Marla came home. If not, we'd really get it. We piled into the car and headed for some various locksmiths and whatever kind of stores sell delicate one-of-a-kind porcelain doorknobs. Racing against the clock was just the kind of excitement I had been looking for and longing to create. The three of us giggled and joked as we picked a substitute doorknob, found the right screws and bolts, and raced home to perform last minute surgery on the damaged door. Technically speaking, we succeeded, and repaired the door perfectly before Marla's return. On a more practical level, we failed with flying colors. Aunt Marla noticed the replaced doorknob immediately, and shared none of our amusement or enthusiasm about the afternoon's exploits.

"That's absolutely it!" She threw her hands into the humid air and escorted her anger towards the kitchen where she began feeding it white shelled pistachio nuts. She continued, "They are going to camp, I'm making some calls and they're going to camp TOMORROW! Do you hear me dammit. TOMORROW. I mean it Fred, that's it."

"I know, I know you mean it." Their mutually angry tone echoed a familiar sound and reminded me of home. Of my parents. Not simply the words of anger flowing between them, but the sense of exhausted experience with a life of constant fighting.

"That's just it."

"Okay, Marla, whatever you want." He turned and walked upstairs. I wanted to follow him but stayed paralyzed watching Marla and the pistachios. She threw the empty shells in the sink with one hand while grabbing full shells with the other. She held steadfast to her decision with the same determination she used to shell each nut. I continued staring at her in silence, devastated and defeated.

The next morning, Uncle Fred drove us, teary and terrified, to a local day camp somewhere on the outskirts of Hollywood.

"I'll be back at 3:30 to get you girls, okay? You'll be fine. And, who knows, you might even have some fun." He tried to reassure us as we cried and were shuttled off with

the other kids.

I clung to my uncle as he gently pushed me away from his suit leg and towards the other children. I remember the image of leaving him in the parking lot as if I left him there this morning. The mental picture continues to stand out as a symbolic memory of how I had changed since my parents separated. And how vulnerable I had become. Him standing stiffly in his dark blue suit, me clinging to him as he carefully guided me away, Kathyanne gracefully capturing the hand that Fred let go. I felt like I couldn't let him leave. Afraid that, if I did, I wouldn't see him later like he promised. I was afraid he'd forget to come back. Afraid that he'd break his promise and Kathyanne and I would be stuck somewhere on the random roadside in Florida, forced to fend for ourselves. During our sudden shipment south we had enjoyed playing with him. We felt homesick and con-fused. Our trips to his office or our adventures searching for doorknobs gave us necessary moments of distraction. We needed him and his patience and we didn't need this camp.

I'm not even sure if it was really a camp. It smelled much more like a gas station and I remember spending most of each day in a huge playground with no camp-like activities and next to no adult supervision. None of the organized sports, gymnastics or arts and crafts that filled our more protected experience back at Camp Arrowhead. And none of the friendly counselors with long braids and overalls who reminded me of the neighborhood babysitters my parents sometimes called when Norma was busy or on vacation. Instead, I remember a grisly old camp director named Mrs. Haggis. (Years later, I learned that "haggis" is also a Scottish delicacy consisting of calf lungs.) She had pink puffy sprayed hair and aqua eyelids and she seemed to despise children. In my memory, she looks like a sinister cross between a porn vixen and that puppet "Madame" from Hollywood Squares. A vision of her wide-open hand swiping an unsuspecting red headed child in the back of the head when he failed to clear his lunch tray is a defining memory from this truly bizarre pit-stop of a camp. I was determined to prevent Kathyanne from leaving my sight, even for a minute.

On our fifth or sixth day there, Kathyanne and I were playing together on the outskirts of the camp, sitting quietly on a remote patch of playground dirt, when a contingent of fashionably dressed girls approached and surrounded us. Most of them were wearing halter tops that were the same color as their shorts. I can't remember how many girls were included in the circle because the ringleader's presence takes up so much mental space. She was thin, blonde and naturally tan. Delicate blonde eyebrows perfectly framed her clear blue eyes. Clear, blue, confident ice. Her peach halter top had a strip of lace down the middle and she was as pretty as my favorite Barbie doll. I hoped foolishly for a moment that she was coming over to invite us to play. But the human Barbie wouldn't have been caught dead socializing with the likes of us.

"Hey you." She pointed at my neck. She couldn't point directly at my head, because it was trying to look away.

"Yes." I couldn't even look at her. Not only was she about to embarrass me, but the humiliation was going to occur in front of Kathyanne.

"We all want to know why you two are wearing those funny shorts."

"I —" I started to answer, then realized I had no idea what to say.

"You wore them yesterday and today and they're so ugly. Don't you know how to dress? Don't you know how to show your little look-alike here how to dress?" The cut-off denim look may be fashionable today, but our jean shorts were dark and stiff and super long, resting just above our knees. Interestingly, at our more upscale Philadelphia camp, fashion did not seem nearly as important as here along the dusty Florida highway. We stood before our campmates humiliated. Two pale and pathetic farmers.

"I don't know." My voice sounded washed out, timid and as thin as my thighs. I could hardly recognize myself. Kathyanne was picking up handfuls of dirt and letting it slide through her fingers. She carefully pretended not to notice the Barbie brigade, gazing steady on the dirt in her hand, my ugly jean shorts mirroring her own. "Come on." I reached for her dirty hand and she took it gently, as we walked away, timid but together, staring straight down.

To save money, my mother's friends had given her bags and more bags of their older children's outgrown clothing. I loved inheriting these hand-me-downs. Wearing my older playmates' used shorts and tee shirts and dresses made me feel close to them and connected to their recent history. It also made me feel older and adult-like in a positive, sophisticated sense. Nothing like the heavy adult sadness I felt when I learned of my parents' plans to separate. Becoming more grown up in the fashion arena felt liberating and hopeful. I may have resented my initiation into the dark and terrifying world of grown up sadness; but I adored my entrance into the world of big kid fashions. Each new world had opened up to me as a result of my parents' separation. The sadness I could do without, but the clothing I treasured. Knowing that this shirt or those shorts once belonged to my older neighborhood friends whom I looked up to in a big way, just imagining them wearing the clothes during their slightly more grown-up lives created an exciting mental image of maturity to come. Some of it may have been behind the ever evolving nineteen seventies pre-teen styles, and most of it must have been an exceptionally awkward fit for my undersized skinny self, but who cared? I never considered my fashion sense or lack of it. I felt perfectly stylish in my secondhand attires until this devastating moment. By humiliating us, the perfect Barbie girl was also humiliating our mother and her efforts to give to us while under terrible financial strain. The cruel Barbie's words contaminated my confidence in front of Kathyanne. And I hated the girl even more for contaminating the hand-me-down system that had been working so well for my mother and for us.

After a few more lonely days as a social outcast at this depressing camp, I was in much worse troublemaking shape than when we enrolled. I decided I was going to let Uncle Fred in on some of what we were learning during our fun-filled, unsupervised days. As camp closed up shop for the day, Uncle Fred pulled into the camp parking lot chatting away with one of his business associates from NCR who was sitting with him up in the front. Kathyanne and I piled into the back, ready as ever to hit the road.

"Hey girls," he greeted us cheerfully as he began to drive. "This is Mr. Grant. He works with a company that hires my company to help out with electronics." Uncle Fred shifted his gaze from us to Mr. Grant. They were both dressed in dark suits and I thought that Mr. Grant looked like Mr. Rogers. "Bob, I'd like you to meet my lovely little nieces Elisabeth and Kathyanne."

"Hi there girls. It's nice to meet you."

"Hi," Kathyanne and I said at the same time.

"How was camp?" Uncle Fred asked with upbeat energy. As if he hoped that his enthusiastic voice might increase our own enthusiasm about the camp.

"Good." Kathyanne pleasantly replied. To this day, when she is not up for a lengthy discussion, Kathyanne lets you know it. Regardless of whom she's talking to and what they are asking her about, she simply replies, "Good". Her agreeable but empty one word reply clarifies beyond reasonable doubt that all is well, but she's in no mood to elaborate. Uncle Fred and the Mr. Rogers guy smiled at how cute Kathyanne looked and sounded saying "good." And I sat quietly preparing to share a joke I picked up while dangling from the camp's rusty jungle gym earlier that day.

"Hey Uncle Fred," I stated.

"Yes sweetie," he answered in a perky wholesome voice as we continued along the highway.

"Why did Lee Majors kill the plumber?" I innocently asked.

"I don't know, why sweetie?"

"Because he screwed the wrong faucet! Ah ha ha! Get it? Isn't that funny? He screwed the wrong faucet!!!" Truth be told, I didn't get it. I knew it had something to do with the fact that Lee Majors, the six million-dollar bionic man, was married to Charlie's favorite angel, Farrah Faucett, but I definitely didn't get it. Still, I laughed cheerfully and repeated my punch line, "He SCREWED the wrong FAUCET!" The tires screeched and the car swerved out of our lane. My Uncle Fred's shocked eyes surged far from their sockets. The Mr. Rogers business guy buckled his lips and tried not to laugh. I knew I'd done something wrong. I knew that it was a bad joke to tell, so I told it with passion. I had no clue what it meant, but I had a feeling they got the joke even if I didn't. My vulgarity was intentional and effective while the joke's meaning escaped me completely. My attempt as a comedian marked the finale of our days at camp, and we were back to passing our time with Uncle Fred where I felt certain we belonged.

I never have quite lived that joke down, and for the following five or so years before he and Marla eventually divorced, Uncle Fred often greeted me by asking if I had any idea why on earth Lee Majors killed that ridiculous plumber.

My miscalculated cries for attention persisted. Two and a half years following my parents' separation, and six weeks following our deportation to Florida, my parents agreed to the terms of their divorce. The fact that the papers were finally served, signed, sealed and definitive made no difference. Our return from Florida made no difference. I couldn't stop.

Early that fall, my grade school class took an afternoon trip to the Philadelphia Free Library. We watched a movie about trains and listened to a lecture about the Dewey decimal system. Then each student tackled the assignment of picking a book from the card catalogue and finding it on our own. Imposing wooden rows of miniature drawers towered over our fourth grade class as we scurried about flipping through titles in search of a desirable book. I chose Roald Dahl's Charlie and the Great Glass Elevator. My *father read many of Dahl's books to Kathyanne and me, and we'd been saving this one for last. My dad had a rule that entailed a refusal to buy us toys in exchange for an enthusiastic willingness to buy us any book we wanted. I knew he was planning to buy this one for us, but I didn't feel like waiting. We all lined up around the checkout stand and took turns flashing the librarians our newly acquired membership cards. Each student checked out a book and stepped outside, and our teachers began lining us up in twos and preparing for the chilly walk back to school. As they led the way, I turned to my friends Liz and Melissa and found myself talking them into a little adventure.*

Why not explore an alternative route from the library to the school? I felt easily confident that our inefficient teachers were taking us out of the way, pointing out various fountains and statues here and there. It was too cold to be wasting our time seeing sites, and I grew determined to follow my own route back from Logan Circle to 25th and Lombard. Liz and Melissa eventually agreed, reluctant yet willing, to my charming little plan. So, when no one was looking, we slowed down and ran behind a large and conveniently located stairwell. The rest of the class continued on without us.

A strange thrill possessed me, and I couldn't resist the excitement of leaving the group. Branching out on our own on this clear and crispy autumn afternoon provided a false sense of independence. Something like the first time our parents let Kathyanne and me go to a restaurant by ourselves. We were staying at the Diplomat Hotel in Florida, where all visiting children wore plastic photo identification name tags at all times. Our parents were sitting at the pool just outside the restaurant, and gave us permission to go in and order our own burgers and fries. All we needed was the room key, they explained. A full-length window enabled them to keep an eye on us throughout the meal. Between our photographs and names pinned on our bathing suits, and our parents monitoring through the glass, we weren't exactly on our own. But the thrill possessed us nonetheless. How mature and sophisticated we felt ordering and enjoying our lunches, and requesting our chocolate milkshakes <u>during</u> the meal rather than afterwards!

The thrill of skipping out on our class had both a sense of independence and defiance attached to it. My parents hadn't given me permission as they had back at the hotel. But the same sensations of conquer and pseudo-maturity made it impossible to care about the consequences. And impossible to turn back to the class once Liz and Melissa expressed that they felt less enthusiastic and actually quite tentative. Determined to sell them on our misbehavior, I assured them that our decision was an excellent one and to just follow me. To trust me with this precious once-in-a-lifetime opportunity to bust out. We cut through the park, chased some pigeons, and pooled our change so we could stop at the corner store for some ice cream. We forgot all about the cold as our crime generated heat from within. Our autonomy was as liberating as it was ridiculous. At least my autonomy was liberating. In retrospect, Liz and Melissa were well-intended, misguided victims of peer pressure.

While they hesitated with every step, and even had difficulty choosing an ice cream flavor, I savored each and every rebellious minute. Who needed the teachers to tell us which way to walk? Making such decisions for one's self felt far more self-satisfying. Surely we were entitled to this little slice of autonomy. We strolled the city streets through Rittenhouse Square, and my friends began to relax a bit and share my enthusiasm. By the time we reached the school, drippy ice-cream cones in-hand, we were pleased to find that we had beaten the group. We soon discovered the less pleasurable information that our worried teachers had taken the entire class back to the library to look for us and had telephoned our principal in a panic.

Before we knew it, our parents had been contacted, and the group of furious teachers and annoyed classmates arrived having concluded their two hour journey back to the school. The excitement and freedom of our joyride of a walk home was fading fast, slipping away before our embarrassed eyes. I was sweating and queasy and dreading the thought of my mother's reaction to all of this commotion I had suddenly stirred. Liz and Melissa refused to look at me as I apologized and quietly told the principal that it was all my fault.

"You may have encouraged this," she looked down at us, standing and waving her angry adult index finger attached to a long red nail. We sat uncomfortably around the thick grey formica table in her office looking up at her as she continued. "But it takes three to tango, young lady." Her big angry voice was agitating my nine-year-old nerves. We received some sort of school sanctioned punishment. A punishment then embellished by our respectively perturbed families. I can't recall the specifics of my discipline, though I do recall spending the evening in my room feeling horribly guilty and embarrassed. I remember asking myself why I had caused such unprovoked trouble for my class and my friends. I had about as little insight into my actions as I had on that afternoon in Florida when I described, while *having little or no idea what on Earth I was talking about, how Lee Majors had killed the plumber for screwing the wrong "Faucet". In both cases, I knew my dismissive actions would anger others. But, like the chocohalic Augustus Gloop visiting Willy Wonka's factory and diving into the forbidden chocolate sea, I simply couldn't help myself.*

When reflecting upon my own childhood, it seems pretty clear that my own episodes of misbehavior grew out of a reaction to my parents' separation. Their conflicts caused my sister and me pain, which I expressed by behaving badly. At the same time, re-living these experiences from an adult perspective generates new insights into my childhood. For example, it is revealing to me that I felt safe enough to misbehave. My parents were going through an awful time, but I knew, deep down, that I was loved unconditionally. This knowledge gave me room to rebel and express my feelings about the separation in a manner which reflected that I, too, was going through a really difficult time. I caused a lot of trouble and my unruly behavior is clearly evidence of the downfalls of divorce. However, it has been essential to my adult happiness that I re-visit and re-tell these stories to include the character building evidence that I felt loved and protected enough to express myself and mirror my parents' turbulent process of adjustment.

Reflecting on who you were as a child will help you Face the Mirror and examine what traits and patterns are not working for you as an adult. As you re-think your childhood experiences and behavior, make sure that you take good care of yourself. Find a quiet, safe, space to follow the tips and suggestions contained in this book. Take your time, and make sure that you discuss your observations with a person you trust if you cannot discuss the material with either parent. Ideally, you should discuss the results of the tips and suggestions with <u>both</u> parents. If you cannot discuss your findings with either parent, <u>or</u> with a trusted friend, please consider counseling in order to safely complete this phase of the Five Step Guide. A mental health professional can help you by being a supportive sounding board and providing insights as you take the necessary steps to overcome the ramifications of your parents' divorce on your life and relationships. If you <u>can</u> talk with a parent or a friend about the material you review during this step, but you find that you are very unsettled by what you learn, or if you experience symptoms such as sleep disturbance, loss of appetite, mood fluctuations, anxiety, or difficulty concentrating, you should also seek professional help in order to safely complete this step. The next exercises can be painful and unsettling. You need a solid support system in order to get the most out of this book and in order to take good care of yourself.

Tips and Suggestions:

- Write down your memories of how you learned that your parents were separating. Ask yourself: How old were you? Where were you? How were you told....or not told? Were you surprised?
- Make a list of the ways that you remember responding to your parents' separation. How did you react? How did you change? How did your siblings react? How did your siblings change?
- Make a list of anything that you remember regarding how your parents and any other parent figures responded to the ways that you and your siblings changed and/or reacted to your parents' separation.
- Read all of your writing about these memories aloud, then read the lists aloud and write down all of the feelings that came up while you were reading.
- If possible, discuss these memories and the feelings they bring up with either or both parents. Remember, you are the best judge of whether or not your relationship with your parents can sustain such discussions. If they can, talk to them! If you know or fear that they cannot, write each parent a letter detailing everything you remember and how it makes you feel. Even if you do not feel comfortable sending the letters, you can read them aloud to someone that you trust. Expressing these feelings, whether to your parents directly or in the form of a letter, will free up important energy that you can then direct toward taking the subsequent steps.

chapter four

■

PINPOINT HOW YOUR
PARENTS' DIVORCE
AFFECTS YOU
AS AN ADULT

■

The second phase of Step Two focuses on pinpointing how your parents' divorce affects you in adulthood and what you need to change in order to have a happier adult life. In order to answer this question, you must Face the Mirror and discover the underlying pattern or patterns that characterize your failed relationships ("your relationship M.O."). What leftover remnants from the pain of your past are carrying over into the present and repeatedly affecting how you select partners and experience relationships?

As other respected research on adults with divorced parents has already proven, many adults with divorced parents are consciously hesitant to commit. The survey results fully conform to these findings. Joelle, a twenty-six-year-old respondent whose parents separated when she was seventeen, stated:

> I'm very skeptical about the institution of marriage...so many people are unhappy in their marriages but stay in them because they're afraid to leave...I just got out of an almost four year relationship, and, for the most part, it was wonderful, but I knew that I didn't want to spend the rest of my life with him. I don't really romanticize marriage in the way many people do. While I still believe

in finding "the one" and having a good marriage, I don't have a sense of urgency to find this, and I am very happy alone.

Barbara, a happily married subject who wed at age forty, explained:

I believe that it took me longer to be prepared to be in a permanent relationship...I learned that I only wanted to be with a man whom I would defend and speak highly of to people, someone that I could respect.

Edward, a happily married subject whose parents separated when he was eleven, shared a similar response:

I think [my parents' divorce] is why I married later in life. I'm much more mindful not to do the things my parents did. I try to be much more hands-on with my kids.

Julianne, a happily married subject whose parents separated when she was ten, reflected on her mother's influence and explained:

My mother hammered into my head not to marry early or make her mistakes. I'm just very aware.

These subjects represent the many adults with divorced parents who are aware of how their history makes them hesitant to commit. But fear of commitment is often more complicated than a conscious reluctance to take a healthy relationship to the next level. It can also involve a pattern of choosing flawed relationships and trying, at times desperately, to save them. If one succeeds in prolonging the relationship, then one remains in a dysfunctional situation where intimacy is impossible. The unconscious goal is achieved, as genuine commitment does not occur. If one fails (as is usually inevitable), the breakup can be interpreted as evidence of personal flaws or defects, thus perpetuating an illusion that one simply is not cut out for an intimate, satisfying relationship. So, again, commitment is out of the picture. As we have already discussed, people who follow this pattern may tell themselves (and others) that they <u>embrace</u> commitment, as they try so hard to make their relationships work. However, trying to save a relationship with an unsuitable partner is not a form of embracing commitment—it is a form of <u>avoiding</u> intimacy.

I vividly remember my sessions with Darla, a brilliant doctoral student who explained that she was eager to help her overwhelmed mother and filled multiple roles in her household after her parents separated. During therapy, she revealed her primary adult symptom:

> I'm still too darn eager to please! I experience each date as if I am being interviewed and I'm willing to do anything and everything just to get the job. Why can't I be the INTERVIEWER for a change?!?

Similarly, I worked for many months with Latisha, a gorgeous science teacher whose father struggled with terrible depression following his divorce. He remained depressed for years and only seemed happy during the brief periods when he was dating someone. This client felt terrible guilt about her father's depression and pinpointed how her parents' divorce affected her as an adult when she admitted to sharing some of her father's traits:

> Boyfriends are my anti-depressants. The worse the relationship becomes, the more things deteriorate, the more willing I am to make it work. Then when it ends—and believe me, it always ends—that's when the depression hits hard.

These clients, like many of the survey subjects, reveal a strong urge to please romantic partners, even when the relationship is clearly not working. In other words, they over-commit to unavailable partners. Whether you fall into the pattern of consciously hesitating to commit, over-committing to unavailable partners, or any other pattern in relationships that is not working for you, it is essential that you take a clear look in the mirror and admit what your patterns are and what aspects of these patterns you need to change.

Years ago, I worked with Martha, a recent college graduate. Facing the Mirror and pinpointing how her parents' divorce affected her in adulthood was central to her process of developing enough self-respect to take better care of herself and, eventually, to choose better relationships.

As I worked with Martha, I gained many insights into the difficulties adult children of divorce face. Therapists are generally trained to talk less, and listen more. We are taught to allow the client the safety and space to figure out their own answers. The goal is to communicate an underlying message that the client can become his or her own therapist and take the therapeutic process out of the therapist office and into their lives. I follow this rule, but get the sense that I am still more talkative than the typical therapist. The amount of talking I do tends to vary from client to client.

Martha was a recent college graduate and a poet, and I was struck by the way she was able to sort through her struggles with little or no intervention from me. She looked the part, with long wavy curls flowing behind her as she strolled into my office, rings on each finger and each thumb, and funky black clothing from head to toe. Martha explained that she was initiating therapy because her boyfriend, Sammy, had cheated on her, and she didn't know what to do.

When I asked about her relationship history, it turned out that all of Martha's previous boyfriends had cheated on her, but she lacked awareness of her part in the problem through choosing the cheaters. Her parents had separated when she was five and her mother discovered that her father was having an affair with his secretary. Interestingly, her parents never divorced and remained married, living separate lives. Her father stayed involved in Martha's life, but on a limited basis, while having two more children with his secretary. Martha's mother remained single, did not date, and had dinner with Martha's father every year at Christmas and on her and Martha's birthdays.

Martha and I spent weeks Re-Writing her Story. During this time, we discussed her memories about her parents' marriage and their eventual separation. Martha needed to explore both her feelings about her father's infidelity and his second family, and about her mother's choosing a man like her father in the first place. In addition, Martha explored the confusing, painful reality that her mother had not asked for a divorce. Martha explained that part of why she wanted to stay with her cheating boyfriend was because her mother really liked him and he helped her mother do projects around the house. Martha's mother told Martha that Sammy was a good guy. She told Martha to stop questioning his whereabouts. Martha explained that when her father "worked" until two in the morning on a regular basis, her mother never questioned a thing. From Martha's perspective, her father's professional success and ability to provide financially filled the void left by his physical absence. Martha's mother had "nothing to worry about in the money department" and she focused on her financial security and the material benefits that went along with it. Martha eloquently summarized the messages her mother gave her about relationships with men as "a bad relationship is better than no relationship." Once Martha had fully explored her past, she began to Face the Mirror. When we discussed what it was like, going off to college, Martha described how hard it was to leave her mother behind. She then recounted, in her poetic style, a freshman year experience that helped Martha begin to pinpoint how her parents' divorce was weighing her down.

"I tell you, from the beginning, college felt overwhelming, isolating and odd. I missed my mom and hated picturing her all alone in the house. One of my first conversations at the school that lasted longer than three minutes occurred when I ran into my freshman English professor near my dorm. We had had our first class earlier that day, and there he was alone on a bench, looking long, thin and significantly bizarre."

"Bizarre in what sense? Can you give an example?"

"Well, the thin skin beneath his eyes was wrought-iron black, and he wore this pale, tired clothing. Everything about him seemed desperate and afraid. His face was angular and much too long. He called to me from the bench, by name, which surprised me because we'd only had one class. He never looked at me head on. But I'm telling you, from that day forward, throughout the first semester, I constantly felt his leering stare. I'm telling you, I SHIVERED with discomfort when he stopped me to say hello. But, then again, I had been shivering with discomfort throughout the whole weird week of orientation. Missing my mom, feeling like I deserted her, and I kept trying, desperately, to pull myself out of my shell. I had this great English teacher back in high school. He totally encouraged me and got me into poetry. So, I figured, why not give this English professor guy half a chance? My gut told me he was bad news and to avoid him. But there I was, accepting his invitation for a walk through campus."

Martha looked at me as she took a breath and slowly exhaled. I was struck, as usual, by the vivid details of Martha's descriptions as she painted a rich and disturbing portrait of her professor.

"Go on, continue," I proclaimed.

"Well, he was just strange, plain and simple." Martha held a coffee cup as she continued. She held the cup in one hand while she twisted the brown paper cup holder back and forth with the other hand as she spoke. "He looked much younger than most of the other professors, but old in his posture. Bent over, and drained. And he told me that he was new to the school, so then I wondered if his oddness was merely an extension of the same nervous jitters inhibiting me. Maybe he had my same trouble being the new kid and wouldn't normally seem so weird. I tried to give him a chance and ignored my sense that he was a total creep. We walked and chatted and he asked me to take a look at a draft of his incomplete reading list for our course. I gave some thoughtless, fleeting, uneducated suggestions. I suggested authors I had heard of, but knew nothing about. Or authors I'd already read. Eventually, after over an hour of conversation, I excused myself and pretended I had plans to meet friends in the cafeteria. He asked for my phone number and I lied and said I didn't yet know it by heart."

"So you ignored your instincts to avoid him all together, but you followed you instincts to say no about the phone number."

"Yeah, at least I knew that much. As I walked away, I tried to forget the strangeness of our conversation. I knew a boundary had been violated, but I pretended I was just imagining and overreacting. I'm telling you, I should have IMMEDIATELY scheduled a meeting with a dean and asked to switch classes. Better yet, I should have said something to someone. But what would I say? 'My professor is odd looking and a freak, give me a new one? Better yet, fire him?' Instead, I pushed the incident out of my mind." Every once in a while, Martha would project her voice with added volume and dramatic flair. IMMEDIATELY popped out of her description as if she were presenting at a poetry slam.

"It's worth noting that you could have tried to switch classes but didn't. Maybe you could have told the dean that you weren't comfortable with his asking for your phone number," I interjected.

"Good point, why didn't I think of that?"

"Well, why didn't you? Why do you think you knew a boundary was violated, but you didn't address it?"

"Good question. Probably because I grew up without many limits and without much *guidance in the boundary department. I KNEW that it wasn't right that my father stayed out as late as he did, but no one else seemed to have a problem with it. I was allowed to sleep at my boyfriend's house by the time I was fifteen, and he could stay at my house as well. Deep down, I KNEW it was wrong, but my friends thought it was so cool, so I just went with it. I focused on the coolness of it all, kind of like how my mother focused on the nice cars and fancy jewelry. But, back to my professor, it gets way weirder. When I arrived in his class the following Tuesday, it turned out that he had structured the reading list to meet many if not most of my uneducated and erratic suggestions. I was TOTALLY uncomfortable."*

"And how did you deal with your discomfort?"

"I'll tell you how I dealt with it, I blamed myself. I wondered what I did wrong. Had I been wearing an inappropriate outfit? Was my lipstick too bright? Were my efforts to look New York-y and fit in giving off the wrong vibe? Did I say something or do something suggestive that inspired his obscure and subtle yet highly disturbing flirtation? Was it even a flirtation? I couldn't figure it out. In retrospect, it seems obvious that I should have done something."

"Since you are mentioning something obvious from your past, I'm wondering if that obviousness can apply to anything in your present."

"You mean is there something now that's obvious? Oh, I get it. It's obvious that I should dump Sammy. But I don't. Why is that?"

"I don't know. Why is that?"

"I must REALLY lack confidence. Confidence to know that professor creepo was out of line. And confidence to give Sammy his walking papers. I KNOW that, but I can't DO anything about it."

"It's one thing to know something intellectually. And we can't change without our intellectual insights. But it is another thing all together to feel it in your heart and to act on it."

"That's it EXACTLY. I KNOW it, but I don't FEEL it."

"So what do you feel?"

"I FEEL that a bad relationship is better than no relationship. I FEEL it and I want it to stop. I mean, back to the creepo professor, I didn't say or do a thing. Instead, I just tried to ignore and avoid him throughout the semester. I knew each student was required to meet with him individually, but I put the meeting off until the professor called my

name in class and explained that I needed to schedule a meeting before the fast approaching deadline for the final term paper. The thought of being alone in a room with him gave me stomach pains. Being in class with him was bad enough. My gut instincts knew without question that he was extremely odd and out of line. Still, I ignored myself. I ignored my intuition and scheduled an appointment."

Martha's breathing was growing louder, and she bit her lower lip in a hesitant pause. I became a bit concerned about pushing too hard.

"Do you feel comfortable talking about the meeting? Or is it too much right now?"

"No, it's important, I want to do it. I arrived in his office with my books, my pens, my class notes and literally PUSHED myself into the room as all better judgment begged me to turn around. He looked up from his newspaper and stood for a moment before sitting. His hair was greasier than usual and his khaki pants seemed rattier. He had the tired look of a washed up hippie who had marched in one too many peace marches. Seriously, his griminess looked alive and contagious and I worried about catching it from him just by being stuck in a room all alone with it. He and his greasy head loomed closer as I squirmed in my chair. He squinted slowly and stared at me without speaking. His eyes looked angry and longing, like a child banned from dessert. Sitting here now, Elisabeth, remembering him after years of trying to forget him, I think of that transsexual murderer in the film Silence of the Lambs. Remember that character?"

"Yes, I do."

"That twisted straggly-haired skin collector who kept young innocent girls in a ditch, starving them and preparing them for slaughter. So he says in his sleazy voice 'Well, you've gotten around to meeting with me after all, thanks for fitting me in. How's it going?'"

Martha continued her heavy breathing as she recounted the scene, word by word. She used her intuitive dramatic skills to distinguish her words from his, making herself sound meek and helpless while he sounded like a whispering lion, ready to pounce.

"He slid his chair from behind the desk and moved it closer to mine. 'Oh nothing.' I said, or something like that, 'I mean, fine, it's going fine. Just busy I guess.' His sense of personal space lacked any regard for my own, as his lanky body leaned forward. 'I see.' In case you are wondering, he smelled like an ashtray soaking in cheap cologne. I wanted to puke and was dying for our meeting to just be over already. 'I have this terrible urge to kiss you, or at least date you, and I haven't been able to shake it.' I sat straight in my

maroon leather chair feeling as wooden as its weathered frame. Had he just said what I thought I heard him say, or was I having a nightmare?"

"You must have been terrified."

"Now that's an understatement. *He just went on talking as if I agreed with him."* Martha bravely continued. *"'It's frustrating, you know. I'm the youngest male instructor at the college, a woman's college, mind you. Plus, I'm new, so they watch me like hawks, you know. I don't have the doctorate, but I've published at a young age, so they hired me and, you know, warned me about getting involved with students. But I feel like we made this incredible connection right from the beginning, I see it in your eyes and that kind of chemistry doesn't just happen every day.' Obviously, I'm not getting this right, word for word, but I do remember he kept saying 'you know' and I just wanted him to stop! Especially because I didn't know. I didn't have the slightest CLUE what he was talking about or how to get the hell out of the room and as far away from him as possible. The way he described himself as so young and being watched like a hawk—it felt like he was flipping things all around. As if he was excusing his behavior by describing his problems. I swear, that happens to me all the time."*

"What happens?"

"I listen to someone's excuses for crappy behavior, and I blame myself. I tell myself the situation is my fault, and I let it go on for too long. So then he says, 'Well, what do you say?' I didn't know what in the world to say to that, so, with sweat running down my neck, my trembling hands gathered up my un-discussed term paper notes and dropped my pens. He reached to pick them up, as his head fell far too close to my knees. I stood up quickly and bolted out of the room."

"Did you talk to anyone about what happened?"

"Come to think about it, I have never mentioned it to anyone, until now. I was so ashamed, and again, what could I say? My creepo professor bent his head down too close to my knees?"

"Well, what if you had complained to a dean about all of it, the reading list, his desire to date you, the whole thing."

"Honestly, I can look back and see how I should have, but it didn't even occur to me at the time. The fact that I was a paying customer attending one of the most expensive schools in the world never even crossed my insecure mind! I mean he hadn't done anything, really. But, on the other hand, he had. I missed the remaining two classes of* *the semester and left a half-written term paper in his mailbox. I received an A minus in the class and started spending more time at home. I hated the college and do wonder if I might have felt differently about the whole thing if my freshman English experience could be magically erased from my first semester memories. For sure, the humiliation about the whole mess didn't help my struggle to fit in and adjust to college life. He never once touched me, though I had a clear feeling he was about to. If I'd stayed in the room, he probably would have. What was the matter with him? What was the matter with me? Did he think I encouraged him? Did something happen to him? Did I make it happen by going on that walk through campus? Why didn't I follow my instincts from the beginning and switch classes?"*

"If you step back and analyze yourself, why didn't you follow your instincts and switch? Why do you think you didn't do something to protect yourself from him?"

"I can see it now, okay, the way my mother doesn't like herself enough to get a divorce already. The way I don't like myself enough to leave Sammy. The way it never occurred to me to talk to someone and do something about the professor from hell. You want to hear the worst part? He got fired the next year for harassing another student!"

"Well, if you can see it, you can eventually do something about it."

"God, I hope so."

Martha worked hard to explore how, following her parents' divorce, her mother lacked the self-esteem to divorce her father and build a new life. Instead, her mother communicated the message "a bad relationship is better than no relationship" and Martha internalized this message and acted on it in her own adult relationships. By acknowledging this relationship between her parents' divorce, her mother's lack of self-esteem, and her own, Martha Faced the Mirror and could begin to work to change her self-destructive choices and behavior. Her mother was not thrilled when she left Sammy, but Martha insisted that she deserved a faithful boyfriend. She eventually pushed herself to date guys who were nice to her. Interestingly, the happier Martha became, the more her mother was forced to look in her own mirror and eventually divorce Martha's father. Once Martha was happier and respected herself, she built a more independent life, and spent less time coddling her mother through her loneliness. As a result, Martha's mother lost a paralyzing crutch. Today, Martha is happily married and works as a reporter for a newspaper. In her spare time, she continues to write beautiful poetry.

Martha's inability to address her professor's harassment was symbolic of how she lacked self-confidence, both in herself and in her relationships. As the vignette reveals, Martha traced how this lack of self-confidence was connected to her parents' divorce, her father's subsequent absence, and her mother's unspoken but pronounced message "a bad relationship is better than no relationship." Martha worked hard to Face the Mirror and pinpoint the difficult and relevant truth that her parents' divorce and its fallout had caused low self-esteem and great difficulty with respect to advocating for herself.

I vividly remember the first time that I, personally, Faced the Mirror and took ownership of how my parents' divorce was affecting me as an adult. I was finishing graduate school, and my devastation about being dumped by a boyfriend combined with my over-responsibility for juggling my various family members during the graduation ceremony took over what should have been a joyous and celebrated occasion.

I was twenty-five and graduating with a Master's Degree in Social Work from the University of Pennsylvania. An unimportant relationship had ended a couple of weeks before graduation. Unimportant from the perspective created by time, yet critical in the midst of the breakup. My boyfriend had dumped me, telling me he wasn't ready for a serious relationship. He said he had the feeling I was getting too serious (he was right) and thought it was better just to call it quits. A devastating blow to my tentative ego. It certainly wasn't the first time I'd been disappointed in the romance department. And whether I'd been the one to end it, or whether the guy was the one to pull the relational plug, the final result was always the same. During the weeks following this breakup, as with any other breakup, I felt numb, alone and heartsick. No matter how excited I should have been about graduating and beginning a challenging new job, all in the same week, I felt like a total failure. Twenty-five and all washed up. All washed up with no hope for the husband, kids, home, happily ever after package of my dreams. No matter how many times my mother glowed as she told me how proud I made her, I could not locate or experience this pride in myself. Twenty-five years earlier, my mother had graduated from the same social work program at the same school.

"What a tribute that you chose this profession and this wonderful school. I

couldn't feel more proud, you're growing so much and you don't even see it."In retrospect, my mother was correct on all three counts. For sure, her many professional accomplishments, her book, her private practice, her years as a newspaper columnist and her love for her career as a social worker had indeed inspired me to follow in her footsteps and choose social work as my profession. Also, as she said, I may have been "growing". Sadly, however, she was right, I couldn't see it. "Shrinking" resonated as a far more suitable term.

My mother and I sat together in the living room on the night before graduation as she continued to try to comfort me. "Really, Elisabeth, try to see all of the good things. You're young and smart, with wonderful friends, a new job, a family who loves you. And you have the kind of independence I never had. Really. It's much better to grow up and get your life together before you get married. Try to see that. I was just a child when I married your father, and you don't need to make that same mistake. The world's so different today."

"So why do I feel so terrible? And every time another friend gets married, I feel even worse. Even more left out. It just seems easier for everybody else and I can't imagine it ever happening for me."

"Listen, you have your whole life to get married. It's more important that you figure out what's got you so upset. Because you know it's not really about the guy. You didn't even know him. You didn't even give yourself time to figure out how you felt about him, you know, to see whether it was real. It takes time to get to know each other."

"You and Stan didn't take much time to get to know if it was real."

"That was different, Elisabeth, we were both much older and more than ready to find life partners."

"I'm ready to find a partner. I am, it just never ever works out."

"Part of you is ready, but part of you is trying too hard and not making good choices." She spoke soft and straight, interspersing my sobs.

"How was I supposed to know? When we first met he said he never felt this way before and he took me on so many nice dates. He said I was perfect. How was I supposed to know he didn't want a serious relationship?"

"Sometimes we really want things to work and we don't see the signs. Really, I did the same thing with your father. I should have seen that it never could have worked. But in those days you had to get married. All of my friends were already married, there was so much societal pressure and I just didn't see the signs." She paused and took a deep

breath, as she tried to make eye contact with my downward glance. I wished with desperation that she could refrain from bringing my father into the mix. She may have had obvious, valid reasons for doing so, but it irked me nonetheless. "I guess you really thought it was right. And I'm so sorry he hurt you like this. I can't stand for you to be hurting this way." I continued to cry, hoping that my mother could say something to make the breakup disappear and reverse itself back into the relationship. Whether it was a good relationship or not. Whether we knew each other or not. "Please, Elisabeth, this is not about the guy. You hardly knew him. It's simply not about the guy." More of the unwanted truth I remained unable to hear.

"It is about the guy, mother. Please don't try to tell me that this is about my father and the divorce. Everything with my father is fine and this situation, right here, right now, is most definitely about the guy. And about how no relationship ever works out and I end up feeling so excluded. At least when you were with my father the two of you had a social life together. I know it was a bad marriage, and I'm sorry you had to go through all of that. But you met people through him and the two of you had plans on the weekends with other married couples. You had children together and you were a part of things. Seriously, at this point, I'd take a bad marriage over feeling like this, I don't care. Anything's better than being alone all of the time."

"Elisabeth. Listen to me. You don't even sound like yourself. You're so much stronger than this. Really. What happened to the little girl who told me to get my act together and stop begging your father to come back? What happened to the passionate child who demanded I stop feeling sorry for myself and gave me the strength and courage to go on during the most terrifying time in my life? And where's my beautiful daughter who led her classmates home from school on her own path rather than follow the teachers? I couldn't help but be so proud of you for that. Of course I couldn't say it at the time, but secretly I smiled and shouted to myself 'now that's my girl!!' You were going to follow your own drummer no matter what. Please remember yourself. You have so much passion in you and don't you let this guy or any guy take that away." I looked down and found myself holding the wooden arm of my chair. Grabbing onto one of the many pieces of furniture my mother had found to replace the things that were split up in their divorce agreement. Clasping. Holding on and desperate for some sense of stability. For some semblance of grounding. Like I'd seen my mother hold on so hard and so often, so many years before. Her past perfectly reflected in my present sadness, refusing to admit that this

major outpour of emotion was clearly and comprehensively not about the guy.

I completely ignored my total failure to consider how I felt about him. All that mattered was how he felt about me. Or, more accurately, how he said he felt about me. I chose one wrong relationship after another and assumed that my necklace of breakups represented evidence of a profound personal defect. Looking back to this, or any failed relationship, I can see that the guys who pulled away from me did so for very real and solid reasons. They were not people with whom I could have built a mutually satisfying relationship. We usually wanted very different things. Only I never gave myself a chance to consider whether our values and dreams (not to mention our personalities) were compatible. I was way too caught up with wondering what was wrong with me and why I couldn't make it work. Just as my mother and father looked great on the surface but had nothing in common and were never right for each other in the first place. I was forcing myself to repeat a pattern of choosing men who would obviously disappoint me and choosing relationships that were clearly never right from the beginning.

When things didn't work out, and we didn't live happily ever after as I irrationally expected, I forced myself to relive, again and again, the pain associated with my parents' divorce. Always trying to make up for lost, irretrievable time. Always trying to work through my sadness by reliving it. Looking for a guy and a relationship to fill me up and take away the pain. Never allowing myself to look beyond the deteriorating situation at hand and consider ways to build contentment and happiness from within.

Most of my family came to the college to celebrate graduation day the following morning. A perfectly clear, crisp day and everyone was there for me. My mother, Stan, my stepsister, Lizz, Kathyanne, my classmate and friend, Louise, who had graduated the previous year. My mother's overly enthusiastic group arrived two hours early to get good seats. My father, Susan, and my step-brother, Matthew, also came, offering equally high levels of praise and encouragement from the other end of the auditorium. Cheerful, loving family favor supported me from every corner of the room. I counted to myself and questioned my unrelenting sadness, as the graduates began lining up along the stairwell just outside the auditorium.

"One… two…three…eight people all together. Eight people whom I love and who have offered unguarded, limitless support. Why do I feel so lonely surrounded by so much love? Why do I feel so depressed when I should be feeling pleasure and pride?" I wished

I could just snap my fingers and stop myself from focusing on the tension between my parents, and derive some happiness from the celebration at hand.

Students lined up in alphabetical order, preparing to walk into the auditorium. Adjusting our caps and flipping through our programs, we awaited together in a state of collective anticipation. Depressed and spaced-out, I floated through the line searching for my proper alphabetical place. I saw from the program that I would walk behind Tasha Conley. I knew her from my professional practice class last semester, though we had never really talked. We held brief, academic exchanges when our class broke off into the small process groups so common and integral to the social work educational method. All about process and group dynamics. We said "hi" to each other when passing in the hall. But we had never exchanged a conversation independent from our assigned mini group discussions on such topics as what we thought was a key point of a particular chapter or how we viewed our "professional function" in a given clinical scenario.

A few weeks before graduation, I showed up for practice class and took my usual seat in the middle of the long table, just across from Tasha's usual seat on the opposite side. I noticed Tasha's absence as I took my seat. Her non-appearance seemed strange since it was our review session prior to finals, and she rarely, if ever, missed class. Our professor began the class by addressing Tasha's absence and announcing that her father had passed away over the weekend.

"He had been sick for a long time, and was in his seventies," Professor Lowe delicately explained. "I spoke with her yesterday and she seems to be doing okay considering the circumstances." A classmate seated next to me began shaking her head and gazing down at the chipped formica table.

"I can't believe it," she whispered quietly but loud enough for those seated on either side of her to hear, "I've known her since orientation. Her mother died just last year. She was in my research class and I remember when it happened. I can't even imagine."

I hadn't seen Tasha since Professor Lowe's announcement and wasn't quite sure if I should say anything. "Perhaps a moment before the procession isn't the right time. I'll say something later, or write her a note." I advised myself as I looked for my spot in line.

Tasha was already in her place and I whispered an awkward hello. It's difficult to describe how she looked. Words cannot quite convey her. An understated and dignified beauty sparkled from within and highlighted her from the rest of our group. She lifted her chin slightly, looking eager yet content. She stood perfectly still, yet the space around her moved with borderless energy. An inner and expectant glow reflecting outward. Refined pride glowing peacefully, as groups of students around her chatted in small circles, laughing about their hangovers from the night before, and discussing post-graduation plans. Tasha returned my hello and I asked her if she was planning to stay in Philadelphia. I felt sad for her, but she didn't seem a bit sad for herself, and I didn't know what else to say. She said she planned to move to Pittsburgh where she knew a couple of people. I told her a bit about my new job managing a Justice Department grant to try to improve the community response to child abuse. She congratulated me, and I asked her if she had plans for later in the evening. I planned to have an early dinner with my father, Susan, Matthew and Kathyanne at Friday Saturday Sunday, a hip but fancy local restaurant. Then, Kathyanne and I would leave a bit early and hook up with our mother, Stan and Lizz for a late dinner at the Garden, locally famous for its Dover sole, profiteroles and elegantly landscaped outdoor dining space.

Tasha answered me in an upbeat and matter-of-fact tone.

"Well, my friend from college came in last night. She's the only one who could make it." Tasha adjusted her cap and fiddled with her camera. "I think we're going to go out dancing or something. We'll see. I'm not really sure." She seemed to derive genuine pleasure from her day and her plans. Her one friend was enough. Her one friend was all she had, and that was just fine. Tasha seemed determined to enjoy a good day well earned. I struggled to contain my emotions as I contrasted our lives. She looked so unassuming and brave.

She broke our silence by asking me to take her picture. The request took me by surprise and I hesitated for a moment before receiving her camera. She stepped away from the line and towards the banister. A gracefully dimpled smile surfaced naturally, without effort. It must have been the same radiant smile she'd had since she was a little girl. The kind of little girl whose weightless and infectious ease could bring unfiltered delight to everyone she knew, especially her parents. She stood perfectly straight, cap and gown as flawless as her posture, unfettered dignity radiating from her gentle and upward looking smile. I kept having the strange thought that she did not look anything like an orphan. As if I had any idea what an adult orphan was supposed to look like. I think this odd thought was related to feeling surprised by how the tragedy of her father's death did not seem to undermine her day. Meanwhile, the non-tragic disappointment of my recent break-up was clearly dragging me down.

Tasha seemed to smile into the camera for herself, for her independence and pride in her accomplishment. She also seemed to be smiling for her parents, as if she could feel their pride from within. I had eight enthusiastic audience members waiting in the auditorium armed with at least three or four cameras. Never in a million years would it have dawned on me to bring my own camera to graduation. It went without saying that various albums would be lovingly compiled by others in order to record my day. Tasha had one friend, one camera, and casual, open-ended plans. A world apart. I kept wondering if Tasha could possibly feel as brave as she looked. Did she experience any of the aloneness I remained unable to shake? If so, no one could have guessed it. From the outside, nothing could touch her. Her parents' love emanated from within her, and she didn't need an external crutch. She honestly sparkled. In spite of her losses, she seemed to reach inside and find contentment and joy in her heart. As I observed Tasha, through her camera's lens, she helped me begin to understand that one's deepest, fullest happiness must be built from within.

In regard to my own academic life, I was unable to look on the bright side and see the big picture of my accomplishments in graduate school. Rather than feel the love all around me, from both of my families, I focused on feeling stuck; stuck in terms of a relationship that didn't work out, and profoundly stuck in the middle of my parents and my two separate families. In my twisted frame of mind, my recent break-up felt like just one more piece of evidence that I wasn't capable of growing up. As if my slot in life was to forever bounce back and forth between my parents, feeling endlessly trapped in a perpetual middle, unable to break out and grow beyond it. Finishing a demanding graduate program and finding a challenging new job seemed totally irrelevant.

Slowly, awkwardly, I began to Face the Mirror and examine my personal contribution to a series of failed relationships. I acknowledged my self-destructive relationship M.O. of choosing unsuitable partners and telling myself that my serial break-ups were evidence that I was better off alone, devoting my emotional energy to juggling and balancing my divorced parents. My mother couldn't have been more right when discussing my most recent breakup. I didn't want to see the signs. I ignored the times he made fun of me in front of my friends. I ignored how he usually seemed like he'd been out for a few beers before we ever began our seemingly romantic dates. I ignored the fact that I ran into him a few nights after our first date stumbling down 20th street, alone and significantly buzzed. I ignored the fact that he insisted on calling me "babe" even when I asked him not to. I saw what I wanted to see (Wharton student, reasonably cute, nice restaurants, compliments) and sadly, yet on some levels intentionally, I set myself up to get hurt.

Just as my mother described, I let my eagerness for a relationship, any relationship, blind me into making stupid decisions. And, just as she explained, my passionate and earth-shattering reaction to his predictable change of heart was absolutely not about the guy. It was about the ways I wasn't comfortable choosing someone who would be genuinely nice to me. With respect to Facing the Mirror, it was also about the way I was stubbornly focusing too much of my emotional energy on juggling my parents.

Perhaps there was a time when the dynamics of their divorce did indeed plop me smack in the middle of their problems. Of course, this is a somewhat predictable and painful part of any divorce involving children. A dynamic that can be exacerbated by a brutal combination of custody disputes, financial tensions, and profound anger that characterizes the divorces that fall on the most bitter end of the spectrum. My parents' divorce fits this bill. But almost twenty years later, as I stumbled through graduation, I was the one focusing on how to balance my two families on separate sides of the auditorium. I was unnecessarily stressed out about whom to talk to first and I was taking on this pointless balancing act in spite of the fact that no one was requesting any such effort on their behalf.

Sadly, I had unknowingly convinced myself that it was better to choose unavailable partners. By doing so, I could continue to end up on my own so that I could continue to be fully available to make sure that all of the balls of my parents' juggling act would stay in the air. Rather than enjoy the day and feel the pleasure of the love around me, I kept myself loyal and devoted to another place and time, moving back and forth between two worlds and never letting myself just stay in one place. Facing the Mirror and acknowledging this pattern made me feel exposed and unsettled. Slowly, though, my discomfort with the mirror and its reflection has been outweighed by a gradual but solid development of an ability to do things differently.

As Martha's and my story reveal, Facing the Mirror and pinpointing how your parents' divorce affects you as an adult is not easy. It can feel awkward, painful and discomforting, but it is a necessary part of the process of overcoming your parents' divorce. In order to pinpoint how your parents' divorce impacts you in adulthood, and how it influences your "Relationship M.O.", follow these next tips and suggestions.

Tips and Suggestions:

- Write down a list of personal goals. These goals should represent areas in your life where making change would be good for you. *Make sure that you are listing things that YOU intend to change about yourself, not things that you want OTHERS to change about themselves. Your list may be as long or as short as you like; just see what comes up when you sit down to write, and remember that you can always add to your list.*

- Use this list of goals to write a paragraph or two that describes "your relationship M.O." By reflecting on your list of goals, describe how you operate as an adult. What are your great strengths? What are your limitations? What are you most proud of? What will you need to work on in order to have a happy life? What leftover remnants from the pain of your past are carrying over into the present and repeatedly affecting how you select partners and experience relationships?

- Refer to your list of goals and your paragraphs about "your relationship M.O." Write about all of the ways that the areas you need to work on may be connected to your parents' divorce. *Remember, it is essential that you explore the possible relationship between past pain and current behavior that does not work for you. You will gain much better insights about WHY you do what you do. Then, you will be in a stronger position to stop doing it and find a mutually rewarding relationship.*

Step Three: Confront Your Commitment Phobia

Step Three is the centerpiece of the five-step process. In order to have a happy relationship, you must identify the specific ways in which you avoid commitment. As the research indicates, many adults with divorced parents delay and avoid commitment. Fear of commitment is often much more complicated than a conscious reluctance to take a healthy relationship to the next level. Many times, it involves a pattern of choosing flawed relationships and trying, at times desperately, to save them. Frequently, it involves choosing partners that are, in subtle or in obvious ways, unavailable. Some available partners are eventually open to increased levels of commitment, and this can be consciously or unconsciously terrifying to someone who has never seen a committed marriage up close.

Step three is a two-part process that involves:

- Evaluating your choices of partners in your romantic relationships, and
- Evaluating how emotionally present you are in your romantic relationships.

As you read the next couple chapters, think long and hard about your dating and relationship history. Many clients with divorced parents with whom I have worked over the years initially insist that they do NOT fear commitment. However, if asked about their relationship choices and their approach to relationships, the answer to this question can change. For example, Patty, a thirty-nine-year-old happily married survey subject, initially explained:

> I did not avoid commitment…I just was the one who always left…I was a serial monogamist who finally got some therapy and found the right guy.

Patty later re-visited this question and explained:

> I guess I am sort of in the yes category. I avoided commitment by leaving…I did choose unsuitable partners. That is why I would leave them. They all had addictive personalities and one was mildly abusive.

Similarly, when Allyson, a forty-one-year-old happily married subject whose parents separated when she was between one and two years of age, was asked whether she ever feared or avoided commitment, she answered:

> Yes! I didn't really realize it as such until therapy. I would either get with someone unavailable or pick the nice ones to pieces.

Remember, in order to Confront Your Commitment Phobia, it will be necessary to expand your definition of commitment phobia to include times that you may have rejected kind and available partners or worked hard to save relationships with unavailable or unsuitable people. If you already know that you avoid commitment, the following two chapters will offer a template for you to categorize this pattern so that you can begin to address it. Even if you tell yourself that you embrace rather than fear commitment, keep an open, honest mind. Consider rethinking your initial response to include the possibility that you, too, may avoid commitment by virtue of the partners that you choose and by your approach to romantic relationships.

chapter five

■

DO YOU CHOOSE
CANDY BARS INSTEAD
OF APPLES?

■

The types of partners you choose is a subject of major importance. Many adults with divorced parents have a pattern of choosing partners who are not good for them. Interestingly, they frequently do not marry these unhealthy partners. Instead, they may struggle in an unhealthy relationship or a series of unhealthy relationships for years. Fortunately, some conclude their series of relationship struggles by choosing a partner who is very different than past partners, and happily marrying.

Joelle, a twenty-six-year-old single woman whose parents separated when she was seventeen, explained her dating history:

> I've been choosing unsuitable partners, but I'm perfectly aware of how and why they're unsuitable for me, and I have no intention of pursuing anything long-lasting with these unsuitable men.

Similarly, Dana, a happily married woman whose parents separated when she was nine months old, recalled a dating history that was "tumultuous at best." Then she explained:

> If I dated a functional man, I could literally feel the walls closing in around me... I secretly loved unavailable men. I say secretly because

I didn't even know what a huge role they played in my dating life. I loved to look like the good one dating the mess. That way, when things fell apart no one blamed me. Also, you can't fear having the rug pulled out from you when there is no rug.

Sara, one of my clients with divorced parents, introduces the concept of Candy Bars and Apples—Candy Bars symbolize unhealthy partners and Apples symbolize healthy ones. Her story emphasizes the importance of confronting and overcoming commitment phobia by learning to choose healthy partners.

"If I'm so in love with Rob, then why the hell am I e-mailing Brian?" Sara shook her head and clenched her fists. She paused to inhale slowly. Sara did not flinch as her cell phone rang and she reached the petite peach gadget effortlessly from her purse, glanced at the small screen, shook her head and ignored the call. "I was the one practically begging to get engaged, remember? And now here we are planning this wedding while I e-mail my ex. My ex who cheated on me, stood me up on a regular basis and couldn't keep a job. What am I thinking?"

Sara and I began meeting months before she broke up with her ex, Brian, so I not only remembered her readiness to become engaged to Rob, but I remembered her descriptions of Brian. And the memories were far from pleasant.

When she started therapy, Sara's weight was so low that she was experiencing noticeable hair loss. Her hollowed grey complexion tugged on perfect cheekbones, sinking her lovelorn face. Her fashionable clothing swayed loosely as she dragged herself into my office each week, thin as a hanger, with lazy strings of brown bangs covering her cheerless expression.

Weight struggles were nothing new to Sara. As a child and teen model, she struggled with massive weight fluctuations, shooting commercials and magazine spreads when she was thin enough, and receiving her mother's cold shoulder during the months she was too heavy to get work. Sara's mother had also modeled during her teens and early twenties, and their home was peppered with life-size photographs from her mother's prior career, a shrine to faded but not forgotten beauty. Work for her mother dried up in her mid-twenties and she seemed intent upon re-living the modeling experience through her daughter. Sara remembered her mother telling every photographer and agent who would listen about her glory days on the runways and magazine spreads of yesteryear.

Single and jobless, Sara's mother relied on her daughter's modeling income for all the extras. While Sara's father sent regular, generous support payments, her mother had expensive tastes. Designer sportswear was a must, as were month-long Caribbean vacations where Sara and her younger sister missed weeks of school and her mother would spend long portions of each day in the beauty spa. When Sara's weight was low enough to model, all this was possible. And during the months that Sara was out of work, her mother avoided eye contact and warned Sara that if she didn't watch it, she'd "end up on the streets."

Sara's parents divorced when she was five and her sister, Becca, was one. As an emergency room doctor, Sara's father kept chaotic hours. His night shift schedule changed one evening without his wife's knowledge, so he arrived home at 10:00 when he wasn't expected until midnight and found his wife in bed with another man. (A cliché-worthy used car salesman from the next town.) Sara's father moved out in a state of shock, the used car salesman moved in, and Sara's mom marched Sara to the local talent agency to launch her modeling career. While Sara's young career flourished, the relationship with the car salesman did not, and he moved out at about the time that Sara's parents' divorce became official.

Sara's father relocated to take a position at a hospital about three hours away. He received an offer to run this facility's emergency room and needed the extra income to support his children's household and his own. He came to get the girls every weekend and, while Sara described fond memories of these two-and-a-half day visits, she also recalled hysterics on Sunday evenings while driving back toward her mother's home.

"I didn't want to leave him, his home felt so much more stable and loving. I just hated being dumped back into the world of my mother's criticism. Never being thin enough. Or pretty enough. Learning to apply my own makeup by the time I was eight. How gross."

For most of Sara's childhood, she spent weekends with her father and lived with her mother during the week. Over time, her father happily remarried a kindergarten teacher named Lillian, and her mother remarried an accountant named Ron. Both parents had additional children with their second spouses and so, by the time Sara was twelve, she and Becca had three half brothers. Sara's father's marriage was a stable and loving one, and Sara continued to look forward to her weekend visits. While she got along well with her stepfather, Ron, her mother's household was never structured. At her father and Lillian's, Sara enjoyed family dinners and homework supervision. With her mother and Ron, it was a free-for-all. The adults drank heavily, while Sara diapered her baby brother, Robbie, and sat with Becca, watching multiple hours of television. Sara's modeling career continued, off and on, as her weight continued to fluctuate. Sara admitted that it was painful to see her father and Lillian's sons having the kind of childhood she longed for. At the same time, she identified the stability of her visits with them as her anchor.

"I've always loved Bret and Jay, and it made no difference in terms of my love for them that we had different moms. But when I saw all of the framed photos of Dad, Lillian, Bret and Jay, it hurt. Bret and Jay didn't have to work as kids to help support their mother's shopping sprees. And, once they were older, they had someone telling them to do their homework. Someone supervising and encouraging them. They were genuinely like kids, while I always felt like an eight-going-on-thirty-year-old, a twelve-going-on-forty-year-old."

"The clinical term for a child who must grow up without experiencing childhood is a parentified child. Such children who, usually in response to some family tragedies like a death or divorce, take on the role of the parent while the parent takes on the role of a child," I told her.

"Exactly," she nodded. "I was the parent, and my mom and, to some extent, Becca and Robbie, were my kids. Now, I see how much time Lillian spends helping supervise Bret and Jay with their homework and I think, no wonder I didn't do well in school! They are the kids and Dad and Lillian are the parents and that's how it should be. I used to think I was just dumb, and that's why I never excelled. But how can you excel if you don't try?"

"I don't think it's as simple as that you just didn't try," I went on. "The fact that your home lacked structure was just one piece of the puzzle. As you are saying, the lack of structure was compounded by your role as the parent. By all of the energy you spent earning money for your mother. Missing school for your mother's trips. Trying to monitor her drinking."

"Our weeks were total chaos," Sara spoke softly. "But at least my dad was helping us on the weekends. Without that, our grades would have been disastrous. Each weekend we had homework supervision and a stable home. We got to be the kids and be a part of a real family. Now I realize that was my means of survival."

During Sara's junior year of high school, her mother began an affair with a science teacher from Sara's school who was, at the time, teaching her younger sister, Becca. Initially, Sara and Becca were in the awkward position of knowing that the science teacher was spending most afternoons in their home while their stepfather, Ron, remained clueless.

"It was such a relief when he finally figured it out, and we could all stop covering for Mom," Sara shuddered at this memory, "Poor Ron caught them in the act. And the world's biggest shock to him was nothing more than deja vu for us. Same scene, different victim."

"And you covering for your mother, the expectation that you help her hide the affair—"

"Just another form of parentification." Sara jumped in, turning her head, raising her petite fingers and twisting her wrists in an apparent attempt to swat away her hurt feelings. "I was always covering for her in some form. Covering her finances, or covering up her lies."

"And how do you think that affected you?"

"Well, I sure do have a history of picking guys who are just about as much of a baby as Mom. So I guess I'm parentified in the romance department too. How about that." Sara's head continued shaking like a pendulum, gazing away as she answered quietly.

Sara soon mirrored her mother's affairs with an inappropriate liaison of her own. Just after she learned of her mother's second infidelity, Sara, sixteen at the time, began a romance with Ted, a twenty-eight-year-old mechanic and father of two. Sara recounted how she would sneak out of her house each evening and stay with him in the mouse-infested bachelor pad in which he had been living in since his wife kicked him out of the house.

"Every night, I climbed out of his bed, raced home, climbed through the window. And no one ever noticed. My grades were atrocious. I went from all B's and C's to all D's and F's and it is a miracle I was able to enter twelfth grade. Thank goodness for summer school. The worst of it all was that the guy, Ted, barely acknowledged that I was alive. We first met at his garage when I took Mom's car in for some work. Of course I had to take the car in, since Mom SO couldn't be bothered. Anyway, we hooked up in this random shed behind the shop. He suggested I meet him at his place that night. And we never even went on a date! What a jerk! But there I was, night after night."

"How long did this go on?"

"*Gosh, I don't even remember. One night, I had come by and he was there with another girl and that was the end of that.*"

The mechanic was the first and Brian was the last in a substantially long line of relationships in which Sara found herself cheated on and treated badly. Ending her relationship with Brian was no easy feat. But Sara grew to understand the parallels between her relationships with men, and her relationship with her mother.

"*Come to think of it, Brian and Mom are two peas in a pod. They both thrive on making digs at me. My ears, for example. My mom calls me 'elephant face' or 'Dumbo' for short. And Brian calls me 'the alien'. Mom wanted me to have them pinned back but I was too scared of the procedure. Anyhow, they both forget when we have plans, so I basically expect to be stood up whenever I'm planning to see either one of them. They both spend way more of my money than I do. I guess I chose a guy like Brian, because I'm so used to being taken advantage of and criticized it just feels like home.*"

"*Well, when something is familiar, it usually feels much more comfortable on a gut level, even if it isn't good for us.*" Sara looked down, nodding, as I wondered about her level of commitment to Brian. "*So, being with Brian feels like home, do you picture yourself staying with him?*"

"*That's kind of a weird question, because I definitely don't.*"

"*Because...*"

"*Because, as far as I can remember, I never pictured myself staying with any of the losers I've dated. I always know these relationships are going to end and, for the most part, that's fine by me. And what's more, as far as I'm concerned, my dad must have seen signs of my mother's self-centeredness and dishonesty. Yet he forged ahead and married her anyway. I'd never go down that forever path. I may put up with a lot of crap, but I've always had this vision that I'm just killing time, whether it's with Brian or the mechanic guy or whomever. That's part of why I'm here, to figure out what I'm doing pursuing a guy I wouldn't marry if you paid me a million bucks.*"

Sara's words speak to the heart of what distinguishes Sara and so many adult children of divorce. While Sara struggled terribly in her relationships, she would not make a long-term commitment in which she would essentially repeat her parents' marriage and put herself in her father's role while Brian played the part of her self-centered mother. On one level, children of divorce frequently struggle throughout dating and early relationships. They frequently find themselves in turbulent, tumultuous relationships, or in no relationships at all. At the same time, many seem programmed on a deeper level to eventually draw the line.

Why is it that children who grow up in divorced households are able to break dysfunctional patterns rather than repeat them? With so many other traumatic family situations—substance abuse, physical abuse, sexual abuse, emotional abuse—it is shocking to observe the extent to which children growing up in such households are likely to repeat, in some form or another, the pain from their past. How is it that so many adults with divorced parents DO NOT repeat their parents' mistakes? Obviously, this question is complicated and difficult to answer with certainty.

Maybe the fact that the very nature of divorcing implies acknowledgment, on the parents' behalf, that they are capable of making a mistake is an important piece of the puzzle. Maybe the honesty that divorce entails helps children avoid repeating these same mistakes. With most other dysfunctional family patterns, the acknowledgment of the problem is not as likely to exist to the same extent and can remain covered up and contained within the family walls. One of the most interesting survey responses touches on this very issue, as a happily married adult with divorced parents explains:

> ...I like to think I model my marriage on a second marriage. In a first marriage, you make all your mistakes and learn what not to do. So I make an attempt to be honest and not hold grudges and keep open communications.

This subject, whose parents separated when she was nine and divorced when she was twelve, is literally spelling out what she learned from her parents' mistakes and how she learned it through witnessing a second marriage. Like Sara, she admits to struggling in her dating life prior to meeting her husband:

> As an adult, prior to marriage, I really think that I didn't have a whole

lot of confidence. I had low self-esteem for a long time. Until I met [my husband] I had a hard time having relationships with people. I wasn't open and I feared I'd be discovered for being a fraud. I decided to stop and shake it off and get over it and let it go. And I made a commitment to myself to not be angry and not be negative and like myself better and like men better.

This subject and Sara seem to share some key similarities that touch on the potential dividend of divorce and how to avoid repeating your parents' mistakes. Like this subject, it was as if Sara was acting out her parents' past, (perhaps as a way to come to terms with their divorce), and yet she refused to fully embrace this kind of relationship. Instead, she appeared wholeheartedly determined to change course. By refusing to commit to the unsuitable partners she chose to date, Sara seemed resolved to figure out a way to break her parents' pattern and chart her own course.

Sara figured out that she had been far more comfortable with guys who treated her as her mother did, and far more comfortable in romantic relationships that mirrored those of her mother's. However, removing herself from this familiar dynamic took weeks of preparation and hard work. And Sara was extremely motivated and eager to change. Just as important as Sara's goodbye to Brian was the following year in which, in spite of male suitors too countless to record, she did not date at all. She simply learned to enjoy her own company.

In our later meeting, I saw a new person.

"It's amazing how much more energy I have these days, now that I'm not drained from feeling bummed out and rejected all the time," Sara smiled.

Sara's appearance was completely transformed. Her posture went from slumped over sadness to peppy ballerina. Her hair filled in, her skin lightened up, and she started to smile. "I never pictured myself as someone with the potential to do anything that didn't revolve around how I look. I always knew that once the modeling jobs dried up, I'd start waiting tables. And that's just how it went. Yes, I've done reasonably well in the restaurant business, but I never imagined I'd enjoy tutoring as much as I do. Or that I would love the evening classes in early childhood education. It turns out that I have a knack for working with kids. Who knew? They really respond to me, and I know how to connect on their level. Plus I have a lot of patience. Probably from all of those years of feeling hurt—I could never push a kid too hard in any direction. I've been on the receiving end of that and it affects my tutoring style."

Sara started working towards her college degree while volunteering in various school settings. In addition, she took "cooking for one" classes. The classes helped Sara improve her eating habits and discover she had a flair not just for teaching, but for food. Rob had enrolled in the same class and we discussed him during sessions as they slowly got to know one another.

"So, there's this cute guy in 'cooking for one'. Not cute, 'bad boy' cute like Brian, but 'nice guy' cute. In high school, my friends used to joke that Ted, that older mechanic guy I hooked up with, was a candy bar, and what I needed was an apple."

"A candy bar?" I queried.

"You know, you see it. It looks great, but you know you'll regret it afterward and it will make you feel sick. But you just can't help yourself. You've gotta have it. So the older married guy was a candy bar, Brian was a candy bar. But Rob is an apple. He looks healthy, tastes okay, good for you, but you don't crave it with the same longing. I go for the candy bar every time. And now, shockingly, I think I'm craving an apple."

"Maybe the hope is that by understanding why you are so drawn to the candy bar . . ."

"You mean how I'm used to it because my mother's a candy bar too?" Sara's manicured eyebrows lifted with her questioning smile.

"Exactly. By seeing why the candy bar has such pull, even though it makes you sick. And pushing yourself, coaching yourself on some level to feel more comfortable incorporating some apples in your diet, the hope is that apples, over time, become more familiar. And so you start to crave them. And then they should start to taste even better. Maybe they even start to taste like candy apples!"

"Candy apples, now that's a new twist on the menu. I like that!"

Sara and Rob enjoyed a slow-paced, friendship-based courtship. Unlike her past relationships, where sex happened quickly, Sara and Rob took their time and got to know each other. Rob had a small web page design business, and he and Sara volunteered in the same tutoring program. He brought her flowers frequently (a first for Sara), and enjoyed planning their free time together. They signed up for scuba diving lessons and took long bike rides together. They took turns cooking for one another, and Sara described

Rob's encouragement and support when Sara decided to begin taking night courses at a local college to work towards a degree in early childhood education.

Over time, their relationship became more serious and they started talking more about the future.

"Rob says he knows he wants a family, and he knows he wants to marry me. He's just not ready. Whatever that means. It's hard for me to believe that he's not ready and I am. Especially given how this relationship is so unlike my others. Remember when I used to cringe when he showed up with flowers? Or when it bugged me that he called when he said he would? The whole apple thing was so hard to get used to. And now I can't imagine life without him. And I can't even imagine why I ever liked candy bars in the first place. Rob is a part of my family. Sure, my mom has nothing but petty things to say about him, but she has nothing nice to say about me either. My dad and Lillian love him. And so do all my brothers and Becca. What is he waiting for?"

"You know, it's not as if you have been together for years and he's refusing to even discuss the topic. When he says he wants to marry you, how does it make you feel?"

"Annoyed that he won't just propose already."

"Is that all you feel, annoyed?"

"Well no, I also feel happy, just picturing it and knowing that he's picturing it too."

"Do you tell him that?"

"No, but I guess I could. I guess I could try to be happy where we are and happy that I'm an apple gal."

"Remember how hard it was to get used to enjoying your life without a guy?"

"Well, yes, so you are saying that enjoying what we have is the same? A be in the here and now kind of thing?"

"Perhaps. A lot of people fear commitment. You hear about it more with men, but you know from your own experience, and from all of those great episodes of Sex and the City, that women fear it too. Rob's parents had a tough divorce and maybe he fears commitment just as much as you do. You just express it in different ways. In fact, you have expressed it through your appetite for candy bars."

"The candy bars ensured that I'd never get serious."

"Right, and Rob is coming forward, putting his cards on the table, and saying he needs a little time."

"I guess he deserves that. He says he thinks he'll be ready soon, and that I'm the only one for him. I guess I can hang back and let that be enough."

So Sara hung back, enjoyed her relationship, and within a matter of months, Rob proposed. From Sara's description, everything was perfect. The proposal, the ring, the new condo they were signing papers to buy. But, as her wedding plans moved forward, Sara began experiencing severe anxiety. There was tension between Sara and her mother about wedding finances and plans, and tension about who would say and do what and how the ceremony and reception would unfold. Rob's parents were also divorced and there were many questions about how to ensure that each parent would have a role and a place. As Sara and Rob planned their wedding day, she was shocked to find herself sending an e-mail to Brian.

"I just popped onto my e-mail and, next thing I knew, there we were, chatting away," she confessed at our next session. "Of course, it's not the same thing as talking, but he wants to talk. He wants to see me. Says I shouldn't rush into anything and asks why I didn't learn from my mom's love life that marriage is for losers? He says he loves me, now that's a novelty coming from him. Says I'm the one. Imagine that, bad boy Brian, professing his love."

"And what's your reaction?"

"I hate to admit it, but I'm having a twinge of a craving for a candy bar. A part of me is wondering if maybe Brian's the candy apple. Maybe that's where I belong—not forever, but for now. With a bad boy turned good. That's what I always hoped with Brian, and with other bad boys before him, that I could turn him around."

"If you could turn him around, what would you get out of that?"

"Well, I don't know, just the thought of it feels healing somehow. Like sewing up a wound."

"What kind of wound? And from where?"

"You know, the wound of all the times my mother put me down or took my money or didn't show up for something important. I guess we've been over this before, haven't we?" We nodded together. "It's not about Brian, it's about my mom. But, why now? Why am I craving the candy bar now?"

"Why do you think?"

"I'm scared?" she offered.

"Are you?" I asked.

"Of course I am," she grimaced. "I'm about to do this thing. This thing that my mom messed up twice. And I'm with this wonderful man. What if I can't make it work? What if the wedding is a disaster?"

"Look, the wedding will be complicated, but it's an opportunity to set the stage for how you and Rob want a relationship with your parents to be in the future. You're *setting the stage. It's also an opportunity to have your family put your needs first. And, therein lies a possible opportunity for healing. There's plenty we can discuss about your wedding, but first, let's talk about the question of the relationship and making it work."*

"Yeah, let's, because my real concern is the marriage. What if I blow it?"

"Well, looks like you may be blowing it right now. Trying to prove something?"

"Yes, I'm trying to prove my worst fear, that I'm cursed like my mom and any relationship I touch will implode."

"So why would you try to prove such a thing?"

"I guess it all comes back to fear of commitment, doesn't it?"

"Maybe it does." *Sara had such a strong psychological sense. What a reward to watch her figure things out for herself.* She reclined slowly as her eyes grew tearful, "I think I'm scared now that Rob's not scared. It's as if now that he's on board, there's nothing to stop us and it all feels much more real! I can hardly take it, and then there's Brian. Well, I guess Brian becomes an easy back door."

"Back door to where?"

"Back door to everything familiar—to the way things were until I looked back on my past and started trying to develop a taste for apples."

"Well you have opened the back door with your e-mails, and the question is whether to walk through it."

"Yeah, that's the question. I guess I just need to keep working to envision myself as someone capable of a happy marriage. I see it with my dad and Lillian and with Rob's mom and her husband. And those models are key. I have to believe we can do it. And if I just keep talking to Rob, we'll be fine. I always feel better when we talk."

So, rather than seeing or further communicating with Brian, Sara and Rob kept talking about their feelings, thoughts, fears and dreams. At this point, they have been married for six years and have twin daughters whom I have seen on the holiday cards that Sara sends each year. Their satisfying relationship and life together didn't come easily. Nevertheless, with a lot of work and planning, they had a magnificent wedding and have an even more magnificent relationship and family.

Sara's story is similar to that of so many other children of divorce with whom I have worked in the past. Her parents' divorce obviously traumatized her emotionally, and caused great loss with respect to her emotional life and ability to perform academically. She gained insight and linked her dissatisfying string of "candy bars" to her mother's abusive treatment of her, as well as to her mother's abusive treatment of various men in her mother's life. However, while Sara struggled terribly in young adulthood, her father's happy marriage became a role model she would not have experienced had her parents stayed together. And Sara's life with Rob was a clear reflection of her relationship role model–a genuine love story.

Had Sara's parents stuck it out and stayed together, perhaps Sara would have had better grades and a less turbulent childhood. Perhaps she would not have become parentified through her obligations to care for her mother at a young age or been pushed to miss out on childhood experiences in order to make money through modeling. At the same time, it is important to point out how Sara may have also been more vulnerable to marrying a "candy bar" just like her father did when he chose Sara's mother. Instead, following her painful young adult struggles, she sought help, learned where, why and how she was choosing poor partners and eventually found a committed adult relationship that could offer her great happiness. In that sense, Sara broke a dysfunctional family pattern of unhappy first marriages and she positioned herself to have an honest, satisfying and rewarding marriage.

By Confronting Your Commitment Phobia, you can begin taking control and ownership of your relationships and your choices. Many of my clients express great relief when they realize that they are active participants in their failed relationships. It's quite common to think that you just have bad luck, bad karma or even that your status of coming from a divorced family somehow dooms you to a lifetime of unsatisfying relationships.

Steve, a young lawyer, came to therapy to adjust to the rejection by his girlfriend of five years. As we worked together, Steve confronted his commitment phobia and began realizing that the woman who rejected him (like all of his former girlfriends) was an unfaithful, unkind, unsuitable partner. He took ownership of his series of failed relationships by confronting his attraction to candy bars and explained:

> It's quite liberating, actually. I swear I never realized how drawn I was to women who treat me like dirt. I've gone all this time just getting

hurt, again and again, and assuming that it's just bad luck. I've assumed that my father had bad luck too, and that's why he married a cheater who left him and broke his heart. It's much better to realize that I'm the one who is doing the choosing, so I'm the one responsible for this mess. Maybe now I can finally do something about my crappy love life.

Like Steve and Sara, you, too, can Confront Your Commitment Phobia by reflecting on their stories and working on these new ideas.

Tips and Suggestions:

- Create an Inventory of Romantic Relationships by writing a page about five different people whom you dated. *You do not have to have been in a committed relationship with all (or any) of these people. What matters is that they are five people whom you dated who are significant to you in some way. If you cannot identify five people, just list as many as you can.* What qualities do you remember most about each person? What are their best qualities? What are their worst qualities?

- Review each page of your Inventory of Romantic Relationships and make a list of any common qualities that your past partners share.

- Make a list of the qualities that are most important to you in a relationship. Then, go back to your Inventory of Romantic Relationships and see what qualities the people you choose to date share with the ones you identify as most important. Highlight the qualities that you claim are most important to you but which are NOT present in any of the people in your inventory. Have you genuinely prioritized these qualities?

- Ask yourself, with each person listed, is he or she a candy bar or an apple? Write "candy bar" or "apple" at the top of each page depending upon your answers.

chapter six

■

DO YOU PREFER
RENTING OVER
BUYING?

■

This chapter will examine the importance of how you operate in relationships and how your level of emotional investment relates to possible commitment phobia. Many adults with divorced parents tend to approach relationships as if they are temporary. They will, sometimes knowingly, spend months or even years in relationships that they know will not work out. Similarly, they will frequently choose dating situations with significant barriers to intimacy, such as long-distance relationships. Approaching a relationship as temporary, for whatever the reason, can be a perfect excuse to withhold commitment and to remain emotionally disconnected.

I once worked with a young real estate broker named David. David's professional success clearly emphasized the value of BUYING real estate. But, when it came to his romantic relationships, David had a strong preference for RENTING. David began therapy in his early thirties when he entered into what he described as his first "real relationship." When I asked him what he meant by a "real relationship", David explained:

> This is the first time I've ever been faithful. The first time I've wanted
> to be faithful. Also, this is my first relationship with someone who

actually lives nearby. In the past, all of my relationships have been long distance. Well, there was one exception, but the one time I dated someone who lived nearby, she was married.

David explained that he and his girlfriend were very happy and that the nine months that they were together was the longest stretch of time that he had ever spent in a committed relationship. He was struggling, however, with a strong impulse to end his relationship, and he could easily connect these conflicts to what it meant to him to grow up with divorced parents. David explained that after watching each of his parents experience two divorces, he went through his twenties assuming that his parents' failed relationships meant that his own relationships would inevitably fail as well. David agreed to participate in my survey and explained:

> I am learning to see my parents' relationship failures as a "map of how not to do it."... I continually fight the tendency to view [my relationship] as temporary. I feel as though I am often looking for the next relationship. My past taught me to get the short-term happiness and jettison the long-term complexities...In the past, once the relationship began to proceed beyond something uncommitted and casual, I began to look for an exit.

Many survey subjects discuss this same pattern of viewing relationships as temporary. Sally, a thirty-nine-year-old single woman whose parents separated when she was fifteen, explains:

> I never pushed for commitment in any of the relationships I was in. I think I was very guarded...I suppose [I rejected available partners] but availability is not really the criteria I use in picking a mate.

Frankie, a twenty-two-year-old single woman whose parents separated when she was one, reveals:

I rarely give anyone a chance to get close…I have a subconscious rejection mechanism…[I] always pick the unavailable ones. As soon as they become available I usually get turned off.

Darla, a twenty-six-year-old-single woman whose parents separated when she was eight, admits:

If I fail at a relationship that was doomed from the start, then it wasn't really my fault. I try to pick those who I am attracted to…who just happen to be those who are unavailable.

Jennifer, a twenty-five-year-old single woman whose parents divorced when she was thirteen, acknowledges:

I date often and find something wrong quickly when the man tries to be more serious and committed.

Paul, a twenty-four-year-old man whose parents divorced when he was two and whose mother divorced again when he was fourteen, described great pleasure in his "extremely loving and respectful relationship" with his girlfriend of five and a half years. However, he explains:

We both have divorced parents and both would tell you that we don't believe in marriage, but we are also very committed to each other. I think that growing up with many sour relationships has instilled in me a desire to have open, honest and true relationships. I hope at all times to be choosing to be with my partner and I don't try to ask or demand my partner to commit to loving me any longer than she wants to…I think I learned that I don't really understand marriage. I see that it can be necessary to be legally bound to someone, but I'm very frightened of asking someone to love me forever, and I'm frightened of telling someone that I will love them forever.

Twyla, a twenty-seven-year-old single woman whose parents separated when she was fifteen, reveals:

> I entertain flirtatious relationships with men who are oftentimes unavailable—married co-workers, classmates, etc. Not that I would ever cross a line, but I have recently identified that I am more comfortable with guys who aren't "dateable". I think I am more comfortable with unavailable men because it means that I don't have to TRY.

Katie, a happily-married subject whose parents separated when she was eleven, remembers:

> The more someone was interested in me, the further I ran away!

In this chapter, we will use concepts of *buying* and *renting* as metaphors to explore the degree to which you are emotionally invested in your relationships. Please keep in mind that we are talking about mature adult relationships that occur in one's twenties, thirties and beyond. We are not talking about puppy love and relationships that happen in high school or college. (As the following chapter describes, high school or college relationships may lead to long-term, mature, adult relationships. But the advice in this book does not directly apply to relationships that occur during teenage years.) This chapter discusses the importance of being emotionally present to the degree that suits the relationship. This chapter is not designed to encourage you to plan to marry each and every person you date. It is meant to encourage you to explore your availability within the context of your adult relationships. And to explore the availability of the partners you choose. My work with a young woman named Kimberley introduces this concept. Renting symbolizes a pattern of being emotionally absent in relationships, while buying symbolizes being appropriately present and emotionally invested. Kimberley's story emphasizes the importance of confronting and overcoming commitment-phobia by learning to be appropriately emotionally invested.

Typically, I begin the first meeting with a new client asking them why they are seeking therapy. And, typically, the new client gets right down to business and tells me.

"So, what brings you here today, and how can I be helpful?" I asked Kimberley my opening question, as she leaned back into the cushion behind her and answered with abandon.

"It's the strangest thing. My husband and I found our dream house, and I couldn't sign the paperwork. We had to postpone our meeting with the realtor on Friday, and we lost the house. I was freaking out all weekend and couldn't get it together to make the offer so we lost out to another bidder. I couldn't go through with it. I'm questioning our whole marriage and everything about Ray. All the while, I'm hating myself for what I'm doing to us." Kimberley's large brown eyes bulged in a panic as she pressed her palms into the sofa, locking her elbows as if struggling to sustain herself in an upright position.

"Why might you be questioning the relationship? What is it about Ray that you're questioning?"

"God. I don't know, that's why I'm here, and that's why I'm so pissed at myself. Ray is the greatest guy in the world. We met in college, freshman year, and that was it for me. I've never been with another guy and never wanted to. Now, suddenly, I can't move forward."

"Has this ever happened before? What I mean is, did you, for example, have questions about the relationship during your engagement or at any other point?"

"No, not at all. I'm a freak; it makes no sense at all. I'm just a freak."

"Well, has anything changed recently, either with you or with him or with the relationship?"

"Yes. And here's the truly twisted part. There's been a major league change for the BETTER! Ever since I've known Ray, he has had a drinking problem. At first, it was just typical college stuff. We went to UVA together and all of the guys in his fraternity liked to party. Don't get me wrong, so did I. We all drank, to some extent, and had a lot of fun. Soon, though, I realized that with Ray it could go too far. He'd black out, do crazy shit. Like one time he punched his fist through a window and got all cut up. At first, I thought that being out of school would make all the difference. And, I'll admit, life did calm down. He stopped doing stupid things and blacking out. And even when we were in law school together he didn't get too crazy. But it was still five to seven beers a night, no matter what." Kimberley went on to describe her efforts, over the years, to convince Ray to get help. "He's the sweetest guy you ever want to know. And he is nothing but good to me. Still, his drinking always bothered me, and I asked him—maybe a hundred times—to *get some help. When he refused, I totally stopped drinking in the hope that if I couldn't speak the message in words, I could communicate it by my actions. No dice. Turns out that what they say about drinking and drugging is true. Alcoholics can't quit for someone they love, they have to quit for themselves."*

"So how did Ray quit? What happened?" I asked.

"He lost a client at work. Missed an important meeting because he overslept and forgot about it. Then, the next morning, Ray woke up and stumbled right through his hangover and into a day treatment program. He says it was the first time that his drinking interfered with his work. I'm not so sure that's the case. I happen to think the drinking interfered with his work for a long time. Just not in a fashion so dramatic as sleeping in with a hangover and losing a big account. But the point is, he had to quit on his own terms, for his own reasons."

"And since he's sober?" I pressed on.

"Well, we've always been best friends. But, since he's been sober, we're even closer. He talks a lot more and is much more affectionate."

"And what's that like for you?"

"I should love it, right? But it's freaking me out."

"Why do you think that is?"

"Well, I hadn't considered it until now, but maybe, even though I would ask him to quit, well maybe I liked the way his drinking kind of kept us down to earth. Yeah, we're making money and rising up that ladder. But behind closed doors, we have this dark side. And that kind of kept it real."

"Kept it real?"

"Yeah, kept us from forgetting our roots. Ray's parents are both drinkers. And so's my mom. None of them make the kind of money that we do, and Ray's drinking just kind of kept it real."

"Real, like down to earth, and like you still have stuff in common?"

"Exactly."

"So, can you say a little more about the importance of keeping it real?"

"Well, my parents divorced when I was five, and my dad totally ditched us. Me, my mom, and my brother Stevie. Growing up, I maybe saw him once a year. And my mom never got over it. She barely leaves the house. To this day, she can't call a plumber, Stevie had to step in and do it all. Seriously, Stevie was calling plumbers and changing light bulbs by the

time he was ten. Mom, Stevie and I struggled to make ends meet, while Dad hooked up with this young, light-skinned hottie from his law firm and turned all Jack and Jill on us."

"Jack and Jill, the social club?" I had a feeling I knew what Kimberley was referring to, but I wanted to be sure that I was following.

"Yeah. The woman he left to be with, Lisa, well, she's this Atlanta socialite. And all that bourgeois society stuff is important to her. My dad was just making partner and he totally disappeared into Lisa's glamorous world of the bourgeoisie."

"I guess your dad and Lisa don't really keep it real, do they?"

"No, they really don't. So, yes, that's part of why it's important to me to lay low and not get too carried away with myself or money or any of that. And Ray, he's the only one I've ever opened up to about how tough it was to grow up without a dad. Ray has always been my advocate, and I know he's on my side."

I asked Kimberley to tell me more about what drew her to Ray in the first place, and she emphasized her ability to be herself and to share her feelings about her parents' divorce. She also talked about how having parents with drinking problems gave them something in common.

"Ray talked to me about his parents' drinking as if they were the only ones with a problem. And, in some ways, he sounded believable because his parents are bitter, mean drunks. Ray, on the other hand, well okay in college he did crazy stuff, but since then he just gets quiet and goes to sleep. And Ray, he's always there for me in a way that his parents were never there for each other."

Kimberley described their honest friendship and devotion. She shared some of Ray's story, and then more of her own past. Kimberley's story was laced with a window into an elite African American society that consumed her father, step-mother, and eventually their two daughters (Kimberley's half sisters). Through the divorce, Kimberley and Stevie were clearly demoted to the outer periphery of their father's high-fashion life. As Kimberley spoke, what unfolded was a heartbreaking tale of a little girl abandoned by a father who acted as if he had suddenly become too good for her. Kimberley's father checked out, while her mother attempted to cope with her divorce through drinking, so Kimberley was left with not one, but two absent parents.

There were, however, two bright shining lights in Kimberley's childhood. Her father's parents meant everything to her and Kimberley referred to them as her "fairy grandparents".

"They lived close by and Stevie and I practically lived over there. We went over every day after school and when Mom was super drunk or depressed, we'd stay over, sometimes for days. Dad broke their hearts too by becoming too good for them. And, looking back, I think they dealt with it by making sure that they were there for Stevie and me."

Kimberley described how her "fairy grandmother" taught her to sew and to cook and to knit. And how her "fairy grandfather" helped her with her homework almost daily. In the coming weeks, Kimberley recounted the debilitating pain of her father's exit. His minimal contact, forgotten birthdays, broken promises, cancelled vacations, and unreturned phone calls. At the same time, her descriptions also conveyed how her paternal grandparents seemed determined to fill the void left by their son's exit and exacerbated by Kimberley's mother's drinking and depression.

Kimberley and I began meeting twice a week, and Kimberley told Ray that she could not go through with the purchase of a home until she got to the root of why she felt so paralyzed and full of panic. Ray expressed great frustration and disappointment, but he told Kimberley that he would wait for her to sort things out.

"After all," *Kimberley explained in a quiet, questioning voice,* "I did wait through eight years of marriage for Ray to get sober, so I guess he can wait for me to get through my freak out."

According to Kimberley, she had a relatively easy time committing to Ray, in spite of his drinking problem. And, while she found it strange and, in fact, baffling, that she would suddenly hesitate and freak out now that the barrier in their relationship—the alcohol—was resolved, I was not so surprised. Most people whose spouses abuse a substance find themselves struggling to adjust when faced with the sobriety they thought they always wanted. My task was to collect as much information as possible about what aspects of Ray's drinking may have worked for Kimberley in the past. We'd established the appeal of keeping it real and not coming across as being, in any way, like her father. And one could analyze this further and hypothesize that being with an alcoholic (like her mother) was a way for Kimberley to demonstrate her loyalty to her mom. But I wanted to know if there were additional reasons that Ray's drinking problem might have an unconscious pull. In order to uncover the answer, and determine what therapists frequently refer to as the "*secondary gain*", *I asked Kimberley to give me as much detail as possible about what their marriage looked like before Ray stopped drinking.*

"*Well, our life looked pretty much like this: we'd get home from a long day's work, and Ray would break open a six pack and turn on the television. My mom would call, and I would sit on the phone with my mom, listening to her tell me how Stevie doesn't come around enough and how lonely she is and what random necklace she bought on the home shopper's network and what sale is happening at her job. She started spraying perfume at a local department store about ten years ago and she pretty much spends her salary on stuff at the store and then justifies it by telling us how great her discount is.*"

"*Did you want to spend this much time each evening on the phone with your mother?*" *I asked, leaning toward her.*

She shook her head. "*No, but I hate the idea of her being lonely. She really needs me. She hates that I left Atlanta, never lets me hear the end of it. So talking on the phone makes me feel like I'm not abandoning her the way Dad abandoned us. If I try to get off the phone, I feel so guilty I can't stand it.*"

"*What about?*"

"*About making more money and having a life. So I'm obligated to give her time to vent about her unpaid bills and endless job search for something to do for a living other than spray perfume at strangers.*"

"*And what's Ray's perspective about the phone calls?*"

"*Well, before he stopped drinking, I think he barely noticed. In that sense I guess the drinking worked for both of us. He could zone out with his beers. And I could zone out with my mom.*"

"*So, it's not just the alcohol that kept the two of you from being more intimate.*"

"*No, I guess my nightly phone dates with Mom caused me to check out on Ray just like Ray checked out on me. And now that he's checked back in, the calls don't fly so well. That's for sure.*"

"*No?*"

"*No, Ray gets really bummed about it. I have to admit, he'll make dinner reservations or want to watch a movie together or just talk, and I tell him I need to call home and he gets bummed. He's worked really hard to change. He's in A.A.; he's seeing a therapist. He's realizing how insecure he was before he got sober and my always putting my calls with my mother before my time with him sure doesn't help."*

"It's interesting that you refer to your mother's as 'home'."

"Well yeah, Atlanta's home."

"And how long have you lived in Washington D.C. with Ray?"

"Since law school, I don't know, ten years or so."

"And yet Atlanta's home?"

"Yeah, Mom lives in a real house. Not super fancy, but the one thing Dad made sure of was that she could stay in the house. She's still in the same house they bought together when Stevie was born."

"A real house?"

"Yeah, our little apartment is great, but it's not a home. It's a rental and, you know, temporary." Kimberley paused and took a deep, slow breath. "So maybe that's it. Maybe that's a part of the whole house thing. If we get this new house together, it's as if we're really making a home."

"And."

"And I'm afraid of that. It's as if before, when Ray was drinking, we were just two kids PLAYING house but the REAL home was always Atlanta. And now he's ready to grow up, and make a grown up life together. Until now, a part of me thought that I was this do gooder, sticking it out and suffering and wishing that Ray would get it together and stop drinking. But I guess, in a weird way, his drinking did work for me. It kept things real AND it allowed me to meet my mom's needs and not feel quite so guilty about being here in D.C.. It's as if his drinking let Atlanta continue to be my home."

"It sounds as if you were both renting in more ways than one. Sounds like you were just renting the apartment, and, on some levels, just renting the marriage. And now Ray's ready to become a buyer."

"Exactly, it worked for me to rent my life and be, you know, less invested. And..." Kimberley paused, perked straight up in her seat and leaned forward.

"And less permanent?"

"Yes, and if I buy a home with Ray, I need to buy the marriage for real. And make this—by this I mean Washington D.C. and my life with Ray—I need to make this my home. I don't know if I can deal with that."

"You don't know if you can deal with what part? With that level of intimacy?"

"Right, it feels too close."

Buying versus renting became an important theme in my work with Kimberley, as she pushed herself to identify her own commitment phobia and explore her reluctance to invest in the very situation—Ray's sobriety—she claimed she always wanted. As she described her nostalgia for some of the wild times of Ray's inebriated past, I was reminded of Monica Ali's quotation from her novel Brick Lane. *I shared Ali's words with Kimberley:*

". . . There are two kinds of love. The kind that starts off big and slowly wears away, that seems you can never use it up and then one day is finished. And the kind that you don't notice at first, but which adds a little bit to itself every day, like an oyster makes a pearl, grain by grain, a jewel from the sand."

Ali's eloquent prose brought Kimberley to tears as she responded, "It's as if Ray and I started out with the first kind of love. All wild and crazy and out of control. And now we're struggling to move towards the second. I want that second kind, the more mature love; I want that with Ray but I'm not used to it."

"Well, you didn't observe it between your parents, so it's not exactly familiar."

"No, I didn't observe it between my parents, or between my dad and Lisa. Dad didn't let Stevie or me in enough to observe anything, and how mature could their love really be if you desert your kids like that? I did see mature love with my fairy grandparents, though. They were so good to each other. And no alcohol in that house, that's for sure. Not since Grandpa quit. They kept it real and were madly in love."

"Your fairy grandfather used to drink?" I was surprised by this detail, given the extent to which Kimberley sang his praises and described him as a "model man".

"Hell yeah, years ago, drank like a fish. But that was way before my time."

"So he and Ray have something in common."

"Yeah, they are two alcoholics who were so darn kind-hearted that their women stuck by them and they eventually recovered. They don't exactly fit the mold of the typical drunk, but I'm learning through Ray's experiences at A.A. that alcoholics come in all shapes and forms. Hadn't thought of them as similar until just now, but you're right. They really are. Two kind, huge-hearted, teddy bear men."

About six months after Kimberley's self-titled "freak out", she found herself ready to buy the house, buy the marriage, and buy into her life in Washington D.C. with Ray. They now have a four-year-old son and a six-month-old daughter.

Kimberley experienced great resistance from her mother as she started spending less time on the telephone and more time on her marriage, but Kimberley continued to set boundaries and put her marriage first. She insightfully described their relationship once they "bought" the marriage:

"Man, relationships are work. I never realized that because my parents just never engaged. But with Ray, I find that I get out of it what I put into it."

We still meet, from time to time, when Kimberley feels overwhelmed by, for example, a request that her mother come to visit for a month when she and Ray invited her to stay for a long weekend. Kimberley still struggles with questions about how to navigate her decision not to leave her children alone with her mother due to her mother's continued heavy drinking. The pain of her father's rejection and limited involvement in her life continues to hurt. In other words, remnants from her parents' divorce, like her father's abandonment and her mother's loneliness, clinginess, and alcoholism, continue to affect Kimberley's adult life. I once asked Kimberley how she thought growing up in a divorced family affected her choices with regard to adult romantic relationships. Her thoughtful response echoes many adult survivors of divorce in its optimism, strength and honesty:

"Well, I had to grow up so fast. I was kind of a loner and never opened up to anyone about the whole broken home thing. Then, I found someone I could really talk to, and who would tell me that my dad was an ass for ditching us, and that was it for me. I now see how a lot of our early relationship was supremely troubled. How the distance worked and let me keep taking care of my mom. But we got through that. The way I see it, without all the hurt in my life, I probably wouldn't cherish everything I have in my marriage to Ray."

In spite of the parts of her life that she wishes were different, Kimberley and Ray developed a mature approach to their marriage and have created a satisfying relationship and an inspiring family.

One of the most notable adults with divorced parents in our current popular culture is the character Doctor Meredith Grey on the television show based on her name, and her psychological anatomy, *Grey's Anatomy*. This character has captivated audiences as she struggles with her estranged relationship with her father (who did not keep in touch after her parents' divorce), grieves the death of her self-centered, Alzheimer's-stricken mother, and appears perpetually unable to be present in her on-again, off-again relationship with the character affectionately known as Doctor McDreamy. When McDreamy is unavailable due to his marriage to another doctor at the hospital where they both work, Meredith does not question her love for McDreamy and seems wholeheartedly devoted and hopeful as she begs, in one of the show's most noted episodes, "choose me."

However, once her desires come to fruition, and McDreamy leaves his wife and chooses Meredith, she becomes paralyzed with fear. She seems profoundly unable to be emotionally present in the very relationship she claimed she always wanted. Once McDreamy is able to be present with Meredith, she struggles internally and summarizes the themes of this chapter by stating, "the more available he gets, the more I pull away."

In order to Confront Your Commitment Phobia and determine if you prefer renting over buying, consider how emotionally invested you are in your romantic relationships. Also, reflect on the partners you choose and their levels of investment. Here are some tips and suggestions below to complete your Inventory of Romantic Relationships and gain a comprehensive picture of your approach to intimacy.

Tips and Suggestions:

- Go back to your Inventory of Romantic Relationships from chapter five. Re-read each relationship description and write about when you realized the relationship would not work out. How long did you stay together once you made the realization that the relationship would not work out?
- If you stayed in any relationship that you knew would not work for over a month, write for at least fifteen minutes about why you stayed as long as you did.
- Consider each relationship description in your inventory and list any significant obstacles—such as geographic distance—that may have prevented intimacy.

- Write about why you may have overlooked the obstacles on your list.
- Honestly evaluate your level of emotional presence and commitment to each relationship and determine, with each, if you were renting or buying. Then write the word "rent" or "buy" on the top of each page next to the word "candy bar" or "apple".
- Examine whether you tend to "buy" with "candy bars" or with "apples" and whether you tend to "rent" with "candy bars" or with "apples". If you are renting with apples, why are you leaving behind potentially healthy partners? If you are renting with candy bars, are you just having fun? Or are you choosing unavailable partners because you fear commitment? If you are buying into relationships with candy bars, you must evaluate the underpinnings of this destructive behavior. Investing whole-heartedly in relationships with unhealthy partners is not a recipe for intimacy, it is a recipe for avoiding commitment. *Remember, unless you are buying with apples, you are probably experiencing some form of commitment phobia.*

Step Four: Calculate Your Dividend

Step Four infuses the process of learning how your parents' divorce can actually help you have a happy relationship with optimism and energy. Calculate your dividend by focusing on any potential good that has occurred as a result of your parents' divorce. By doing so, you are making lemonade from the lemons that comprised your parents' divorce and positioning yourself to have a new perspective on your past and a new approach to your present life.

Step Four involves a two-part process:

First, take an inventory of any and all good relationships that are in your life as a result of your parents' divorce. While you are at it, take stock of any bad relationships that are in your life as a result of your parents' divorce and see if you learned anything of value from these relationships that is potentially relevant to your adult life.

Second, seriously consider if there are any ways in which the commitment-phobia identified in Step Three may have been adaptive and protective. In other words, ask yourself: how has it worked for you to remain single and delay commitment? What have you learned from your relationships and experiences thus far? Are you more emotionally mature than your parents were at the time of their marriage?

chapter seven

■

ACKNOWLEDGE THE IMPORTANCE OF RELATIONSHIPS THAT RESULT FROM YOUR PARENTS' DIVORCE

■

Now we will consider the importance of evaluating all of the relationships that you have experienced (mainly step-parents, half-siblings, step-siblings and persons with whom your parents had a romantic relationship) that are a result of your parents' divorce. It would be difficult to find an adult with divorced parents who would say that their parents' divorce did not drastically alter their childhood. When considering how the life of a child with divorced or divorcing parents is altered, it becomes clear that most of what occurs during that period is NOT pleasant, nor a positive. You may see vulnerable sides of your parents that are not flattering; you may be over-stimulated with too much information or with too many relationships, and you may be brought into the middle of your parents' disputes. The list of unhappy aspects is long. However, my work with many adults with divorced parents and the results of my recent survey demonstrate the importance of certain significant relationships that result from your parents' divorce. In spite of the pain that flows from almost every divorce, many adults whose parents divorce can identify a dividend. Frequently, this dividend is connected to key relationships that resulted from the divorce.

Why is it so important to acknowledge these bright spots in an otherwise dark picture? Because in order to overcome the negatives of your parents' divorce and the ways that it has affected you, it is imperative that you be able to create a comprehensive calculation of any ounce of good that has flowed from an otherwise tragic and formative event. Hopefully, re-telling your story in Step One should help you understand the reasons why your parents divorced more fully. Facing the Mirror and then Identifying Your Commitment Phobia in Steps Two and Three should help you explore the trauma and tragedy associated with your parents' divorce and how it may carry over in ways that do not work for you as an adult. It is equally important to take the time to calculate the meaning and potential value of any relationship that you would not have experienced had your parents stayed together. These relationships may have had a major impact on who you are. It is important to reflect on them and calculate whether and how they may carry a dividend.

As I talked to and researched adult children of divorce, I did not directly ask if their parents' divorce had an upside. Nevertheless, many men and women directly or indirectly referred to a dividend of their parents' divorces. Brent, a happily married forty-year-old man whose parents separated when he was six, summarizes his dividend:

> The divorce had a silver lining. I had the most amazing childhood experiences growing up in two very different countries. My American home with my dad offered all that is good about a classic suburban upbringing. My foreign home with my mom was on the beach with fishing, snorkeling….diverse cultures and much more right at our doorstep. These foreign experiences have shaped my world view, values, interests and career. In short, without the divorce I wouldn't be the same person in some ways. The divorce brought two new and wonderful adults into my life (stepmom and stepdad), both of whom, together with their extended families, enriched my childhood in many ways.

Kathy, a forty-one-year-old happily married woman whose parents divorced when she was thirteen, identified a similar dividend with respect to her parents' remarriages:

Both my parents are very happy with their current spouses. They both found people who love and support them. They have both grown into more fulfilled, loving, and kind people. Their second marriages have challenged them both deeply and have made them look at their lives and actions; they are much better parents and people.

James, a forty-one-year-old unmarried man in a year-long relationship he views as serious and long-term, explained that both of his parents have been happily remarried for many years. And with respect to his approach to relationships, he proclaimed:

> I have a healthy combination of realistic expectations and idealistic, romantic expectations. I think I have a very balanced view of romantic relationships and what it takes to be happy in a marriage. So, I think, in a lot of ways, I've learned good lessons from my parents.

Many of my current and former clients spend some portion of their work in therapy focusing on and evaluating the importance of relationships that resulted from their parents' divorce. Gregory, a young teacher, found that calculating this dividend of his parents' divorce was the cornerstone of his healing process.

Gregory, a happily married twenty-eight-year-old from the Midwest, began therapy when he moved to Washington D.C. to teach at a local charter school in the northeast section.

"I always knew I wanted to teach," Gregory explained, "but I didn't expect that when I finally paid off my loans and could afford to start teaching, I would end up feeling depressed."

When a client reports feeling depressed, I believe it is essential to review their symptoms, evaluate the severity of the depression, and, if necessary, refer the client to a psychiatrist for medication. As we discussed his symptoms, Gregory explained that he was sleeping well, eating well, getting along well with his wife and his friends. He continued to enjoy socializing and enjoyed riding his bike to and from the office and mountain biking on the weekends. Gregory did not appear to be in need of a psychiatric referral, but he explained that he could not shake the sensation of feeling "down in the dumps." When I asked him what he felt depressed about, he had difficulty answering.

"I wish I knew. Sandy and I moved here six months ago. I started teaching in September, I love it, by the way, but I just feel like I'm dragging. I love my life, my wife, D.C., the school, the kids I teach, it's all great but I'm definitely down."

"When did you first notice feeling down?" I interjected.

"Soon after the school year started, I would say." Gregory cracked his knuckles and shrugged. His thick hair matched his dark skin, and he looked like the kind of guy whom fourth graders would adore. Bold smile, cool, colorful T-shirts, calm but jovial disposition —a perpetual youth to the Peter Pan degree. "It's not something that anyone other than Sandy would notice. But I'm not myself. It was her idea to come talk to you. Not really my kind of thing. But I know something's wrong."

"Greg, can you think of any reason that starting to teach would trigger these feelings?"

He shook his head. "No, as I said, I've always wanted to teach, and I love the kids. I mean, if you want to be inspired, come check out these kids. They're smart, fun, motivated, and many of them have none of the advantages I had growing up. The parents, some of them can be tough to deal with, but I can handle that. And it's worth it. I tell you, even with the most challenging kid. You find him challenging. Then you meet his parents and you suddenly realize the kid is amazing. You wonder how such difficult parents could end up with such an incredible kid. I'm doing EXACTLY what I've always wanted to be doing. I love it, I'm good at it, and I'm totally down. Go figure."

"So, it doesn't seem to be the teaching itself, that's the problem."

"Definitely not. It beats investment banking for sure. Sandy and I are both thrilled to have that part of our lives behind us. Teaching is not the problem, trust me."

"Well, sometimes even the things we love the most can illicit difficult feelings. Or painful memories. Is there anything going on at the school, or with any of the kids, that you find yourself thinking about after hours?"

"Anything going on at the school? No, not that I can think of. With the kids? Well, let's see. I will say that I'm remembering more of what it's like to be nine. I guess that's been a little weird."

"Weird? In what sense?"

"In the sense that nine is a pretty great age for a lot of these kids. But not for all of *them."*

"How about for you? What was being nine like for you?" Gregory's eyes frowned as his mouth smiled.

"Ahh, such a therapist's question. 'So tell me about your childhood.' What was nine like for me? It was like when the shit hit the fan. That's what it was like."

It soon became clear that Gregory's experiences with his students were causing him to re-visit memories of his parents' separation when Gregory was nine. His experience reflects a psychological phenomenon commonly observed in parents with young children. When someone has experienced significant trauma during their childhood, they will frequently re-visit this trauma when their oldest child (or the child they have the most in common with) reaches the age that they were when the trauma occurred. Seeing one's child at that same age causes them to remember more about what it felt like to be that specific age, and, as they remember the age, they re-visit the traumatic experience. Gregory was experiencing this same phenomenon by teaching children who were the same age that Gregory was when his parents separated.

One child in particular, a young boy named Kai, elicited painful feelings in Gregory as the child struggled with his parents' recent separation. Kai reached out to Gregory and found, in his fourth grade teacher, a wonderful resource. As the young boy attempted to adjust to splitting time between two households, Gregory reflected, for the first time, on his own, very similar experience. Gregory was a source of support and a marvelous advocate for his young, vulnerable student. However, Gregory was troubled by how tired Kai seemed and by the declining quality of his homework assignments. In response, Gregory organized a series of meetings and encouraged Kai's parents to re-negotiate their separation agreement to find a schedule that was more consistent for Kai and involved less frequent back and forth shuffling between households. While Gregory was a natural and committed advocate for Kai, he lacked adequate personal insight about how helping Kai was bringing up unexplored pain from Gregory's own past.

As Gregory's sessions continued, he remembered his own hectic visitation schedule and his difficulty shuffling back and forth between his parents' different households and their very different sets of rules. As soon as Gregory figured out WHY he was down, his mood improved dramatically, and he was able to take a look at his own past. He continued to help Kai and his support of his student stopped bringing him down.

Remembering his parents' divorce was painful and difficult for Gregory, as one would expect. However, Gregory and I met weekly and he was committed to getting the most out of his therapy. He was always on time, always smiling (a trait that is common, perhaps, in greater society, but somewhat uncharacteristic of the typical psychotherapy client), and he took to calling me "Shrink". The tone of our conversations was somewhat lighter than the norm, but Gregory set this more jovial tone, and the levity clearly worked for him.

Our discussion of the importance of the relationships resulting from his parents' divorce was particularly enlightening. Gregory was discussing a meeting with Kai's parents and I shared that I was struck by the ease with which he could connect with both of Kai's very different, very difficult parents.

"I think dealing with difficult people has always come easily to me. Not that I seek them out. But when I have to deal with such types, I can handle it."

"It's one of your most striking qualities. The kids in your class come from so many different backgrounds. And you seem comfortable with everyone. Even the more challenging parents."

"Well, Shrink, I know that you're going to ask me why I'm that way. Before these meetings I might have chalked it up to my natural charm and good humor, but I do honestly see it a little differently now."

I smiled. "So, please explain." I tried to ignore the fact that he was calling me "Shrink" so that I didn't laugh and lose the opportunity for more serious reflection.

"As you know, both of my parents re-married. My mother's husband was a charac-ter. A good guy at heart, but a spit-fire and a definite character. We're talkin' one major machismo dude. My father's wife was extremely high maintenance. Also a good person, but you never met anyone wearing so much make-up or so into shopping. And all of their kids are great. My stepfather's children spent the first half of their lives in Spain, so that certainly made our household different than the norm. Different languages being spoken all the time. At first, I hated it. But I can tell you that it was good for me. Plop me down anywhere and I feel comfortable. I can talk to anyone and I think being comfortable with different people and different environments will be essential to my success as a teacher. If I'm honest, I can only thank my parents and my stepparents for that. My dad always says he could throw me down, anywhere on earth, and I'd find my way home and make friends along the way."

Gregory calculated the dividend of his parents' divorce and connected his professional success to his comfort with working with so many different kinds of people. Understanding how his ease connecting with different personality types related to some of the key relationships that resulted from his parents' divorce helped Gregory overcome some painful feelings about his past. As we worked to make sense out of these feelings, I was struck by how much Gregory benefited from his work as a teacher. He put incredible amounts of energy into his teaching and his students. He also caused me to remember how my tenth grade English teacher did the same for me. She reached out and made me feel special. In the process, this remarkable teacher helped me calculate my own dividend.

"Elisabeth, may I speak with you for a minute?" My tenth grade English teacher, Connie, requested casually, as her class ended and my classmates and I stood from our desks and headed for the door. I had standing lunch plans with my good friend, Sandy, who looked at me and smiled.

"I'll meet you later, come find me at Yonnie's."

"Okay, I'll see you there." Sandy left the room along with my other classmates, as I walked over to Connie's desk in front of the blackboard.

"I don't want to keep you from anything."

"Oh, no, you're not." I could tell from Connie's carefully turned up smile that, while I had no idea what she was going to say, it wasn't anything to worry about.

"I was actually wondering if you and I could go to Yonnie's for lunch, I wanted to talk to you about your paper."

"Sure." I'd never had an actual meal with a teacher, just one-on-one. Her request made me feel as special as the day, years before, when my parents informed my grade school teachers that they were separating, and my first grade teacher, Nancy Langsford, gave me the popular divorce book for kids called My Dad Lives in a Downtown Hotel (Scholastic Books, 1973). Connie was my favorite teacher. Sandy and I used to say that we hoped we'd be just like her when we were older. Wearing stylish long skirts and having always perfect hair. Sandy and I looked a lot more like each other (dark hair and fair freckly faces), and not a bit like Connie. But it was certainly nice to pretend.

Yonnie's, an artsy-crafty delicatessen around the corner from our high school, was a regular hangout among my friends. A series of marble tables, each slightly different from the other, were scattered closely together in a space about the size of one of our classrooms, but with much lower ceilings and all kinds of artwork. A dramatic range of still lifes, nudes and landscapes left barely any blank space on the walls. The chairs at Yonnie's were different from each other too, scattered about with a chaos that paralleled the artwork, producing the creative feel of a student gallery. Or perhaps a coffee house ahead of its time. Perfect for uncalculated hours of free periods and lunches ordering scrambled eggs with cheese and hash browns. We'd inhale our meals in minutes, and wash down the food with a forbidden cigarette if we were reasonably sure no teachers were around.

As we walked into Yonnie's, I hoped Sandy wouldn't be smoking. I knew she wouldn't want Connie to see. Luckily, she wasn't. She was tucked in the back corner with a group of our friends, and she noticed Connie quickly enough to refrain. Connie and I sat up front near the door. We faced each other closely at a small round marble table across from the counter. Yonnie waved and said hello as we were seated. He was tall and friendly with handsome features and skin lightly glossed with the shine that comes from hours of standing over a grill. He never seemed to mind our teenage gab session lunches, day after day. I had a feeling he'd tell the waitresses that we were all young at one time or another, and what was the big deal about our taking up a table or two as long as we paid and didn't make too much of a mess.

I noticed Connie quietly noticing who was and who wasn't smoking back at my table of friends, and I tried to give off the vibe that I'd never smoked a cigarette in my life. My high school friends could be divided into two distinct categories: those who were proud to smoke in front of any and everyone, and those who smoked to fit in, knew their parents would flip out, and tried to conceal their smoking from any and all adults. Sandy and I obviously fell into the latter, closet smoking category. I hoped Connie assumed I never smoked, and I slowly shifted my focus away from my friends and back towards her wondering what we were about to discuss.

"I wanted to take you to lunch to thank you for the paper you wrote." The assignment had been simple and straightforward. Write a chapter from your autobiography. We just finished reading Beryl Markham's West with the Night (North Point Press, 1982) all about life as a woman and a pilot, well before women were pilots. I could think of little or no comparable adventure in my own life. Nothing like flying a plane.

But the word "chapter" made me think of beginnings and endings, which gave me the idea to write about something that had ended. I decided to write about my mother's only romantic relationship after the separation and before she met Stan. My mother first met Steve, a psychiatrist and attorney, in New York at a psychotherapy conference. The paper described a one-year chapter in my life when Steve, my mother, Kathyanne and I spent a great deal of time together. I titled it, appropriately, although not creatively, "Steve".

I wrote about our Amtrak train trips from Philadelphia to New York for weekend visits. He'd taken us to see Broadway shows, and introduced me to the fluffy puffs of bread served in Indian restaurants. I described my excitement when Steve bought me my first camera and taught me to load the film, advance it for each picture, and unload in the dark so I didn't mess anything up. He had a beard and reminded me of a Jewish Santa Claus. Only with sadder, more serious eyes. Sometimes I'd look at him and wonder if something was bothering him. But then I'd end up doubting that since someone couldn't possibly be so kind and bothered at the same time. I remember asking him what he was like when he was little. He said he cared only for comic books and the movies. He'd laugh and say that Kathyanne and I were much better looking, better behaved children than he ever was, and that we were an absolute pleasure. When my mother was annoyed with me for not wanting to share with Kathyanne, he'd say he grew up an only child and commented that he doubted he could share as well as me.

He never took my side in any of my disciplinary conflicts with my mother, but had a diplomatic way of helping me feel that, even if my mother was right and knew best, at least I had a point. At least my gripe was worth hearing. Even if I had to share my book or allow my sister to beat me at Monopoly every once in a while, at least my protests had some value or nugget of meaning. He'd say something like, "It must get frustrating to have such skill in these games and be told to play below your ability. I know it's a pain and you're really a generous sport about it." His simple summary of my side of the story was all I needed. He helped me to feel grown up and good about myself, and I knew that he loved me.

When Steve's relationship with my mother ended, I had trouble making sense of it. I remember my mother explaining to me that they would always have good feelings for each other, and that we could always have the happy memories of our time together. They just couldn't work some grown up things out, so they had to say goodbye. My paper came out like a tribute, an acknowledgement of the happy memories of Steve that I treasured. But it was also about the years following, through my mother's remarriage and our new life. On each birthday, a bouquet of flowers and a long letter arrived from Steve. Each message asked current, thoughtful questions like "had I kept up with photography?" (I hadn't). Or "was I still taking gymnastics?" (I wasn't, I'd switched to ballet and jazz dance). Or "what new book was I reading in school and, by the way, had any teachers assigned the Dicken's classic A Tale of Two Cities (Penguin Classics)?" (They had, and I loved it). His letters felt like they were written from one adult to another, even though the first was sent to me when I was about ten. Like our exchanges when he was in my life, his words made me feel grown up and taken seriously. Though I went through a time of missing him terribly, I never felt deserted or forgotten. The thought and time funneled into each of his script written letters spelled out his care for me, and, in the midst of my new life, his care and letters were enough. Not too much, just enough. A perfect mix of memory and consistence.

Connie explained that my writing about his letters to me was actually quite timely and relevant to her own experience. She explained that there was a young boy in her life, whom she knew in the same way that Steve knew me.

"Reading your paper helped me to know better how I want to handle some difficult questions about what to do with my feelings for him in spite of the fact that my relationship with his father has ended. I don't want him to feel obligated to have a relationship with me, but I don't want him to feel abandoned. Your paper really comforted me, really. Thanks for writing it." I smiled, imagining how special Connie must be to this boy, as Steve was to me.

"Steve's writing to me has always made me feel special," I explained. "I can't remember if I wrote it that way in the paper, I mean, I have enough parents as it is. My mother and father and Stan. And my father's started dating someone great. She's fun and smart and has two sons around my age. I think he's going to get married. I have enough parents as it is, that's for sure. But the letters make the relationship different. Something special where I know he's thinking of me and interested to know what's going on in my life."

"That's what's so complicated, I know this boy has enough parents too. It's so hard to know how to avoid intruding but keep the kind of relationship that would be best for him. I mean, I don't have children, and he's the closest thing to a son I've ever had." I thought about how Steve didn't have children either, and it made me sad. I knew that both he and Connie would both be such wonderful parents. "I could see him all of the

time, he's this sweet wonderful boy, and so smart. But I know that keeping up that kind of relationship would just confuse him." I looked down at my fork and pressed my hand lightly into the prongs, wondering what it would be like to see Steve after all this time.

"I hadn't really thought about it that way, I mean about what it would be like to see him instead of to hear from him through the mail, but I guess you're right. If I had continued to see Steve, I might have been confused, and once my mother married, I think it wouldn't have made sense at all. But his letters never confuse me. I save all of them, and, it's hard to explain, but it's like they just make me feel like he cared, and cares."

"And I'm sure he does, I'm sure he really does." I looked up from the fork and noticed that Connie was crying, only for a second. She didn't even wipe off the two or three tears. They just faded. Our conversation made me feel even closer to Steve. Not just through remembering and discussing him, but through realizing that Connie was treating me with the same level of encouragement. Taking me seriously in a style that's different from what a parent can do. Mature parents need to be responsible for too much. Curfews, grades, and all kinds of growing pains. They can't talk with you like semi-adults, but Steve could. In the backdrop of our written relationship, he could communicate with me in a style that helped me build confidence. Connie was speaking with me in the same way, and the parallel brought me closer to Steve. And closer to Connie. They both addressed me with a mature honesty my parents couldn't; my parents had to be parents, not honest friends. Once again, an adult was able to connect with me not as a friend, and not as a parent, but somewhere in the middle. I realized how lucky I was to have Steve in my life. As I re-evaluated the relationship, I realized it had ended only on one level. It had changed into something different, and continued on. Perhaps as you look back on relationships born of your parents' divorce, you will come to a similar positive realization.

While adjusting to the end of Steve and my mother's relationship was difficult, and certainly not the kind of challenge that a child with married parents has to face, the relationship was a positive one, and the experience is a part of who I am today.

Much more significant than my relationship with Steve are my relationships with my four step-siblings and my two step-parents. My mother remarried when I was eleven. And my stepfather, Stan, has become my parent in every sense of the word. He raised me, he disciplined me, he loves me, and the feeling is very mutual. He continues to teach me about gardening and orchids, and when it comes to the strain that having divorced parents causes in the long run, I always look to him as the voice of reason. He is calm, understanding, and very gentle. As gifted as he is a surgeon, he is even more gifted in his ability to care for his family. His children, Lizz and Doug, grew up with us and I cannot imagine my life without them.

My father met Susan about a year after he relocated to Harrisburg for his work. Like my father, Susan was originally from the Harrisburg area. Like my father, she was recently divorced with two children—my brothers, Matthew and Mark. Susan and my father dated for about a year, and then decided to marry. I felt thrilled when they announced their engagement. Susan seemed much more grown up and mature than the other women my father dated. Susan is fun, funny and a great mother. She is also the only one of my four parents who has ever taught me anything about how to cook.

However, I was about fifteen by the time Susan came into my life. My focus was all on my peers, my school and the enamored concept of growing up. Susan, my father, and Susan's sons all lived two hours from Philadelphia in the state's capital, Harrisburg. Naturally, Harrisburg seemed worlds away from my interests, and failed to surface on my teenage radar screen. Since our visitation routine involved my father making multiple trips to visit us, we never felt much direct pressure to visit our father in his new life. And this was just fine with Kathyanne and me. We were both passionately absorbed in our adolescent worlds and not at ages that lent themselves to frequent travel.

Philadelphia, and our life with my mother and Stan, was home. After many years of a hectic visitation schedule of shuttling back and forth between my mother's home and my father's apartment, Kathyanne and I wanted, and probably needed, to have our time with our father take place primarily on our terms, in our environment.

I have often wondered about how our lack of time in Harrisburg may have hurt our father, and how our lack of interest in his life there may have let him down. Clearly, my fear about his potential disappointment is further commentary on the aftermath of divorce. I constantly feel like I come up short with respect to spending time with each parent. There never seems to be enough hours in the day to make up for such shortcomings. So we all tried, and continue to try, to make up for lost, irretrievable time.

Obviously, not everyone is so fortunate as I have been with respect to the positive relationships that result from our parents' divorce. One of my clients, Gabbie, shared with me difficult memories while she reflected on her father's romantic history.

Gabbie began therapy to adjust to the break-up with her boyfriend, Sam. She sobbed through most of our early sessions, as she admitted to a laundry list of reasons she should have left Sam months ago—his drinking, his flirtatious friendships with many other women, his laziness and his lack of a career.

"I can't believe I put up with it all, and just hoped he wouldn't dump me. When he did dump me, I begged for another chance, and he refused. Said he needed his freedom. Whatever." Gabbie had a full, round face and slender, muscular build. She dressed for success and presented as someone you would not expect to be dating a guy who was frequently out of a job. Sam was a candy bar in every sense of the word, and Gabbie easily admitted that she was only renting him. She also admitted to a long history of "killing time with losers" which we soon redefined as "renting with candy bars."

We utilized the Five Step Guide to help her work through the past. This worked well for Gabbie. She seemed energized as she re-told her stories, re-processed her past, faced the mirror and confronted her commitment phobia. She figured out the clear relationship between her mother's dating patterns and her own, and expressed determination to overcome the dating patterns that obviously were not working for her as an adult.

When we began to talk about calculating her dividend, she remembered her father's former girlfriend, and their complex relationship:

"When Helen and my father got together, Helen was only twenty-three. A twenty-three-year-old, blonde-haired, blue-eyed, chain smoking Quaker. She had been adopted when she was two, and I remember her telling me that, until the age of two, she had nothing but her diapers. Can you imagine? It was as if her first two unaccounted years on earth gave her this mysterious allure. Like a beautiful country cottage with dramatic moldings and fixtures and a wavering foundation. Gorgeous and inviting, yet ready to collapse at any minute." Gabbie shook her head and fiddled with her long beaded necklace.

"How would you describe your relationship with Helen?"

"Ever changing. I'd say it evolved from infatuation to anger to discomfort to love to concern. She and my father were together for ten years. That's a long time."

"Yes, it's a long time and a huge portion of your childhood."

"Right. When we first met, her fun, happy, peppy blondeness was a thrilling contrast from my more elegant, refined and devastated mother. I used to compare them like Charlie's Angels. Helen was all fun and Farrah, while my mother was a serious, saddened version of Jacquelyn Smith. Helen loved to sing and make spaghetti and take long hot baths with the bathroom door wide open. Modesty was not her thing." Gabbie crossed her ankles and covered her chest with her arms as if reflecting on Helen's immodesty made her modest. She leaned back and continued. "When we stayed with our father, he'd read to us at bedtime, then Helen would come in and sing. She'd lounge across our trundle beds wrapped up in a towel. She sang folksy stuff like 'Send in The Clowns' from her hippie days. My brother and I chimed in, although we in no way shared her confident groovy voice or her knowledge of the words. The singing was nice, but what really got to me was the ironic twist that we were grooving to my mother's favorite song! We'd sing 'isn't it bliss, aren't we a pair, me here at last on the ground, you in mid air,' and I'd imagine my mother at home, alone and tearful. I'd wonder if she was having trouble sleeping without us in the house. And I wondered if I should be punching Helen for stealing my mother's husband, not to mention her favorite song, rather than laying there all cuddled and cozy, singing right along."

"It sounds like you felt torn about the relationship."

"Really torn. My enjoyment of her groovy songs and playful spaghetti dinners confused up my sense of loyalty. I loved the way she taught us to throw a single strand up to the ceiling to see if it would stick. It may sound random, but I'd never spent so much time with a blonde! Her blondeness felt like a foreign country. And I was drawn to it like honey." Gabbie paused and sighed. She took off her necklace and wrapped it around her wrist. "At the same time, I equated feeling close to her with betraying my mother. Our fun time left me feeling dirty and fallen. The closest thing I knew to a sin. So I dealt with my guilt by telling my mother, in detail, all about Helen's cellulite!!! I didn't want to tell my mother that she always looked so Farrah-like and pretty, so I focused on her fat! I couldn't help noticing her excess layers, since she spent so much time out of her clothing. Swaying into one room and out the other, headed ultimately into her bath. My mother promised me I'd never have to worry about cellulite because the women in our family were blessed with thin legs and narrow hips, even after childbirth."

"How did your mother handle your stories about Helen?"

"She was <u>always</u> interested. I think that's a piece of why I did it. She listened with such overwhelming focus and asked for more details. Just how naked was she? (Totally). Just how many baths did she take? (Many). I would return from visits with my father and Helen and sense that our time away had been tough on her. She'd examine Bobby and me with concern, and ask how our weekend was. And she stared at everything from our eyes to our elbows. Examining each inch of us, with these intense, discerning stares. It was never enough to answer with 'fine' or 'okay', and I quickly figured out that discussing Helen's flaws, mainly her hips and thighs, was a way to sooth my mother's desire for information. A way to connect with her and assure her that she would always be my number one. I could be brutal in my critiques, and it was such a relief to watch my mother relax back into herself and smile. Whatever I could say to help my mother and me bond over Helen's groovy faults was worth saying as a means of easing the transition from my father's place back to home."

Gabbie described how her father and Helen eventually broke up. As her father's career became more high-powered, Helen's alternative aura proved to be a difficult fit. They realized they wanted different things. That's what Gabbie's father explained, but Gabbie had the strong impression that the choice was not Helen's to make. Gabbie and Helen kept in touch for a few years, until Helen married and started a family of her own. Gabbie was torn about the relationship while she and her father were together, but even more so once they split up.

"She wanted to keep in touch, and I was seriously worried about her. She was smoking more than ever, and she seemed, I don't know, unstable. I kept picturing her as a two-year-old with nothing but her diapers! That's how she seemed—so afraid and alone. Plus, how would my mother feel to know that we had lunch every once in a while? She wouldn't be thrilled, I can assure you!"

"How old were you by this point?"

"Fifteen, sixteen. I guess."

"How would you have lunch? I mean, where did you have lunch. How did you arrange it?"

"She would meet me at school. We were allowed to go out for lunch. That way she could keep in touch and my parents wouldn't know. I think my father did know, and was *fine with it. But I never told my mom."*

"Well, it's a lot for a fifteen, sixteen-year-old to worry about—the stability and happiness of a grown adult."

"Tell me about it. It was really stressful. Hoping that she would be okay, a lot like my worry for my mother, over the years. The whole situation was stressful from the beginning. Feeling torn between her and my mother. Not that there ever was a contest, but just dealing with my mother's sensitivity—my mother was sensitive and I'd say she had a right to be—but the relationship was always stressful."

"Does Helen remind you of anyone by any chance?"

"Not exactly, but my relationship with her does. Let's just say that I was torn about her the way I'm usually torn about the guys I date. All these 'candy bars' as you have taught me to call them."

"You know, I once worked with a client who had her own name for candy bars that was a little bit different. She called them 'the strugglers'." I was talking about Madeline (the hairdresser from Chapter One), and hoping that recalling her poignant terminology would be helpful to Gabbie.

"That's it! Sam was obviously a candy bar in that he wasn't good for me. But the candy bars that I choose are a specific type—they are all strugglers. They all seem to be trying, like how Sam tried so hard to get a job. And I want to help him like I wanted to help Helen. I hated to see her struggle—she tried to quit smoking like twenty times and she'd become a total train wreck! Sam too. So Sam and Helen are totally different people. But they are both strugglers and I get wrapped up in an obligation to help them through their struggle. And it's like, what in the hell is the point of trying so hard if, ultimately, I'm the one doing all the work?"

"Good question." Gabbie nodded and gave a tight-lipped smile.

"Still, I don't regret knowing her. There's some aspect of her that's still with me, and it's not all bad. I learned from my father's dating her that it's better to really get to know someone before you marry. Being in love isn't always enough. And I have happy memories of a lot of great times, singing, cooking, skiing. We took great trips together, and it's weird, but I still throw spaghetti on the wall to see if it sticks. And when I do it, I think of Helen and feel really happy."

Gabbie had a clear sense of the downside and the dividend of her relationship with Helen, and was able to push herself on her pattern of care-giving with struggling candy bars. In her thirties, she married a wonderful apple named Tom. "A major apple, non-struggler" was how Gabbie enthusiastically described him in her letter to me, announcing their engagement.

Gabbie's experiences with Helen demonstrate that even complicated, difficult relationships that result from your parents' divorce may have a positive dividend. By re-visiting these relationships once you have gained a more psychologically mature perspective on your past, you will be in the best position to determine your dividends and make the most of them.

Gabbie struggled with the end of her father's relationship with Helen. And Helen's limited maturity exacerbated Gabbie's struggles. My mother's boyfriend Steve seemed extremely respectful of my space and kept in touch with me in a way that was mature and sensitive to my mother's re-marriage and my many parents. By contrast, Gabbie seemed to take on a burden during the years that she kept in touch with Helen. Gabbie's challenges with Helen are symbolic of the many painful experiences that can comprise the scars of a parents' divorce. Like so many children of divorce, Gabbie was over-stimulated by exposure to her fathers' dating experiences and over-stressed by her mother's pain. This pattern of over-stimulation and over-stress obviously contributes to the phenomenon of fear of commitment among adults with divorced parents. Children of divorce enter adulthood with too much information about what their parents did wrong. It's not at all surprising that their information overload makes them scared about commitment and wary of repeating their parents' mistakes.

In spite of the downside, the relationships that result from your parents' divorce can have a dividend worth calculating. As you create the inventory we speak of next, be aware of the unique personal strength that can flow from growing up in a divorced household. Whatever relationships have resulted from your parents' divorce, take the time to reflect on them and how they shape your personality and your adult experience.

Tips and Suggestions:

- Create your Inventory of Parent Figures and Siblings by listing every significant relationship that you have been exposed to as a result of your parents' divorce. *This list focuses on, but is not limited to, your parents' current and former romantic partners and their children. If, for example, your mother's sister moved in with you after your parents separated and lived with you for many years, it may make sense to include your aunt in your Relationship Inventory since you probably know her more intimately because of the divorce.*

- Write for at least a half hour about each person on the list. What are their best qualities? What are their least favorable qualities? What, if anything, have you learned from them? How have they influenced you?

- List as many possible dividends as you can think of regarding the advantages of your exposure to these relationships. *Even if the dividend seems silly or superficial, write it down. All dividends are worth calculating!*

chapter eight

■

SQUEEZE LEMONADE
FROM YOUR LEMONS

■

This chapter will emphasize the importance of identifying the possible upside of fearing intimacy and delaying long-term commitment. Countless adults with divorced parents fumble through years of dissatisfaction and disappointment in the dating department. The leading literature on divorce tends to criticize adults with divorced parents for marrying later than their peers. This literature has failed to explore what adults with divorced parents may have to gain by making important life choices when they are more emotionally mature. Clearly, adult survivors of their parents' divorce display increased levels of fear of commitment. But fear of commitment can be a good thing—a dividend in disguise—as long as one learns to identify it, figure out what it means, and eventually address it. Fear of commitment gives us time to know ourselves before making tremendous life decisions with long-term implications. Describing fear of commitment as a silver lining that can dispel the dreary clouds of divorce is probably overreaching. But fear of commitment can generate an unanticipated and unlikely upside to an otherwise dreadful event. Fear of commitment is a consequence of divorce that hurts and makes dating harder, but carries with it great potential to lead children of divorce to eventually make better choices and build happier lives.

Ellen, a happily married client whose parents divorced when she was four, explained the advantages of delaying commitment:

> My parents' divorce taught me that divorce is pretty damn awful. If I hadn't been so afraid of ending up just like them, I most likely would have married sooner, like most of my friends. Don't get me wrong, I felt left out being single in my late twenties and early thirties, and that was hard. But I'm so much better off. The guys I was dating back in my twenties weren't right for me. Once I came into my own professionally, I started dating people with whom I actually had things in common. Waiting, as I did, to marry clearly paid off. I know I am much better off, and I'm very, very happy.

Recently, Morgan, a single client whose parents divorced when he was ten, reflected on being a bachelor and his desires to meet a life partner:

> Yes, I would much rather be married. But not to any of the women I have dated. And not now. I didn't learn much about what makes a happy marriage from my parents. I only learned what not to do. Then again, maybe that's not such bad information. I know NOT to get married just because everyone else is doing it. NOT to ignore your spouse and live separate lives. And I'm determined NOT to get married until I know myself a little bit better and feel more grounded.

One of the most well-known figures in current popular culture to publicly articulate the dividend of her parents' divorce is the pop singer Christina Aguilera. The public watched this former mouseketeer turned mega pop star as she paraded around in outrageous outfits and over-the-top hairstyles. For many of her young adult years, she was frequently compared to her co-mouseketeer, Britney Spears. During her single years, Spears was viewed as much more wholesome and together, while Aguilera was ridiculed for her unconventional looks and rebellious behavior. Interestingly, Aguilera married music marketing executive Jordan Bratman in November, 2005 and speaks openly about how this loving relationship has changed her life.

Meanwhile, Spears (whose parents stayed married throughout Spears' childhood and did not separate until she was out of the house) has split from her husband and the father of her children, faced custody battles, and suffered publicly with serious emotional struggles. Her life seems to be in shambles. Of course, no one knows what the relationships of celebrities really look like behind closed doors, but it is interesting and sad to contrast the very public paths of these two young and talented singers, one whose parents divorced, and one whose parents stayed together until their oldest child was essentially out of the house. Aguilera speaks eloquently about the divorce dividend:

> My parents' divorce and hard times at school, all those things combined to mold me, to make me grow up quicker. And it gave me the drive to pursue my dreams that I wouldn't necessarily have had otherwise.

Reflecting on Britney Spears and her awful recent trajectory from mega-stardom to public humiliation, it is worth noting that her parents stayed together and then separated after she was out of the house. The issue of parents staying together, unhappily, and then divorcing once their children are older, or not divorcing at all, is an interesting and important one. One way to explore the under-acknowledged, underlying advantages of delaying commitment is to consider the alternative. In addition to considering how many adults with divorced parents delay commitment, it is also worth considering how many adults whose parents stay together, unhappily, are inclined to do the opposite—to marry earlier and struggle less with their decision to commit. My counseling experience with Dan, a father of two, is reflective of my work with several adults whose parents stuck it out through blatantly dysfunctional marriages.

Dan and I had been meeting for over a month before he mentioned the likelihood of his wife's affair. Dan was in his mid thirties and he and his wife, Noel, had two children, Olivia, age six, and Alexander, age four. Originally, Dan explained that he was initiating therapy because he felt "down in the dumps". Not "depressed" he clarified with assured precision, just down. He and Noel had been married for seven years, and they had lived together for five years before marrying. He described feeling very much in love with her, "the girl of my dreams in every way". He smiled like a shy, blushing kid as he described her: blonde, tall, thin and "as pretty as Nicole Kidman." The couple first met fresh out of college as young Capitol Hill staffers, and both had built successful, "life in the fast lane," political careers. His work as a lobbyist following years on the Hill and on various political campaigns was going just fine financially. He was making a small fortune; however, he found his energy and enthusiasm reduced and his concentration frequently wandered.

"I love my job, always have. It's the best work in the world. So it bothers me. No, it scares me that I can't stay focused these days like I used to." Dan's hairline receded into fine dark curls and the anxious expression scaling his long, thin face reflected an agitated look of permanent surprise. While the thin blue skin below each eye suggested utter exhaustion, his fists clasped together with tight excitement and he leaned forward as he spoke, as if he were fully prepared, at any unexpected moment, to pop up off the couch and run a marathon.

"What are you scared of?" I asked, as Dan paused, taking a quick breath before answering me with another question.

"I can't say, exactly. Am I simply afraid of losing my edge?"

"I don't know, are you?" Dan then described the sharp competitive edge his mother encouraged him to cultivate. Ever since he was a kid, Dan felt intense pressure to succeed. His brother was expelled from various grammar schools as well as two different high schools, and the clear expectation placed upon Dan was that he excel and flourish academically. Throughout school, he brought home straight A's, no matter what, and his distinguished academic career included awards, college scholarships, and, upon graduation, a prestigious job on Capitol Hill. Dan continued, describing his boundless scholastic and professional energy.

"The most important thing, in the beginning, was to make my mom proud. And the more recognition my grades afforded me, the happier she seemed. Well, at least my grades gave her happy moments. I became known, in school and in my career, as the go-to guy who could get the job done no matter what. Stress is no problem for me. I've built a career, a profitable one for that matter, out of being able to understand and manage complicated legislative and political issues coupled with my ability to stay calm and focused in a crisis. And if I lose that edge, I'm through."

"Can you place when you began feeling down in the dumps, or when your concentration first started to wane?" Again, Dan hesitated, frowning carefully before answering with questioning reservation.

"How can I say? It's been over a month, for sure, but I just can't say when. It's weird. As if my focus is so off, that I can't focus on your question well enough to answer it."

"Well, has anything changed recently?"

"Good question. And the honest answer is, I don't know." I asked Dan to spend some time thinking about whether he could pinpoint anything in his life that had changed that might possibly have precipitated his symptoms, and he agreed to give this question some thought.

In the meantime, we discussed his family history and various aspects of his current experience. Dan described a strong and devoted relationship with his mother. He painted her as quiet and kind, pretty, but not beautiful. He smiled, remembering and recounting how she always had time for him. Sometimes, he admitted, too much time.

"She definitely lived for me. My brother, Sam, was too much of a partier and she just couldn't control him. I, on the other hand, wanted nothing more than to make things easy on her, and she was all about my success. She knew everything I was studying and reading and was more than eager to drive me to debate team practice and wherever else I needed to go. She went on and on to her friends about every award. You know the type, best mom on earth, just a little bit over-absorbed into my world."

Dan remembered how, while his parents had been married for over fifty years, he felt little or no connection to his father.

"Dad worked crazy hours as a traveling salesman and was forever on the road. That's all fine and well, but even when he wasn't traveling for work, he was barely around. He was about the most handsome guy you'd ever seen. Seriously, everyone said he looked like Brando in On the Waterfront and the ladies just loved him. They beyond loved him, worshiped is a more suitable term. My mom loved to tell me how he had so many girls in high school. Said she just couldn't believe it when he started coming around. Oh, so, where was I?"

"You were describing how your dad wasn't around." Dan's descriptions echoed his concerns, as he struggled to sustain his focus. Focused or not, his voice contained constant energy and urgency.

"Right, so he'd go in these phases where he'd stay out all night. And Mom would come wake me up and just cry. It was this on and off kind of thing, as I remember it.

There'd be weeks where he would essentially disappear, staying out night after night. Then weeks where he was around and Mom would just pop back into her subdued but cheerful self and act like nothing in the world was the matter. And I knew to go straight along with her act. I also knew that it was just a matter of time before Dad would start disappearing again and Mom's tears and desperation would kick back in. We both knew he had other women."

"How?"

"It was just something in the air." Dan turned each palm upward, cupping them together and bouncing them slightly as if he could feel dense air in each palm, heavy and bursting with his father's infidelity. "Plus, Mom would find receipts from romantic restaurants she'd never dreamed of dining in herself. Or from Tiffany's which they clearly couldn't afford."

"Did she ever confront him that you remember?" I asked quietly.

"No way. Not a chance. In fact, the few times that I bad mouthed him during her tear-filled, gloomy, late nights, she defended him. Even slapped me once when I called Dad a washed up, good-for-nothing cheater."

We continued to explore Dan's past, and the desolation of his parents' marriage became an overriding theme. Then, on the morning of our fifth meeting, Dan came into my office and began speaking before giving himself permission to sit. I looked up at him and felt confused by his hesitation to sit. His towering stance tugged his drooping eyes lower, while his resolute elbows pointed outward as if they were charting an escape.

"I first suspected that Noel was seeing someone about three months ago when, out of nowhere, we completely stopped having sex. At first, I thought it was just my imagination, or that she was over-worked, over-tired. The whole kid thing. But we went years without sleep when our kids were babies, and Noel always managed to keep her career booming while our sex life barely missed a beat. So why now? I planned dinners and a romantic getaway where she refused to join me at the last minute blaming her work. But now I know for sure."

"How's that? How do you know?" I asked. When I first began practicing, most of my clients learned of their partners' affairs (or were caught in affairs themselves) through the discovery of unusual cell phone activity. Frequently, a bill would arrive for a cell phone that was thought to be cancelled, and all the calls on the statement would be to the same mysterious number. Currently, e-mail has replaced the cell phone as the most typical affair busting evidence, so I anticipated Dan's response.

"I got desperate, couldn't take feeling so cut out with no explanation. So what do I do? I log onto her email and it's all right there in her Yahoo! account." Dan finally allowed himself to be seated. Sliding down onto the sofa slowly, poor Dan seemed to resemble a scared, sinking ship. He rubbed his index fingers under his eyes and then began to slowly massage his neck, looking down as he continued. "So it's a guy I know. He's younger and single and there they are on email, professing their love. I'm sitting there reading, spying is more like it, watching my whole perfect little world disintegrate before me. How could she do it?"

"I don't know. You would probably be able to answer that question better than I. Was your little world really so perfect? I mean, were you genuinely surprised?"

"Yeah, sort of. Yes and no. But, either way, it really hurts." Dan's gaze stayed with the floor as he lowered his head to his hands and started to cry. "And do you want to hear the worst part? I found out two days ago and I can't even tell her! I feel like I've been hit by a truck, but I can't get myself to bring it up!"

"Have you spoken with her at all?"

"Barely. You know how it is. With the kids you can get into this routine with all of the crap that needs to happen, so we've just gone back and forth about who is taking whom to soccer on Saturday and so on. I've known since the day before last, and she's just continuing to say how late she needs to work, and I'm basically letting her lie to my face. She's so wrapped up in her affair that she hasn't even noticed that I'm just hanging on by a thread! I've just gone along with her lies. What kind of a wimp am I? And what am I doing?"

"It's a good question, what are you doing?"

"I'm going along with business as usual, because I can't even imagine bringing it up and how that would play. I can't stand the thought of putting it out there, so I'm going along with the worst kind of treatment there is. And I swore a long time ago I would never let anyone treat me this way."

"You'd never let anyone treat you this way. When did you make yourself that promise?"

"When I saw how my dad's little flings just broke my mother's heart. Downright destroyed her. Aged her before her time. To me, the worst part was how she couldn't tell him, and we all had to pretend things were normal."

"So, on some level, this situation is familiar."

"*Too familiar. None of us can guarantee that our spouse will be faithful. Her cheating is obviously tearing me apart. But what's really blowing my mind is my own refusal to speak up. I've become my mother! My heart is just as broken as hers, and I'm married to this superstar of a glamorous woman, just as good looking as my dad. And, it turns out, just as deceitful. And here I am, paralyzed!*"

"*Well, sometimes we repeat the very things that are the most painful from our past. Consciously, we may promise ourselves we'll do everything in our power to avoid them. But unconsciously we can be drawn to repeat the most painful parts of our history that remain unresolved.*"

"*Why in the hell would we do that?*" Dan looked at me as if I were a Martian. In some sense I guess I was. We sat there together in the same room, two beings coming from such different perspectives that we essentially did inhabit different planets. He a lobbyist, me a shrink. He harshly questioned my theoretical hypotheses, yet seemed eager to find some possible explanation.

"*Well, one theory is that there's a fantasy attached to our unconscious pull to repeat the past. That maybe if we repeat it, we can fix it or master it in some way. But usually, instead, we just end up repeating and re-experiencing the pain.*"

"*Well, I will say that there's some truth there. I'm sick about Noel, and the whole thing is also making me remember a lot of stuff about my parents that I'd rather forget.*"

"*Like what?*"

"*Like how miserable they were together. And how I never bought their pretense that everything was okay. How they never talked about anything. Never affectionate. They lived separate lives in a sense, but Mom just needed him around and so we never complained. Just went along ignoring the obvious.*"

"*And what else?*"

"*And here I am doing the same thing. And it's true that all I care about is keeping our family together and keeping Noel. I'm trying to think about how to be a better husband as if that's the answer. As if maybe I can win her back. But I know from those damn emails that she's in love with someone else. Or at least she thinks she is. Eventually, I have to confront her, but I can't find the words.*"

Dan struggled with the pain of Noel's affair and with his own resistance to engage in an honest discussion. He explored how his mother taught him, by example, to live in a form of painful denial. And explained, eventually, how his father's distance and unavailability may have led him to choose a partner who was equally detached. When I asked him if there was ever any indication of the possibility that Noel might someday be unfaithful, he initially said there was none whatsoever. Then, a few weeks later, he re-visited this question without my prompting, acknowledging an affair he had discovered when they were first living together, years before they married. Not surprisingly, he learned from a bill that arrived for a cell phone he thought they had cancelled.

"I saw the charges for months worth of calls to the same place, dialed the number, and realized it was someone I knew. I figured we were just young, and she was so beautiful. After all, she was living with me, not him, so wasn't I the lucky one? I thought marriage would cure it, and I decided to swallow it and just let it go."

"Did you ever ask her about the phone bill?"

"No, I couldn't. I was just as stuck then as I am now."

It took Dan weeks to feel prepared to talk to Noel about her affair. And once he did, he asked her to try couples counseling and she refused. Soon afterwards, Noel left Dan and granted him custody of their children. Olivia and Alexander spent most weeks with him, and weekends with her in her new apartment downtown. Dan continued in therapy and experienced devastating pain as he went through their divorce. However, his children remained close to him, and his career began to blossom even beyond his prior success.

"What I need to work on now," *Dan explained during the weeks following the finalization of his divorce,* "is how to be alone. I know, intellectually, that I was most alone in a disconnected marriage. But I had the marriage and I could pretend that I had Noel. Mirage is probably a better term than marriage for what we had, but now it's like I have nothing."

"Well, when a relationship ends, there are multiple levels of loss. You lose Noel, the person. And, of course, there are the losses associated with your whole history with her, all of your years together, it all changes in light of the divorce. Then there's the marriage, the relationship itself. By that I mean you lose the status of being in a relationship."

"Yeah, for me, surprisingly, that part's the hardest. The state of being married gave me a sense of security, albeit a false one, and I sometimes feel lost without it. But I've realized that if I am ever going to be happy with someone else, I need be happy on my own."

Being alone without the status of being in a relationship became a substantial focus of Dan's therapy. Over time, he adjusted to being single, cultivated an interest in photography, developed a routine as a single dad, and felt more comfortable with his independence. When we ended our work together, he said that there were still many things he wished were different, but he described himself as happy. He understood his pull towards Noel in a different way, and hoped to someday have a relationship with someone monogamous and more available. By exploring how his parents' unhappy, unfaithful marriage affected him, Dan realized how he unknowingly repeated his mother's mistakes. He fell for someone a lot like his father and proceeded without caution even though he learned, early on, that Noel was not faithful.

Dan did not hesitate to make a life-long commitment to someone unfaithful in spite of the pain he watched his mother suffer growing up. According to various psychological theories, this phenomenon of repeating the past is common. People are consciously or unconsciously drawn to repeat the painful parts of our past, either to make an attempt to fix them, or simply because they are familiar. Adults with unhappily married parents seem more vulnerable to repeating the past than adults with divorced parents, as they are not forced to face the flaws in their parents' marriage. Over time, Dan overcame significant hurdles, and faced some difficult truths about his parents' marriage, and his own. He then worked hard to be happy on his own, and thus set the stage for a happier future.

Dan's experience highlights a common contrast between adults with divorced parents and adults whose parents were unhappily married but chose NOT to divorce. Dan did NOT struggle during his young adult relationships and he did NOT delay commitment. He DID, however, unknowingly repeat the very pattern that was most painful to him growing up.

Dan's experience with Noel is also emblematic of many divorces in that, often, one spouse wants to save the marriage more than the other. Had Noel been willing to engage in therapy and address their problems, perhaps their relationship could have been saved. Of course, saving their marriage would be the optimal outcome. And, of course, their divorce—like all divorces—was tough on everyone, especially their children. Having never met Noel, I am in no position to genuinely evaluate her willingness to work on her marriage with Dan. From the countless details that Dan described, he seemed genuinely motivated to save their marriage. According to Dan, Noel first refused to acknowledge an affair. Then she refused to give up the affair, and appeared to lack Dan's level of commitment to address their problems and try to make it work.

Dan and Noel's story also raises the difficult but compelling question of what these adults, and their children, would have experienced had Dan remained in the marriage and never raised the issue of Noel's infidelity. We cannot answer this question with any accuracy, but it is certainly a question worth considering.

Some critics of divorce would remind us that Dan and Noel are consenting adults who, together, made a grown up decision to bring innocent children into the world. They might argue that Dan's silence would be in the best interest of his children. His silence would allow his kids to grow up in a home with both of their parents in what some experts have called a "good enough marriage." These experts explain that with a "good enough marriage", children feel they are number one in their parents' eyes and they are not forced to make sense of two separate households with different and conflicting rules, norms and values. These experts argue that a "good enough marriage" is preferable to what other experts have promoted as a "good divorce."

Of course, there are no good divorces. Some may be less traumatic than others, but most cause damage beyond full repair. Consider the relationship between Dan's parents' "good enough" marriage and Dan's eventual choices with respect to a life partner. And consider the possible impact on Dan's kids had they grown up in a family with ongoing but unmentioned infidelity. Isn't the question of divorce vastly more complicated than can be addressed by advising people to stay in a "good enough" marriage for the sake of their children?

In her book *The Unexpected Legacy of Divorce* (Hyperion, 2000), Wallerstein writes of her respect for unhappily married couples of past generations who, like Dan's parents, stuck it out and stayed together. She writes that these couples struggled with all of the "problems that beset modern marriage—infidelity, depression, sexual boredom, loneliness, rejection." While "few problems went away as time wore on…that's not what mattered most to these adults." Wallerstein concludes, "I think you should seriously consider staying together for the sake of your children." She points to one woman in particular who "explained 'There are two relationships in this marriage. He admires me as a wonderful mother. As a wife, I bore him in every way possible. But our children are wonderful and that's what counts.'" Wallerstein praises this woman's perspective and argues that children whose parents stay together are better off than those whose parents divorce.

In *Between Two Worlds* (Three Rivers Press, 2006), Elizabeth Marquardt describes a young woman, Allison, who (like Marquardt) has divorced parents. She also has a loving marriage (like Marquardt) and a child who brings her great joy. Marquardt points to Allison's decision to spend "quite a while" in therapy before having a child as a reason to criticize Allison's parents' decision to divorce. She explains that Allison wanted to engage in therapy to make sure she could be a good parent, and makes noteworthy observations of how Allison's self doubt is emblematic of the wrath of divorce.

It's true that, as the stories in this book describe, children with divorced parents frequently doubt themselves and question their instincts. But isn't it also worth asking whether Allison would be in her loving, happy marriage had her parents stayed together? The divorce necessitated the therapy, and the therapy helped Allison prepare for a good marriage and helped her feel prepared to be the best parent she could be.

Maybe we'd all be better off if people waited to know themselves better and become fully mature before marrying and bringing children into the world. Maybe her waiting period allowed her to identify and overcome her fears about the commitment associated with parenthood. Maybe her waiting, and the soul searching that accompanied it, helped her be better prepared for the enormous, life-long endeavor of raising children. Maybe Allison, like so many other happily married adults with divorced parents, has a more mature approach to marriage than the approach she witnessed growing up. Maybe Allison's children will have it better than Allison had it as a kid. Maybe they'll have it much better. If Allison can create that level of improvement for the next generation, it's worth considering that divorce, as terrible and ugly as it is, can also generate an important dividend.

To be sure, it is helpful to be reminded that many divorces that occur do not need to happen. The most notable unnecessary divorce was a fictional one. During the height of the divorce boom in the 1970s, the film *Kramer vs. Kramer* won Academy Awards, received great acclaim, and achieved broad viewing as a model of what one might describe as a bad divorce turned good. Unfortunately, this film glorified a growing national trend. During the custody court battle, the film depicts great tension between the parents with respect to each parents' strong desire to win custody of their only son. The mother (played by Meryl Streep) wins custody even though she disappeared from her son's life for weeks without making contact. She temporarily abandons her young son, but, before her exit, she was his primary caregiver. She was a typical stay-at-home mom while her husband (played by Dustin Hoffman) was totally absorbed in his work and perpetually unavailable to his wife and child.

The bulk of the film takes place during the mother's absence and follows Dustin Hoffman's character as he blossoms by necessity into a wonderful, loving and extremely available father. At the same time, Meryl Streep's character seems to build a sense of identity during her absence. By doing so, she appears to evolve into a happier person. While the mother wins custody, the film ends with the mother expressing great conflict about taking her son from the only home he has ever known. With the film's conclusion, it seems unclear where the son will end up living, as both parents are able to acknowledge the importance of the other parent's role in the young boy's life. The viewer is left with the sense that these are two adults who are very much on the same page about wanting what is best for their son. The viewer also sees how both parents grow immensely as individuals through the process of facing some of the basic problems in their marriage—his unavailability and her loss of identity. Granted, the Kramers' divorce and its parties are fictional, but they represent a perfect example of the kind of divorce that does not need to happen.

With hard work, couples whose experiences parallel the Kramers should be able to work it out. The shortcomings of the film *Kramer vs. Kramer* symbolize the value in pointing out that some marriages do not need to fail. But overemphasizing the virtue of staying in a marriage solely for one's children takes this concept too far. This message—that people should stay in a "good enough" marriage—can also be dangerous. Someone already feeling insecure, scared and hurt in the wake of dealing with infidelity or emotional abuse in their marriage could easily hear this message and become paralyzed with fear. Assertions about the value of a "good enough" marriage may cause untold numbers of people to stay stuck and emotionally abused. One could even analyze such a message as encouraging and indulging commitment-phobia. By remaining in a flawed situation, genuine intimacy remains impossible, as true commitment does not occur.

The intention of this book is NOT to argue that divorce is okay or that all divorces that occur are necessary. The intention of this book is to argue that every family and every marriage is different and complex and that some of the blanket statements in the existing literature are dangerous. The purpose of this book is to communicate a hopeful message to adults with divorced parents that they can grow from and overcome their parents' mistakes.

In this book, we consider the possibility that, for many families, divorce may be the very worst possible outcome, unless you consider the alternative. Think about the many vignettes in this book about adults with divorced parents struggling in their relationships, delaying marriage and eventually finding happy, healthy relationships. Then consider Dan's story and the confusing messages that children are exposed to when they grow up in households with unfaithful or emotionally abusive, unhappily married parents.

The vignettes, the survey material, the personal and professional observations we have been explaining that lead up to Step Four are designed to explore and document the many layers of tragedy associated with growing up in a divorced household. Now it is time for you to genuinely consider the alternative. It is time for you to gather the lemons that comprise your own personal history of growing up with divorced parents and make some lemonade. Give yourself credit for the many hurdles you have faced by living through your parents' divorce and its aftermath. By following the next tips and suggestions, you can calculate your personal *Divorce Dividend* and use your lemonade to help you begin to forge healthy relationships.

Tips and Suggestions:

- List every painful feeling and bad experience you can think of that relates to your dating experiences.

- Put a check next to any of the feelings and experiences on your list that mirror feelings or experiences that you remember from anything related to your parents' divorce.

- Put a star next to any of the feelings and experiences on your list that mirror anything that either parent has shared with you (or that you observed as a child) regarding their feelings or experiences related to their divorce.

- Ask yourself if your fear of commitment may be a form of reliving or re-experiencing pain related to your parents' divorce. Spend at least a half hour writing about this possibility.

- Ask yourself what your life might look like had your parents stayed together.

- Ask yourself what your life might look like if you married any of the people you listed in your Inventory of Romantic Relationships from chapter five. *Remember, if your parents had stayed together, you may have been more likely to marry sooner. But you also may have been more likely to repeat your parents' mistakes.*

- If you _did_ marry any of these people, evaluate that decision and write about what, if anything, you learned or gained from this marriage.

- List any and every possible dividend of your parents' divorce and your subsequent commitment phobia.

Step Five: Forge Healthy Relationships

Once you have completed steps one through four, you are ready to practice doing things differently with respect to dating. I use the term "practice" intentionally. Approaching Step Five as if you are practicing a newly acquired, underdeveloped skill will be key to your success. Remember, if dating candy bars or renting your relationships is what you have done thus far, then dating candy bars or renting your relationships is what you are finding most comfortable, even if these are not good for you. We are all most comfortable with patterns that feel familiar, and, especially in times of stress, we are vulnerable to reverting to these old patterns. As you learn to stop having dysfunctional relationships and start forging healthy partnerships, you will most likely experience a good deal of anxiety and feel various forms of discomfort.

One way to deal with your discomfort is to approach dating as a laboratory in which you will practice and experiment with change. Remember when you first learned to drive a car? In the beginning, there was so much to think about—stepping on the gas pedal, hitting the brake, remembering to use your turn signals, putting the car in drive when you wish to go forward versus reverse. Driving took a great deal of effort. Over time, however, you learn to think about and employ all of these necessary skills without having to put as much conscious effort into the process.

Perhaps one of the minor consequences of my parents' divorce, in my opinion, was that I did not learn to drive a car while I was growing up. I think it represented a learning task that each parent kind of left to the other and it just never happened. In fact, I learned to drive rather recently in my thirties. I was surprised by how hard it was, how much effort it took and how much I had to think hard about a lot of different driving instructions at one time. My own needed effort reminds me of observing my clients as they work hard, practice and devote so much effort to make necessary changes in order to reach their goal of finding and maintaining a healthy relationship.

Changing your patterns with respect to dating and relationships, I feel, is a lot like learning how to drive. At first, it will be extremely difficult and should be approached as a form of training in which you are your own best coach. Talk yourself through your discomfort. Remind yourself that your instincts to choose the candy bar partner over the apple may provide the instant gratification of doing what is familiar, but it will also lead to heartache, stomachache, and regret. Coach yourself to try satisfying your dating appetite a little differently—to give an apple a try. Take yourself seriously enough to only date people with whom you might eventually fulfill a long-term relationship hunger rather than those who might satisfy a short-term craving. With hard work and persistence, your practice will pay off and you will enjoy a mutually rewarding relationship which leads to a healing commitment.

chapter nine

∎

SHOP THE
RELATIONSHIP
SUPERMARKET

∎

Forging healthy relationships takes practice. As you work on this chapter's activities, you will need to coach yourself to practice dating and work on slowly getting to know different people. By doing so, you give yourself a chance to figure out what you like in another person, what qualities you don't like, what qualities in a prospective partner are deal-breakers and what qualities you might be willing to give up if enough other good traits are present.

The concept of Shopping the Relationship Supermarket was introduced to me years ago, when I was explaining the importance of Step Five to Mary, a client with divorced parents. Mary was a self-described "serial monogamist" who had been in one long-term relationship after another and had never been single. Earlier we discussed the advantages of slowly getting to know different people, rather than jumping right into a new relationship as soon as your current relationship fails. I explained the value of giving yourself a chance to experience different types of people and determine what qualities are genuinely most important, and what qualities you might be willing to compromise on if enough of your other criteria are present. As I presented my "forge healthy relationships through dating" talk, Mary interrupted with a laugh and a smile:

Oh Elisabeth, you make it all sound like there's one big relationship supermarket and everyone's walking around squeezing each other the way they would squeeze fruits and vegetables!

While I would not recommend squeezing people as if they were fruits and vegetables, Mary was on to something. My experience with clients and my own experience strongly indicates the following success formula: you will have more success with dating if you approach dating similarly to the way you would approach a trip to the supermarket. You will have more relationship success if you do not approach dating as an all-or-nothing experience in which another person's opinion, acceptance or rejection is excessively important and relevant to your self-worth. You will have more success with dating if you can enjoy being a solo shopper and can focus on yourself. You will have more success with dating if you avoid over-emphasizing the opinions or approval of others. You will have more success in dating if you shop in the fruits and vegetables section and stay out of the candy aisle. Focus on what you like, what you don't like, and what are the healthiest choices on the current market.

One of the keys to forging healthy relationships and dating different people before you begin a relationship is learning to be comfortable being on your own. It may sound strange, or counter-intuitive, that the key to forging healthy relationships is being able to be happy WITHOUT a relationship, but it's true. The more you can enjoy your own company and your independence, the better position you will be in as you make choices about dating and relationships. The concept of being comfortable on your own underlies the ability to successfully shop the supermarket, as people who always need to be in a relationship usually do not give themselves enough of a chance or enough emotional independence to date different people. It is usually harder for them to reflect on their experiences and preferences. They are generally less objective and more desperate in their approach to dating. Remember discussing my client who complained that boyfriends were her anti-depressants? And my client who said she approached each date as if she were the interviewee desperate to do anything and everything just to get the job? And how she wished she could be the interviewer for a change? That's what

Shopping the Relationship Supermarket is all about—walking the aisles independently and interviewing the selection rather than being the frantic interviewee willing to settle for whatever candy bar happens to be on sale. Reflecting on the importance of dating and building enough independence to feel okay with yourself, even if you are not currently in a relationship, always leads my thoughts to Lisa, a young client of mine. Like Dan, the client I spoke of in Chapter Eight, Lisa's parents stayed together throughout Lisa's childhood. Like Dan, Lisa did not hesitate to commit to marriage. In fact, she actively sought to recreate her parents' lives. Unfortunately, she quickly became unhappy when things did not turn out as she hoped and she wanted to move on.

"I'm ending my marriage, because Greg could NEVER make me happy." Lisa explained with surprising ease and self-assuredness during our first meeting. "But I'm not here to work on my marriage. I'm here to work on my relationship with Harry."

"Harry?" I said with a surprised tone.

Lisa nodded. "My boyfriend. We've been together for over a month now, and he refuses to really let me in. He holds my marriages against me and keeps me shut out of his life. I know I'm here by myself, but what I'm really interested in is couples therapy, I just need to convince Harry to join me."

"Can you tell me about your marriages?" I asked her.

"Sure, Dave and I met when I was starting grad school and we were married for four years. Then I met Greg about a year ago, got separated and eloped with Greg as soon as the divorce was final. In retrospect, I jumped in too quickly. My second marriage was a total rebound from the first. I figured it all out when I met Harry. He's my true soulmate and I'm determined to make it work."

I felt instantly overwhelmed by Lisa's relationship roster. She had been divorced and recently re-married, but she wanted couples therapy with her new boyfriend? Now here was a twist that was new to me. And she was only twenty-seven! Sounded like we had a lot of material to cover!

Lisa was not interested in providing much detail on her first marriage or why she left Dave. She seemed equally disinterested in discussing her current marriage to Greg. Of equal concern was Lisa's disinclination to talk, in any meaningful detail, about herself. Harry was her sole topic of interest. Harry's prior financial success in the cyber-world of internet start-ups—Harry's house in the Hamptons—Harry's rugged good looks. For weeks, I attempted to gather Lisa's personal history and learn about who she was. And for weeks, in spite of my efforts to direct the discussion toward Lisa, I learned a lot more about Harry.

Lisa's heavily processed platinum hair, thick make-up, bubbling blue eyes and well-proportioned features gave her the aura of a wanna-be starlet–a swollen, lost looking version of Cameron Diaz. I noticed that Lisa usually looked upward when she spoke, as if wishing for divine intervention, or at least a second chance. She reluctantly revealed that her mother was a popular local talk show host in her mid-sized hometown. Her mother frequently traveled on location throughout Lisa's childhood and was, in her daughter's words, "a drop dead gorgeous hostess with the mostest."

"Could you tell me a little more about her?" I asked, one of many as of yet fruitless attempts to learn about someone other than Harry.

"Well, just picture the most beautiful, smart, successful woman out there. She's always had it all, love, career, fame, fortune. Well, I guess she had it all until recently when she found out that Dad was cheating and left her after thirty-four years of marriage."

When I initially asked Lisa if her parents were married, she said they were, so I was surprised to learn of their separation.

"It's interesting, when I asked you early on if your parents were married, you said yes; and you described a happy marriage."

"I know. That's because they always have been married, and they always have had a great relationship. They never fought, and they were always the life of every party. My mom is always the belle of every ball and my dad is the CEO of a Fortune 500 company. What more could you want? I'm just not used to saying anything about my parents or about my life that's less than perfect. Maybe it was just an instinct. You asked, and, before I knew it, I was giving you the answer I'd given all my life."

"So," I replied softly. "If your parents were always so perfect, what went wrong?"

"Damned if I know. I'm not kidding when I say they never fought. NEVER. And I'm not kidding about the belle of the ball thing. I've been schooled in the art of cocktail conversation, and I can work my way to the top of any crowd. Country club, night club, Sports Club LA. That may sound harsh or stuck up, but I'm here to be honest, right?"

"Yes. Therapy is definitely most effective if you are honest with your therapist."

"Right, so being the belle of every ball is the best way to describe my parents' marriage. And I learned the art of being the belle of the ball from the belle of all balls. I've always had a boyfriend, I've always been 'the love of his life', and we are always the kind of couple that other people long to be. Affectionate, romantic and noticeably in love. And Harry's no exception."

"It sounds like having a boyfriend has always been pretty important," I mentioned.

"More than important, it's been everything. That's probably part of why I forget to mention my parents' separation. I can hardly picture them without each other. Mom has always said that love is everything. And that life without love is not worth living. She's already in love with someone new, another mega-businessman who reminds me a lot of my dad. He's a long-term acquaintance, actually. It's just like my mom to come out on top. And I know my mom has always been proud of my ability to find love."

"Is that what you were supposed to do?" I asked. *"Always have a boyfriend and make your mother proud by being the love of someone else's life?"*

"Well, what else is there? I know I was unhappy with Dave for months, maybe even years. Maybe even always. But, since we're being honest, I wouldn't dare leave him until I met Greg. Then, when I realized that Greg could never make me happy, and that I'd made a terrible mistake, I found Harry. I know it sounds bad, but if Harry would just open up and let me in, I'd be fine and we wouldn't be sitting here having this conversation. Once I can get Harry to commit to me, or at least commit to therapy, he'll realize we were meant to be, and he's all I need."

No matter how long I practice, and how many people I see, I continue to be struck by the power of a parent's message. Being raised with the mantra that life without romantic love (or at least the façade of it) is not worth living can leave an individual trapped; he or she is a shell of a person so fully defined by their string of relationships that they basically fail to exist without them. Lisa was an example of this problem.

I leaned forward. *"You mentioned your marriage to Dave. When was it that you noticed your unhappiness, and what were you unhappy about?"* With so little to go on in terms of who Lisa was beyond her men, I looked for clues as to what would drive her to leave a marriage that she described as, initially, belle of the ball-worthy. Lisa paused, sighed, and gave her signature skyward glance. The frustrated wrinkle between her platinum brows punctuated the ongoing sense that she'd much rather be talking about Harry than Dave.

She shook her head. *"It's hard to say, I'm so not focused on Dave these days, but I think it was right about when I learned about Dad's affair. My parents' perfect marriage imploded, and I got to thinking about my own supposedly perfect mini-belle of the ball life with Dave. I started wondering about why Dave got up in the middle of the night, maybe four or five nights a week, saying he had work to do. So I logged on while he was at the office (Lisa did not work and had not ever held a full time job). I looked up recently visited sites and learned that my perfect jock-star, mini-mogul husband was addicted to internet porn."* For the first time, Lisa's voice sounded real, and I could hear her shattered sadness. Previously, I could only assume the presence of her unacknowledged sorrow hidden behind her matter-of-fact descriptions, which usually sounded as if she was attempting to imitate one of her mother's local news broadcasts.

"How did you deal with that?"

"How do you think?" Broadcast voice returned with a vengeance. "I got a dog and started spending a lot of time walking it, you know, looking around. Dogs are great conversation pieces. And that's how I met Greg, at the dog park. And then I left."

"What's your dog's name?" I knew it was a strange question, as soon as I asked it, but when she referred to her own dog as an "it" I wanted a little clarification.

"Oh, Bailey. Right, I left Bailey with Greg. I'm not really a dog person and Greg is."

"I didn't mean to change the subject," I said quietly. "Did you ever confront Dave about the internet porn?"

"Not until I hooked up with Greg. That's when I knew for sure that I wanted out."

Roughly five weeks after beginning our meetings, Lisa called to gleefully explain that Harry had finally agreed to join her in therapy. She wanted to give me the good news that Harry would be joining us in our sessions. I had anticipated this possibility, and felt conflicted about how to respond. On the one hand, it is important to respect and respond to a client's needs and wishes, whenever possible and appropriate. But were Lisa's wishes appropriate? Is it appropriate to be in couples therapy with a new boyfriend before your second divorce is final, and less than a year after your first divorce is final? Is it even my place to make that determination? Probably not.

On many occasions during our sessions, I attempted to direct the discussion away from Harry in order to learn more about Lisa. Lisa's resistance to such direction made it clear that, at least for some period of time, she needed to spend our sessions talking primarily about Harry. To me, Harry was much less relevant than Lisa's persistent need to be with someone— anyone who allowed Lisa to continue her ongoing status as "the love of his life" (whomever the "his" may be). Still, Lisa needed to discuss Harry, and so that's mostly what we did.

Had we continued individual therapy, I would have begun to point out to her how much I was learning about Harry, and how little I was learning about Lisa. Unfortunately, Lisa did not seem ready for such input, and she was not pleased with my response to her request that I become her couples therapist. A response rooted in this strong sense that it was more important to focus on Lisa, than on Harry.

On the one hand it is important to respect and respond to a client's needs and wishes. On the other hand, it is essential to resist the temptation to, as the family systems theorists call it, "buy into the client's system." In other words, had I changed the course of our therapy, I feared I would be buying into Lisa's idea, rooted in her mother's problematic message, that "life without romantic love is not worth living." I did not want to, through my actions, perpetuate a notion that one cannot fully exist without a romantic relationship, or that what we were doing without Harry in the room (working on Lisa) would somehow be inferior to what we would do with him in our presence (working on the relationship). While I felt extremely invested in continuing our work, I was already indulging her desire to talk at great length about Harry, and worried that letting Harry become any more of a focus than he already was would mean that I was buying into Lisa's destructive pattern.

My training as a couples therapist dictated that I should refer Lisa to a different therapist to do the couple work. Since I had already been meeting with Lisa, I was not in a position to be objective, and that would not be fair to Harry. Were I to agree to see them as a couple, I would need to insist on meeting with Harry individually for the same number of sessions I had already had with Lisa. I knew this would not be realistic, given the urgency of Lisa's desire to get into couples therapy.

"Lisa, I really think it's best if I'm YOUR therapist. I can give you a referral for couples counseling, but I encourage you to continue your individual sessions with me in addition to any therapy you pursue with Harry. I couldn't be objective with Harry after all of the meetings that you and I have done one-on-one."

"But you already know us. With a referral we'll have to start over. And, besides, I don't have any need for individual therapy. I told you from the start—I need to make it work with Harry, and he's finally on board so we can finally get started."

"Have you ever considered that individual therapy might help strengthen whatever progress you and Harry make as a couple?" I tried to pitch my services by speaking the language of Lisa's emphasis on coupledom, figuring it was worth a shot. "It seems you and

I have a lot to talk about. You have been through a lot with your parents' separation and your own relationships." Unfortunately, my pitch didn't go over so well.

"Well, I'll think about it. But if you won't see me with Harry, I guess I'll just take the name and number of someone who will. Then maybe I'll get back to you once Harry and I get situated."

I gave Lisa the numbers of some good couples therapists, and continue to hope that, in the future, I will hear from her.

Five or six sessions are rarely enough to help a client make meaningful, significant changes—especially if the client mostly talks to you about someone other than herself. Keeping my limited level of information in mind, my overall sense of Lisa is that she demonstrates the uncounted numbers of adults who internalize the unhappiness of their parents' marriages and subsequently pay a long-term price. Her parents prioritized how you present at a country club or a cocktail party as far more important than life behind closed doors. What little I learned about Lisa's first marriage to Dave indicated that she found herself in a marriage much like that of her parents. Lisa said she was "unhappy for months, maybe years." I wondered, in retrospect, if the "months" referred to the time following her parents' separation when she began questioning her marriage and learned about Dave's internet porn addiction. And perhaps the "years" referred to the aspects of her marriage that never worked, but that she did not consciously consider while her own parents were still together. Lisa was given the clear message that what mattered was being the belle of the ball, and that life without a romantic partner is not worth living. She absorbed and internalized this message with unquestioning loyalty.

I wondered whether Lisa would have left Dave had Lisa's parents stayed together. And I wondered in what ways Lisa's two marriages may have been similar to the marriage she observed growing up. I continue to hope that Lisa will recognize her need for individual therapy focusing on herself and that I will have the opportunity to explore these unanswered questions.

When considering the importance of Step Five, Shopping the Relationship Supermarket, Lisa's story is especially relevant. Her compromised ability for self-reflection is like many clients I have worked with whose parents pretended to be happily married. Like my former client Dan's initial reluctance to acknowledge and address Noel's infidelity, Lisa wanted to believe that as long as she had a relationship that looked good to others, everything was fine. And if it wasn't fine, Lisa viewed it as someone else's problem. Whether it be Dave's problem (internet porn), Greg's problem ("Greg could never make me happy"), or Harry's ("he refuses to really let me in"). Lisa was profoundly unable to consider what she may have contributed to the problems in her relationships or in her life. Her parents' ongoing presentation of a perfect, belle of the ball, party life gave Lisa the message that she was no one if she did not have a guy. Lisa lived a relationship life that represented the polar opposite of Shopping the Relationship Supermarket. In other words, rather than giving herself a chance to cultivate an independent adult personality and then slowly get to know different people, Lisa could not end one bad relationship until she found another. In this sense, Lisa barely existed. Her entire existence was so dependent on whatever guy she was with that she never gave herself a chance to develop an independent, full-functioning self. Instead, she drifted around in a chameleon-like manner. While Lisa's likelihood of getting married was quite high, her chances for a fulfilling life, in my opinion, looked unfortunately bleak.

Step Five–Shopping the Relationship Supermarket–is rooted in the belief that it is essential to feel happy in your life WITHOUT a relationship before you can be genuinely happy WITH a relationship. Lisa's approach–needing a relationship to feel good about herself–put her in a perpetual state of dysfunction. She made one bad relationship choice after another. She was so consumed by this pattern that she could not see it and, therefore, could not address the problem. By using the first four steps of the Five Step Guide to increase insights about yourself and your parents' divorce, you position yourself to be happy on your own. And, if you can feel secure and grounded on your own, you are more likely to make better choices when and if you choose to enter into another relationship. If you DON'T choose a relationship at this point, that's great too. There's no need to rush. Remember, once you make a life-long commitment to someone, it is life-long. Enjoy and embrace your time on your own. You will find that you get much more pleasure out of any relationship supermarket shopping you decide to pursue.

If you feel reluctant and resist the idea of being single and dating, you are not alone. Remember how Mary resisted breaking out of her pattern of serial monogamy, joked about my "forge healthy relationships through dating" speech, and coined the phrase "Relationship Supermarket"? Darla, a twenty-six-year-old survey subject whose parents separated when she was eight explained:

> ...Ever since I was fourteen, I have had some type of relationship with somebody. I have never really been alone and even though I might have not been committed, I was [always] dating someone to keep me occupied... For a long time I used to have certain physical characteristics that I felt my partner had to have. If they didn't meet them all, I felt that was reason enough for it not to work. Needless to say, looking back, I probably have passed up at least one great relationship all because...he was too short and too nice...

Similarly, my work with my young client Tanya delineates the importance of learning to be independent and to "shop the relationship supermarket."

"Be single? On purpose? Are you seriously encouraging me to BREAK UP with Julius BEFORE I meet someone else?! Why in the hell would I do that?!? What are you, nuts?" Tanya pointed her index finger toward me with disappointment and possible disgust. She seemed to think I was suggesting something utterly outrageous, and she demanded a decent explanation.

"I'm not encouraging you to do anything other than explore what it means that you're staying in a relationship with someone whom you describe as emotionally abusive. When I hear you describe his jokes about your weight and your looks, or when you tell the story of being stood up at the firm dinner– it's a concern. And I think it is interesting that you plan to stick it out—"I paused to grab a clarifying breath, "in the short run."

"Well, I can read between the lines. When you express 'concern' and say it's 'interesting' that I'll 'stick it out'–I get it. I KNOW that you mean I should end it, and I've already told you I will end it, as soon as I find someone new."

Tanya's relaxed curls swayed slowly, as she nodded once and clarified her preference for staying with Julius in spite of his continuing criticisms and candy bar disposition. Tanya initiated therapy after Julius did not show up for her company's annual holiday party. She described her embarrassment and humiliation looking at his empty seat at a table of colleagues and their significant others. She said that some of her close friends at the office encouraged her to seek counseling to explore her pattern of choosing unavailable, unkind men.

Tanya's parents separated when she was ten and her older sister, Genevieve, was twelve. According to Tanya, their divorce was more than necessary. They were both leading separate lives, and they were both involved in romantic relationships outside of their marriage. Neither of her parents had re-married. Instead, they each engaged in a series of long-term relationships that Tanya described as "collectively doomed from the start."

"What do you gain by waiting it out with Julius until you find someone else?"

"It seems so obvious to me that I'm surprised you even ask. Isn't it obvious?"

"No, many people stay in flawed relationships, and they do so for very different reasons. I'm genuinely not suggesting that you leave Julius. I do, however, think it might help you to articulate what you gain by using the strategy of staying with him until you find someone new."

"I gain not being alone. Obviously. I stay until there's someone else. That's what I do. And I do it because I don't want to be alone. Don't most people want to be with someone? What's wrong with that?"

"There's nothing wrong with wanting to be in a relationship. It's not my place to say it's right or wrong to want anything. I will tell you, though, based on my experience working with a lot of young adults, especially those in their twenties and thirties—in relationships and out of relationships—that it's generally harder to find a healthy relationship if you are already in an unhealthy relationship while you are looking. I'm not saying that it's impossible or that there is no chance whatsoever that you'll find what you say you want by going about it as you always have. I'm just saying it's generally not the most effective strategy for finding a suitable partner."

"And why is that?" I sensed Tanya's interest increasing as she leaned toward me and intensified our eye contact by further opening her inquisitive, walnut eyes.

"Well, I think it's partly because too much of your emotional energy is invested in

your current relationship. Even if you don't want that to be the case. You're walking around with the effects of Julius' emotional abuse, and it can make it harder to meet someone else. That's the first part."

"And the second?"

"The second part is a bit more complex. If you find someone when you are already involved with someone else, a lot of what appeals to you about the new person is really all about the person you are currently with. I once worked with a client named Sherry who wanted to leave her husband, because they had no sexual relationship and hadn't for years. But she did not want to be alone. So she waited and left him when she met someone else. The problem was that, in her new relationship, sex was ALL they had. Her husband had so many good qualities—honesty, stability, a career. She was so focused on the void in her marriage that she chose someone who was really more of a rebellion against her husband than anything else. Her new relationship had great sex, but that was it. To make matters worse, the sex with the new guy seemed great while she was still with her husband, but once she left her marriage, even the sex deteriorated. It turned out her new partner was much more available when she was unavailable. In other words, it appealed to him—on some level—that she was married. Once he had her, he didn't want her with the same enthusiasm. And as a therapist, I see many different variations on this theme of leaving one unhealthy relationship for another unhealthy relationship all the time."

Tanya nodded. "And I can see how I do choose each new guy based on what I don't like about the guy I'm currently with. Maybe what I want gets lost in the mix. Like the movie where Julia Roberts doesn't know what kind of eggs she likes because she always orders the same eggs as whatever her current boyfriend chooses. What's it called?" She paused before answering herself. "Oh yes, 'Runaway Bride'. I see some value in what you're saying, but what do I gain by doing it alone?"

"Perspective, clarity, independence. A chance to stand on your own two feet and figure out what you like, and what you don't like. The Julia Roberts egg analogy is a great one. Being on your own gives you a chance to determine what's most important to you in a relationship. And it gives you a chance to enjoy your own company. Wouldn't you rather go to your holiday party on your own and have fun? Isn't that preferable to a date who doesn't show up? Given what you've been honest enough to tell me about Julius, even if he had shown, he would have put you down in front of your colleagues." Tanya frowned and took deep, slow breaths as I continued. Her light brown skin was beaming with *beaded, modest perspiration. I felt torn between not wanting to push Tanya too hard, and not wanting to downplay her stated pattern of accepting emotional abuse.*

"You would also probably benefit from taking some time to look at why you have this pattern of choosing unsuitable partners. It may relate to some of your parents' patterns. Again, I'm just telling you my experience—but it's usually more effective to work on these kinds of issues while you are on your own rather than while your energy is constantly disrupted by the kinds of hurtful experiences you've described. Look, _you_ mentioned leaving him, not me. I just pointed out that if you know you are planning to leave him, you may want to look at why you feel compelled to stay until there's someone else."

"But I _should_ leave.We both know that.Thing is, I can't even imagine being on my own. It's not what I do. Just the thought of it—picturing myself alone—well I envision myself wasting away. Dying some slow, isolated, premature death all alone in my apartment. Seriously."

While Tanya and Lisa shared a similar pattern, Tanya expressed much more conflict about her Relationship M.O. than Lisa. Granted, it wasn't easy for Tanya to contemplate leaving. At first, she asserted that _I_ had more problems with the relationship than _she_. She resisted my questions about why she wanted to stay in the short run even if she ultimately planned to leave Julius and was simply waiting around for an alternative plan. The more we talked about her current relationship with Julius and her history of growing up in a divorced household, the more Tanya prepared herself to acknowledge her Relationship M.O. and begin to change it. She soon realized that she was delaying commitment on purpose because she didn't like herself enough to be with a nice guy. She knew better than to commit, long-term, to an unsuitable partner, so she remained in renter's mode throughout her relationship history. Her pattern of renting with candy bars allowed her to have a degree of distance from her partners that was necessary for her, given her past and her desire to come to terms with her history before committing to a long-term relationship.

It took time to undertake each of the steps in the Five-Step Guide, and Tanya stayed with Julius throughout the process of the first four steps. However, when she was ready, she ended her relationship with Julius _without_ meeting somebody new.

"I know I had to do this. I get it. But it's no party, let me tell you. I feel so alone. Why is that? I've learned and now believe that you are actually lonelier with a guy like Julius than you are on your own. But this is a different kind of loneliness. I'm not used to *figuring out what to do with myself. I'm used to revolving my plans around someone else."*

"It must feel strange and even unsettling to do this. To be on your own."

"You're describing it exactly. Strange and unsettling. A part of me is excited. But I need an outlet. SOMETHING to replace Julius so I don't replace him with SOMEONE."

"Finding an outlet, or a series of outlets, is a great way to begin enjoying being on your own. Did you have a particular outlet in mind?"

"A couple, actually. But they're both <u>so</u> not me. I want to take hip-hop classes and I want to learn Spanish. Pretty random, don't you think?"

"Those interests don't sound random at all, what do you mean?"

"Don't know, maybe it's just random to hear myself express this stuff out loud. I've had these ideas in my head, but I never thought I would pursue them." Tanya tapped her sandaled, manicured toes and twirled her neatly styled hair. It seemed especially hard for her to discuss her independent interests. If you are used to giving over a lot of your time, energy, preferences and identity to an unsuitable partner, then expressing independent interests can feel as foreign as speaking Chinese. *"A voice in my head says: 'who the hell are you to take hip-hop classes and Spanish? That's what happy people do. That's what normal people do. Find things they like to do, and learn how to do them. That's not you.' My mom always wanted to take singing lessons. She had a gorgeous voice, but she wouldn't even join our church choir! She's always said she was too embarrassed and too old. And you know what, I feel too embarrassed and too old to take hip-hop OR Spanish."*

"Look, it doesn't sound like you had a role model for pursuing interests. And, like your mother, you are acting as if you are all washed up and it's too late to take these classes. And how old are you? Thirty?"

"Thirty-one. Yes, I did not ever see either parent enjoy or cultivate much of an interest in anything."

"So it's not familiar. Sometimes with uncharted territory it helps to take smaller steps. Why not just commit to doing some research on the classes out there, the prices, the schedules. Just take it one step at a time."

"Sounds manageable enough. If I don't have to do it all at once, maybe I can work up to it. I already know where I'd like to take the dance class. And I can take Spanish classes at the Department of Agriculture. My office will even pay for them. I've wanted to do both of these things for years. I'll just get the schedules and take it from there."

Small step by small step, Tanya moved forward. She enrolled in hip-hop classes and

Spanish lessons. During the course of our work together, she traveled to Spain and Bolivia to put her new Spanish skills to use. She enjoyed hip-hop classes so much that she decided to enroll in various other classes at the dance studio. She dated a guy that she met in her swing dance class and, for the first time, she <u>dated</u> rather than jumping into a relationship. She eventually decided that, if she was going to pursue a serious relationship, she wanted to be with someone who was more professionally driven. Tanya's career was taking off and she wanted a partner who would not be intimidated by her professional success, and who had a fulfilling career of his own. So she stopped dating the guy from her swing class and continued dating other people (Shopping the Relationship Supermarket) whom she met on Match.Com and through her friends.

About a year and a half after ending therapy, Tanya wrote to me to tell me that she was engaged to a "wonderful apple" whom she met on a singles trip to Costa Rica. "For the first time in my life, I'm buying instead of renting and Carlos was truly worth waiting for." Tanya wrote to me on her professional letterhead and her management title indicated that she had received yet another promotion. "You were right, by the way, about learning to be on my own. Without having the guts to become more independent and enjoy being single, I never would have had the confidence to sign up and go on the trip where I met Carlos. And without taking my time, I wouldn't have gotten to know Carlos and I wouldn't be marrying the apple of my dreams."

Tanya worked hard to become independent enough to break away from Julius and to stop dating candy bars. She grew to understand that, to do so, she would need to develop her own interests and independent sense of self. She also realized that she needed to choose different kinds of partners. It wasn't easy, it took practice and training, but she continued to push herself, and to enjoy her independence. Once having a guy became less of a necessity, she was able to learn to make healthier choices.

Of course, there are many single adults with divorced parents who <u>do not</u> go from one relationship straight to the next. These adults may not need to place the same emphasis on learning to be comfortable on their own. If you have not forged healthy relationships in the past, and fall into the category of adults who are comfortable on their own, your main emphasis will need to be on putting yourself out there in situations that may not feel comfortable or intuitive. You will need to push yourself to make different choices with more suitable partners. You may need to work on being more present in your relationships and on making more of an effort to meet and date different people and to slowly, carefully, begin to find healthy relationships.

During the period of my life when I struggled to forge healthier relationships, my personal challenge was not as much with being on my own, but with learning to be more present, and more comfortable with dating buyers. I wouldn't say that I dated many candy bars. Though I dated a few candy bars, I frequently dated apples who were not ready for a committed relationship and were, therefore, in renter's mode. And while I didn't need to work on being happy on my own, I did need to work on being more independent while dating. I needed to work on not expecting whomever I was dating to prove to me, to an exaggerated degree, that they were worthy of the relationship.

Forging healthy relationships wasn't easy. And it wasn't familiar. Dating Russ was a very different experience than my other dating experiences. For example, Russ was the first guy I dated who took a genuine interest in my work. More accurately, he was the first guy to express an interest while I, in turn, was able to respond in a positive way. In the past, I was more drawn to relationships where my career never entered the conversational mix. I frequently felt pressure to appear indifferent to my profession in order to remain adequately feminine. And, at the other extreme, I sometimes sensed that the guy I was dating would ultimately prefer someone with more high-powered credentials. In these cases I felt looked down upon partly because I wasn't making much money, but more significantly because I lived so far outside of any kind of a professional fast lane.

When I met a man who asked intelligent questions about social work, I would drop him into the "available" (or "buyer") category and push him away. It wasn't intuitive to date someone who genuinely cared about what I thought, how I felt, and what I did. But, like countless other adults with divorced parents, I married (later rather than sooner) and have a happy and fulfilling marriage. When Russ and I discuss my work, I feel encouraged and accepted and continue to be surprised by his innate psychological sense.

Dating Russ felt strange at first. The experience was noticeably, genuinely different than dating other guys. Reflecting on what was so different, I'm struck by the energetic interest Russ took in my career. His kind, thoughtful questions and comments always remind me of a quotation from Jill Ker Conway's The Road to Coorain:

> *...It was intoxicating not to have to set a watch on my tongue, to be actually found more interesting because of my mind. In his company I enjoyed the experience a [professional] woman needs most if she has lived in a world set on undermining female intelligence: I was loved for what I was rather than the lesser mind I pretended to be...*

On one of our first dates, we ate dinner outdoors on a rooftop café and, as we talked, I squirmed internally as I pushed myself to grow more comfortable with his insightful perspective and engaging presence.

"So what exactly do you mean by a paradoxical intervention?" Russ asked. We were discussing one of my post-graduate courses at Penn Council for Relationships. The instructor had been discussing the concept of paradoxical interventions, rendering our classmates unanimously overwhelmed and fascinated by his explanation.

"I don't know that I quite get the concept, but let me try to give an example." I inhaled and attempted to put together and express what felt slightly beyond my psychological reach. "So, our instructor told the story of a conference where this pioneer in the usage of paradoxical interventions is lecturing to a large room of participants. You know, going into detail and describing how the intervention is supposed to work. So then a psychiatrist attending the conference raises her hand and goes on to describe how an institutionalized patient under her care has, for months, been refusing to shower. The patient is chronically mentally ill, and shares a room with others who were struggling with his odor. Understandably, the patient's roommates and his doctors are pretty concerned."

"Obviously."

"Yes. Well, the lecturer goes through this step-by-step process that basically involves forbidding this patient to shower under any circumstances. The psychiatrist follows the lecturer's instructions, and the patient ends up showering regularly within days. My instructor gave some other examples, weird stuff like having someone who throws up every

time they drive collect the vomit for a fake analysis. To somehow treat the vomit as a good thing. But all with the caveat that paradoxical interventions are tricky, and dangerous, and should only be tried by a beginning therapist if you are getting a lot of supervision from someone experienced in this form of treatment."

"So," Russ paused for a moment, a collective pause communicating his genuine interest and engagement, "can you think of a paradoxical intervention as another form of reverse psychology?"

"I guess so, yes." Why didn't I think of that? I asked myself as I continued. "How is it that you are a lawyer and here you are asking the one question that would have helped clarify the concept for all of us in the class? Why didn't our instructor just suggest that we think of a paradoxical intervention as another form of reverse psychology, plain and simple?" One would never describe Russ as an especially emotional guy. He's not in the least bit touchy feely. Still, he carries this quiet yet piercing psychological astuteness that continues to catch me off guard. "Really, you're a lawyer, not a shrink, so how do you get these things so clearly?"

"Well, the law and psychology aren't always so different if you think about how much they both rely on precedent. Isn't that the essence of each field? Obviously, it's a different kind of precedent. Past case decisions or past family history. But you can't practice effectively in either field without examining and understanding the past." How strange. How strange and beautiful; these words from a lawyer, a soulmate and the love of my life.

Russ's ability to understand and respect what I do, and to connect it to his own career, is just one in a long list of things I love about him. Sometimes I literally shudder at my good fortune. Sometimes I seriously can't believe that I am married to him and that we are going to spend our lives together. My experience teaches me that when you grow up with happily married parents, you tend to expect this kind of happiness. You assume you'll have it, and frequently you find it. (I don't see many people with this background in my practice unless they have been faced with an unexpected tragedy.) Not so for adults who grew up in a divorced household. For many years I (like so many survey subjects and clients with whom I have worked) would never dare to make such an assumption. I assumed the opposite and lived accordingly. And therein lies yet another dividend of divorce. Once you do forge a healthy relationship, it can take you by total surprise, and you are likely to appreciate it wholeheartedly.

Forging healthy relationships is the essential final step to overcoming your parents' divorce. However, please keep in mind that the most important healthy relationship you will forge will be with yourself. Like yourself enough to enjoy your own company. Value yourself enough to pursue your interests and make your life as interesting as possible. Have fun with your independence and, whenever that's hard, remind yourself of the dividends of your parents' divorce and ways that delaying a long-term commitment may work to your advantage. The happier you are, the more grounded you feel in your independent life and your choices, the better position you will be in with respect to choosing healthy partnerships.

Tips and Suggestions:

- If you are not used to being on your own, plan at least two weekly activities that you will do by yourself. Take yourself to dinner, or to a movie. Or just spend a quiet evening reading at home rather than rushing around, making plans. Do not have your solo time involve watching television.

- Spend at least twenty minutes writing in your journal about your independent experiences. What parts do you enjoy? What's difficult about being on your own? Why is it hard for you to spend quality time with yourself?

- Put yourself in at least two situations that force you to meet new people. Ideally, these situations should be recurring and/or should create opportunities for you to spend quality time getting to know new people. For example, take a class, join a club, take a singles trip, or sign up for online dating.

- Set aside time to reflect on and fully evaluate all of the potential partners in your life whom you may be over-looking due to reasons delineated in your Relationship M.O.

- Consider the possibility of being more open to people who have expressed, or are expressing, an interest in you. You may be ignoring or over-looking certain available, suitable partners because they are "too nice," "too boring" or "too perfect."

- Seriously ask yourself if you have been writing off apples that have fallen into your very own backyard. If you have, coach yourself to consider Shopping the Relationship Supermarket in your own backyard.

- Refer to your journal notes, especially from Steps Two, Three and Four on a regular basis. This reference will remind you of your goals and your old patterns as well as the dividends of your parents' divorce.

- Categorize anyone you date in the same way you did when you completed the suggestions in Chapter Five. Coach yourself to avoid candy bars. Remember, you are in training now and *apples* are a much healthier diet than *candy bars*.

- When you are dating someone, be aware of your tendencies to revert to the patterns you have identified in earlier chapters that do not work for you. We are all vulnerable to returning to these self-destructive tendencies. It is important to coach yourself to work on changing the things that have not worked for you in the past. Remember, training is not easy, sometimes you want to quit and call it a day. But winners never quit!

chapter ten

■

SURVEY
SUBJECT
RESULTS

■

The candid, thoughtful answers of the subjects who participated in my survey have informed and enhanced all of the information on the steps needed to forge healthy relationships. There were only two requirements for subjects' participation in the survey:

- that the subject have divorced parents;
- that the subject's parents' separation occurred by the time the subject turned twenty-one.

I utilized the second specification, because people whose parents break up AFTER they turn twenty-one do not spend any of their psychological childhood with divorced parents. There is no set age that defines psychological childhood versus adulthood; however, by age twenty-one most people are generally more psychologically formed than during their teenage years. For the purposes of this book, persons twenty-one and over fall into the category of adults. By age twenty-one, most people are more emotionally separate from their parents than they are during their childhood. (College age persons will frequently tell you that they are "separate" or "grown". But in current American culture, this is usually not the case.) Without spending any of their childhood growing up in a divorced household, people whose parents separate AFTER the age of twenty-one should be considered as a separate category— one in which the parents stay together, presumably unhappily, for the sake of their children.

I made one exception to these eligibility criteria for the inclusion of a subject whose parents separated during her early childhood and never officially divorced. This subject's father had children with, and lives with, another woman and has done so for many years.

Subjects who participated fall into many categories: current clients, former clients, friends, two of my five siblings, friends of friends and acquaintances. The data collection method for gathering this survey's sample is referred to in the research field as a "snowball sample." Rather than purchasing computer-generated contact information to target participants, I simply asked many different people to participate, and to send the survey on to others who might participate.

It is important to note that many persons who received the survey did not choose to participate. It goes without saying that the subject of divorce is painful and complex. Also, I chose to compose a long survey with open-ended rather than multiple-choice questions. The survey's length and open-ended answers encouraged participants to go into depth when describing their experience, and their comprehensive answers enrich each chapter of this book. It is unclear how many potential subjects chose not to respond. I asked colleagues and friends to distribute the survey to adults with divorced parents, but I do not know how many surveys were given to people who met the qualifications, but did not respond. I know, however, that several potential subjects did not respond. Non-responses can presumably be attributed, at least in part, to the sensitivity of the topic. The views of individuals who feel their parents' divorce is too painful to discuss may not be well represented in this book.

Subjects did not receive payment or any goods or services in exchange for their participation in the survey. Most of the subjects completed the survey independently and then mailed or emailed me their responses. However, a small percentage of subjects requested to complete the survey via telephone interview.

It is also interesting to note some of the following quantitative results of the survey.

Of the respondents who participated, 70 percent are female and 30 percent are male. Of the subjects who completed the questionnaire, 75 percent are currently married, 20 percent are single and not currently in a relationship and 5 percent are unmarried, but currently in a relationship. When asked if they view their current relationship as "serious and long-term" or "temporary," nine of these eleven subjects said they view their current relationship as "serious and long-term." Of the subjects who did not say they view their current relationship as "serious and long-term," one subject replied, "I hope it is serious and will be long-term because he is so deeply kind and good." The other subject explained:

> It is serious. However, I continually fight the tendency to view it as temporary. I feel as though I am often looking for the next relationship. My past has taught me to get the short-term happiness and jettison the long-term complexities.

Of the married subjects, all describe their marriage as happy. None of the married subjects say they are not happily married. The average age that the subjects married was close to thirty-two. The median age of subjects at the time of their marriage was thirty-one. The mode ages were twenty-nine and thirty-one. The ages at which the subjects married ranged from twenty-three to forty. It should be noted that one of the two subjects who married when he was twenty-three is currently sixty-five years old and therefore married during a time when people generally married earlier. Aside from these two subjects, none of the other married adults with divorced parents married before the age of twenty-seven. Of these thirty-one married subjects, three subjects had married and then divorced prior to re-marrying. Of the unmarried subjects, four had married and then later divorced. One of the divorced and currently unmarried subjects clarified that both her marriage and her divorce were according to the rules and norms of lesbian relationships. Of the unmarried subjects who had never been married, one subject mentioned that she was once engaged, but then called off her wedding.

The average age of the subjects participating in the survey is just over thirty-seven and the median age is thirty-eight. The subjects range in age from twenty-two to sixty-nine. Nine of the subjects are in their twenties, twenty-six of the subjects are in their thirties, twelve of the subjects are in their forties, none of the subjects are in their fifties and three of the subjects are in their sixties. Thirteen of the subjects were born in Pennsylvania. Five subjects were born in Virginia. Four subjects were born in New York. Three subjects were born in New Jersey. Three subjects were born in California. Two subjects were born in Connecticut. Two subjects were born in Florida. Two subjects were born in Maryland. And one subject was born in each of the following states: Iowa, Washington, Oregon, Maine, Michigan, Illinois, Wisconsin, Washington, D.C., Massachusetts, Arkansas, Colorado and Louisiana. Two subjects were born in France. One subject was born in Germany. And one subject was born in the United Kingdom.

Of the subjects who are currently single and not in a relationship, three said that they do not avoid commitment. A small percentage said that they do avoid commitment, and a fraction gave answers that are difficult to quantify as a definite yes, or a definite no. These answers are:

I just don't go looking for it...I really do want to be loved, but I don't know how to let someone love me.

Although I think I am not avoiding commitment...I have to wonder because all those I tend to attract seem to always be emotionally unavailable...And that being the reason it never seems to work...Not because I'm avoiding commitment...

Yes. And No. I want commitment—I just don't think I attract the right guys all the time for that commitment. To be honest, I am a bit suspicious of the idea of legal marriage—as I was surrounded by divorce and the destruction it caused for all the children involved. My mother has been married twice. My bio father five times and my father three times. I have eleven step-siblings. That is a whole heck of a lot emotionally to navigate through, especially when the parents barely speak to each other. It only hurts the kids when parents handle it so immaturely. My parents could have done a much better job handling their situation by putting us first, by communicating with their ex-partners and putting the kids first. I want children with a man I love, respect and adore and want to be living in a committed relationship with that man. I would love to have a spiritual ceremony and reception. But, being legally bound to a man when there is a 50 percent chance of success/failure really has made me think twice. Especially when kids are involved. Different things work for different people. In this day and age, I don't think it's necessary.

Of the unmarried subjects who are currently in a relationship, some said that they feared or avoided commitment at some point in their past. Others said that they did not fear or avoid commitment in their past. One particular unmarried subject currently in a relationship gave the following answer that is difficult to quantify as a definite yes, or a definite no:

Before my current relationship, I never felt the need to have a boyfriend just for the sake of having one, but I never thought that meant I feared or avoided commitment because I always said that I would only be in a committed relationship if the right guy came along. For as long as I can remember I have been a cautious person in every aspect of my life, so it would not be in my nature to put myself on the line unless it was someone special. I guess it's a fine line between being conscious/cautious and being fearful.

Of the married subjects, the slight majority said that they feared or avoided commitment at some point in their past. Interestingly, three of these married subjects said they would not have realized, at the time, that they feared or avoided commitment as their following responses explain:

Yes...I don't think that it was conscious. I think it was more about me, and the fact that someone was going to discover the true me. And I didn't want to be discovered.

Yes! I didn't realize it as such until therapy. I would get with someone unavailable or pick the nice ones to pieces.

Yes (although I denied it at the time).

A small percentage of the married subjects did not answer the question about whether or not they avoided commitment in the past. Fourteen of the married subjects say that they did not avoid commitment in the past. However, one of these fourteen subjects changed her answer to this question later in the survey as she explained:

I guess I am sort of in the yes category. I avoided commitment by leaving.

The pattern in the surveys in which the majority of the married couples either say they avoided commitment and did not realize or acknowledge it at the time or changed the answer from "no" to "yes" may relate to the theory stated in the book that some persons who choose unsuitable or unavailable partners may tell you that they embrace, rather than fear commitment. Perhaps some of the survey subjects fell into this category at some point in their pasts.

When considering the surveys as a whole, the most important, consistent theme is the degree to which the responses in the surveys are different from one another. The subjects have many different perspectives and opinions about how having grown up with divorced parents affects them as adults. The main point affirmed by the survey results is that every family is different, and that it is difficult—even dangerous—to make generalizations about adults with divorced parents.

In terms of similarities, a striking aspect of the survey results is the degree to which the subjects admit that their history of growing up with divorced parents not only affected them in the past but also continues to play a role either in childhood, in adulthood or in both childhood and adulthood. Every subject identified ways in which their parents' divorce affected their childhood and continues to affect them as adults. In spite of the multiple difficulties that flowed from growing up with divorced parents, it is worth noting some of the positive things that subjects say about their parents' divorce. Brent, a forty-year-old happily married subject whose parents separated when he was six, explains:

> The divorce had a silver lining. I had the most amazing childhood experiences growing up in two very different countries. My American home with my dad offered all that is good about a classic suburban upbringing. My foreign home with my mom was on the beach with fishing, snorkeling, windsurfing, tennis, horseback riding, diverse cultures and much more right at our doorstep. These foreign experiences have shaped my world view, values, interests and career. In short, without the divorce I wouldn't be the same person in some ways.

Carolyn, a thirty-five-year-old, happily married woman whose parents separated when she was twenty acknowledges the major difficulties of having divorced parents, and then mentions an upside as she talks about how her parents' divorce affects her in adulthood:

> [The divorce] made me feel less likely to find a partner I could "make
> it work" with. [It] made me feel like "damaged goods" to a potential
> partner, as now I came from a "broken home." On the positive side,
> [the divorce] was an empowering example (from my mother) that
> one doesn't have to put up with harmful behavior.

Ellen, a thirty-six-year-old who is currently in a relationship she describes
as "happy, we are both extremely committed to our partnership and all that
goes with that...full disclosure, honesty, loyalty, support, physical
connectedness", explains how her parents' separation when she was thirteen
affected her as a child:

> In some ways it was a blessing because they were not a "match made
> in heaven" couple and in others it was very difficult. Consistently I
> felt torn by my parents' competing opinions and needs and I often
> felt as if I was betraying my mother by maintaining a relationship with
> my father despite what he did to her. She could not have been more
> supportive, however.

Ralph, a forty-one-year-old, happily married subject, explains how his
parents' divorce affected his adult romantic relationships:

> Maybe in a good way because I have become the person who would
> do anything to keep a family together. There's nothing more
> important than that to me.

Trent, a thirty-seven-year-old, happily married subject, discusses how his
parents' divorce affects him in adulthood and affects his romantic
relationships:

> Positively. I feel that what happened to my family (i.e. the divorce

and the actions that led up to the divorce) has enabled me to be more prepared in my adult life when it comes to relationships. From a positive standpoint, I am fiercely loyal (both to friends and family) and have a healthy sense of priority – my wife outranking everything else. Negatively, I feel that I am overly introspective (always focusing blame on myself before others) and fearful for the proverbial "shoe to drop" – despite the success of my marriage.

Pat, a forty-three-year-old, happily married subject, reveals:

We saw, I think, divorce as a normal part of modern life. With time and retrospect we see that there are many other solutions and I believe that I do try harder and avoid conflict in my marriage to try to make it successful. This said, I am not afraid of conflict or even divorce since it was not a traumatic experience for me. Divorce is a reality and a solution when a relationship does not work, but not a solution that should be arrived at easily or without exhausting all other possibilities…I am not sure it does affect my adult romantic relationship, but if it does I suppose I give lots of importance to the time I spend with my wife alone. We make a point of getting away alone at least once a year for a honeymoon trip with no kids, friends nor family around.

Not every subject had something positive to say, and not every subject agreed that divorce was the optimal outcome. Roy, a sixty-five-year-old happily married subject whose parents separated when he was seventeen, describes what he learned about marriage from his parents:

I learned to find a wife who would make a wonderful marriage, home and mother for my children so that the craziness I grew up with would stop with [my brother] and me. Unfortunately, my philosophy has not worked for [my brother]—we are estranged, and he is on his fourth marriage. I learned that couples who split and babble about how they are doing it in a way that is fine for their kids are full of bologna. The kids are always hurt, even if they are older. If nothing else, you end up having to take care of both of them during their declines. I learned that it is probably not always true that kids are better off with divorced parents than with parents in a lousy marriage. I feel/believe that I probably would have been happier with my parents staying married.

Many subjects in my survey prioritize their desire for happy, committed relationships, even if they are currently single. Here are some comments of survey subjects which demonstrate the extent to which many adults with divorced parents are determined to chart different courses than those they experienced growing up.

Lucy, a forty-three-year-old whose parents separated when she was ten, describes her current relationship as "happy. I am with someone who respects me and loves me for who I am. ...I think I've finally found real love." This subject explains what she learned about marriage from her parents:

Nothing, except maybe what not to do...Perhaps I learned what a marriage should be...commitment, trust, shared lives, shared vision and goals, communication.

Jeff, a thirty-one-year-old whose parents separated when he was one describes his current relationship as "happy" and then states:

I am learning to see my parents' marriage/relationship failures as a "map of how not to do it," instead of as... inevitable failure.

Maggie, a thirty-nine-year-old whose parents separated when she was thirteen, explains the effects of her parents' divorce:

It caused some loss of childhood and forced me to become self-sufficient at an early age... I feel more affected by the type of people they were back then than by the divorce itself. I feel I have a very different set of values.

Then Maggie describes her own marriage:

[The marriage is] happy. My husband is affectionate, communicative and committed to having intimate relationships with those around him. I believe he developed these traits from his parents who happen to have a wonderful marriage.

The following four surveys completed by subjects who were generous enough to agree to the publication of their candid insights and perspectives will, I believe, add to your own understanding of the aspects of your parents' divorce which influence your own relationships. Take note of the feelings that come to you as you read their answers. Also, make note of your own insights that may arise while you read.

The first subject of interest, Darla, is in her mid-twenties and not married, but is, as she puts it, "seeing someone".

1. First name: **Darla**

2. Age: **26**

3. Ethnicity: **Black**

4. Your age when your parents separated: **8**

5. Your age when your parents divorced:
   My parents never actually divorced, just legally separated in 1989.

6. Place of birth: **Alexandria, Virginia**

7. What is your understanding of why your parents divorced?
   Looking back it was my understanding that my dad couldn't take it anymore... You might ask what "it" is but back then I really didn't know... I still don't know... I just remember them arguing the day he left, other times were very faint... So either they hid their arguing very well or it just didn't happen... To be completely honest... I really do not remember my dad around a lot to argue... I think I just remember that one fight and then he left...

8. How did your parents' divorce affect you as a child?
   I think this question has to be answered in hindsight because as child you never really think of how it affects you... Did I notice any change in lifestyle... Not really... There were a couple of times that the phone didn't work... But that's it... My childhood memories are very slim... I remember things I

did as child, like girl scouts, or the band... But honestly my memories really start when I started dating...

9. How does your parents' divorce affect you in adulthood?

Well one could say that it didn't at all... I mean looking on the outside... I think I have done very well for a person of my age... I have a college degree, my very own place, and a pretty decent job... Umm... But looking past the material things and looking deep inside my parents' relationship or lack there of has a very damaging affect... I look at past relationships and could blame my parents for a lot... I look at something so small as my eating habits and could find a way to blame my parents.. Inevitably the blame is all on me... It's not as if I'm not aware of my issues... Although one could say that not having an example to look up or mimic could have been the reason... But honestly... I think in small and large ways I am mimicking my parents... For example in small ways I mimic my mother by latching on to the first new thing in my life and doing whatever it takes to make it work even if it means sufficing my own happiness... I look at my father and I mimic him by using what money I have and don't have to make others happy and again sufficing my own happiness... Even though the things I do make me happy for selfish reasons... I do it for the fear of being alone...

(Notice how this subject has a clear sense of the ways she mimics her parents' patterns and behavior. She is able to honestly Face the Mirror and understands how her parents' divorce affects her as an adult.)

10. How has having divorced parents affected your adult romantic relationships?

Of course only in hindsight... I see myself staying in relationships longer then needed only because I make excuses about their feelings to satisfy my own selfish want of not being alone... I tend to have trust issues... But not in the normal way... I tend to give all trust up front and they never lose it even when there are obvious reasons that the trust has been compromised... I also seem to have a problem with commitment. Even though I have convinced myself that I'm ready for a committed relationship I tend to go for those who are not emotionally available and I seem to be aware of that... Which, to me, proves that even though I claim to want a committed relationship, I do not give myself a chance. This is all underscored by another issue I have which is failure... I can't fail at a relationship that had no chance from the start.

(These insights about how mimicking her mother's relationship patterns affect her own adult relationships show how she effectively ties her past to her present and sees how her past relates to her adult perspective on commitment.)

11. What did you learn about marriage from your parents?
    I learned a lot of things... I think anyone sees what their parents did and swears to do it differently.. So in that sense... I have learned that money doesn't buy love... I want to give all my love through emotions and not anything of materialistic value... I also learned that in order to be treated and seen as an equal you must also take ownership of your part in the relationship. I also learned not to sacrifice my own happiness and use the excuse that I did it for the ones I love. What I have realized is it bothers me greatly that I really do not know what I should deserve or receive from a marriage.

12. What did you learn about marriage from your grandparents?
    Well, my grandparents from my dad's side I really do not remember... My dad's father died before I was born and my

dad's mother I really did not at all know... I do remember her asking me to call her Ms. Agnes which was her first name... I only have one vivid memory of my dad's mom. I just remember being at her house in her living room watching TV and asking for some lemonade. That is really it... I do remember not being invited to her funeral and being one of the only grandchildren not involved in the funeral or the obituary besides my older sister. What I do remember about my mom's parents isn't much either... When I was young we never really went down to the country and they came to live with us in 1986... I was just five... I do remember my granddad suffering numerous strokes and what I do remember about him was... He was a man who was unable to do anything for himself after his strokes... Before, I used to follow him around attached to his hip... We used to eat sardines together and I helped him make his own cigarettes... What I do remember about him was his brown medicine bag that he carried with him all the time... He died in 1993 and I didn't really see anything as far as a marriage was concerned... Only that in the end my grandparents loved one another enough to stick by one another till the end...

13.   Did either of your parents re-marry? (If no, please skip to question 14)

13a. If yes, which parent? (If both parents re-married, please answer questions 13a, 13b and 13c with information about your mother first, and then your father)

13b. Is your re-married parent still married?

13c. How would you describe your parent's second marriage?

14.   Are you currently married? (If no, please skip to question 15)

14a. If yes, at what age did you marry?

14b. Would you describe your marriage as happy or unhappy? Why?

15.   If you are not married, are you currently in a relationship? (If no, please skip to question 16)
Well I wouldn't say I'm in a relationship, however, I am seeing someone... It started with honest flirtation and I was under the impression they were available but later and even now I know they are seeing someone else and that I am not the first person in their life... My past two relationships have been that way... The one prior to those... I was in a committed relationship, however I still maintain some kind of relationship with my high school sweetheart... So since my high school relationship, I (or my partner) have not been faithful.

15a. If you are currently in a relationship, would you describe this relationship as happy or unhappy? Why?
I would consider myself only happy when I'm with them and all the other time miserable because I'm not sure what they are doing or who they are with... I guess the hard part of this question is why... I mean I think that I am happy but honestly I'm not... I mean it would be nice to be happy all the time; however, that just doesn't seem to be the case... I really can't remember the last time I was happy in a relationship... I mean I think about my high school sweetheart and I think I was happy but honestly... I can look back and realize that it was the same type of relationship my parents had... I mean I sacrificed everything for him and in the end he still left me for someone else...

(Again, this subject makes important observations about the parallels between her parents' relationship patterns and her own. Ask yourself if you have felt any of these same things.)

15b. Do you view your current relationship as serious and long-term? Or do you view it as temporary? Why?

There are some aspects of my current relationship that I would love to be long-term... However the actual relationship has to be temporary because of the situation... They are committed to someone else and I have realized from my parents' marriage that it will never work like this. Even though I'm happy some of the time I deserve to be happy all the time and I deserve to be the only person in their life to make them happy.

16. Have you ever divorced? (If no, please skip to question 17)

16a. If yes, how old were you when you married?

16b. How old were you when you divorced?

16c. What is your perspective about why you married and why you later divorced?

17. How would you describe your dating history?

My dating history isn't very detailed... I mean ever since I was 14 I have had some type of relationship with somebody... I have never really been alone and even though I might have not been committed I was dating someone or was kept occupied... During my college years when I was only involved when I came home I dated others. However, it was nothing really there except sexual relationships and even then I was searching for something more and could never find it... Hence why I would either sleep with them or be intimate and then lose interest once it happened... It just wasn't fulfilling me like I thought it was...

18. If you are not currently in a relationship, do you think that you avoid commitment?

Although I think I am not avoiding commitment... I have to wonder because all those I tend to attract seem to always be emotionally unavailable... And that being the reason it never seems to work... Not because I'm avoiding commitment...

18a. If you avoid commitment, please describe the ways in which you avoid commitment.

For a long time I used to have certain physical characteristics that I felt my partner had to have... If they didn't meet them all I felt that was reason enough for it not to work... Needless to say looking back I probably have passed up at least one great relationship all because he was too short and was too nice... Even with my strong personality I used to say I wanted my partner to be able to control me... He just didn't cut it... He was too nice and too available... Always wanted to spend time with me...

(Like this honest, articulate subject, so many people miss out on relationships with suitable partners because they disqualify them—either for superficial reasons or because they are actually available! This subject's honest assessment of her tendency to reject available, suitable partners puts her in a good position to change this pattern should she decide to forge healthier relationships.)

18b. Do you reject available partners?

Until I looked past the BS... I used to think, how could I reject available partners? There weren't any to reject... But I can remember a couple that I have passed up because they didn't fit that image of the Abercrombie thug guy I was looking for...

I tend to focus on those who aren't available and then latch on tight. **And when they hurt me because they aren't available I either try my hardest to make it work with   whatever time I get, or I blame myself for not being good enough for them to become more available for me.**

18c. Do you choose unsuitable partners? Are they abusive or unavailable?

All the time... It's because of my fear of failing... If I fail at a relationship that was doomed from the start then it really wasn't my fault... I try to pick those who I am attracted to... Who just happen to be those who are unavailable.

19. If you are not currently single, was there ever a period when you feared or avoided commitment?

I've never been single, so it's hard for me to think until now that I was avoiding commitment. However, looking back, the fact that I wasn't ever single is reason enough to think that I avoid commitment all the time.

19a. If yes, please describe the ways in which you avoided commitment.

Well, I avoid commitment by choosing partners who are completely unavailable; however, over the years the capacity at which they are unavailable is falling so eventually I will choose someone who is available.

19b. Did you reject available partners?

Not intentionally. Usually it was because of a physical characteristic, or I slept with them too fast and hated it and completely lost interest... Now, as I'm growing, I'm able to look past the physical characteristics; however, I am still caught in somehow always picking wrong partners.

19c. Did you choose unsuitable partners? Were they abusive or unavailable?

I guess I choose unsuitable partners because somehow I get tangled up in a web where the only reason why they are bad for me is because they're not available, not necessarily because they are a bad person... I've never been in an abusive relationship unless one could say that being with someone who is unavailable hits your self-esteem and creates doubts of one's self so it mentally hurt me...

Like many adult children of divorce, this first subject has had problems choosing and maintaining a healthy, happy relationship. Her insights may help you to recognize similar feelings, actions and reactions in your own life.

The second subject of interest is Dana, a thirty-seven-year-old Arab American who has found a happy relationship and marriage.

1. First name: **Dana**

2. Age: **37**

3. Ethnicity: **Arab American**

4. Your age when your parents separated: **9 months**

5. Your age when your parents divorced: **3 years old**

6. Place of birth: **Washington, D.C.**

7. What is your understanding of why your parents divorced?
    My mother simply says she did not want to be a wife/mother anymore. She was very young when she married and, truth be told, she wanted to enjoy her life.

8. How did your parents' divorce affect you as a child?
    At the age of three months, my mother sent me to live with my grandparents. I had a real fear of abandonment as a child and felt very little security.

(These observations of her sad and difficult story are emblematic of the many children of divorce who struggle with separation anxiety and fear of abandonment.)

9. How does your parents' divorce affect you in adulthood?
    I feel a real need to be perfect. I have a hard time believing that people will stay with me if they discover how flawed I really am. It's a real struggle for me to ask for help as I want

everyone to love me and think I can handle everything.

10. How has having divorced parents affected your adult romantic relationships?

    Prior to counseling, I never believed marriage was a good thing or something that would add happiness to my life. I knew if I did it would be forever so I sort of envisioned myself making the best of the situation. I also believe I dated men that were horrible for me so there was no real fear of losing a good thing (being the one abandoned). Dating inappropriate men always gave me the easy out.

11. What did you learn about marriage from your parents?

    That you could get out of them very easily. My mother taught me that you should never depend on a man for your happiness and that you should leave at the first sign of trouble. Otherwise, you ended up miserable and pathetic.

12. What did you learn about marriage from your grandparents?

    Just the opposite of my mother, that men generally treated their wives horribly (cheated/drank) but everyone stayed and endured the hell to which they had committed their lives.

13. Did either of your parents re-marry? (If no, please skip to question 14)

    Yes, both parents have been married three times.

13a. If yes, which parent? (If both parents re-married, please answer questions 13a, 13b and 13c with information about your mother first, and then your father)

13b. Is your re-married parent still married?

    Mom - YES
    Dad - YES

13c. How would you describe your parents' second marriage?
Mom—Happy but they spend very little time together.
Dad—Same as above.

14. Are you currently married? (If no, please skip to question 15)
Yes—very happily!

14a. If yes, at what age did you marry?
32

14b. Would you describe your marriage as happy or unhappy? Why?
My marriage is very happy. We are very much in love and very
kind to one another. I think that our marriage works because
we both share similar goals and ideals when it comes to
marriage/family. (Which is funny considering we are
complete opposites.) We also discuss problems when they
arise and do not allow issues to fester.

(This enthusiastic description of her marriage is as inspiring as it is
triumphant!)

15. If you are not married, are you currently in a relationship? (If no, please
skip to question 16)

15a. If you are currently in a relationship, would you describe this relationship as happy or unhappy? Why?

15b. Do you view your current relationship as serious and long-term? Or do
you view it as temporary? Why?

16. Have you ever divorced? (If no, please skip to question 17)
No.

16a. If yes, how old were you when you married?

16b. How old were you when you divorced?

16c. What is your perspective about why you married and why you later divorced?

17.   How would you describe your dating history?
Tumultuous at best.

18.   If you are not currently in a relationship, do you think that you avoid commitment?

18a. If you avoid commitment, please describe the ways in which you avoid commitment.

18b. Do you reject available partners?

18c. Do you choose unsuitable partners? Are they abusive or unavailable?

19.   If you are not currently single, was there ever a period when you feared or avoided commitment?
Definitely.

19a. If yes, please describe the ways in which you avoided commitment.
Again, I didn't believe anything could be permanent or stable so I didn't really pursue relationships that would be worth losing.

19b. Did you reject available partners?
Yes. If I dated a functional man, I could literally feel the walls closing in around me.

19c. Did you choose unsuitable partners? Were they abusive or unavailable? **Yes, I secretly loved unavailable men. I say secretly because I didn't even know what a huge role that played in my dating life. I loved to look like the good one dating the mess. That way when things fell apart, no one blamed me. Also you can't fear having the rug pulled out from you when there is no rug.**

This subject writes eloquently of her pattern of "tumultuous" relationships and choosing unavailable, unsuitable partners during her twenties before marrying happily at age thirty-two. Her gutsy descriptions paint a clear, crisp picture of the struggles faced—and often overcome—by so many adults who grew up in divorced households.

Having come through a number of unhappy relationships, this subject points the way to achieving a happy marriage though she has parents who have been married several times and she had to overcome the negative influences of parental divorce.

Meg, a thirty-nine-year-old subject, insightfully tells of the impact of her parents' divorce and the legacy of her grandparents' tumultuous but loving marriage.

1. First name: **Meg**

2. Age: **39**

3. Ethnicity: **Caucasian**

4. Your age when your parents separated: **1**

5. Your age when your parents divorced: **2**

6. Place of birth: **Philadelphia**

7. What is your understanding of why your parents divorced?
    My parents were high school sweethearts. They got married and had three kids within three years. I think they got divorced because that was just too much for them to handle at that time.

8. How did your parents' divorce affect you as a child?
    I thought it was NORMAL. I thought all families were divorced. My parents were married for such a short period of time that I never really knew them married. As a child the divorce affected me less than as an adult.

(This observation clearly reflects the divorce phenomenon of the nineteen seventies and its impact on so many children who grew up in communities where divorce was unfortunately perceived as commonplace.)

9. How does your parents' divorce affect you in adulthood?

As an adult you have to deal with many things when you have divorced parents. You have separate holiday celebrations, separate evenings out, separate meeting the in-laws, separate time with grandchildren. Generally, you have to spend more time with your family because your parents are divorced. You have to see your dad, your mom and your in-laws.

(This subject makes frank, honest observations about the long-term consequences of divorce. Even once you achieve a healthy relationship, your parents' divorce will likely have lasting ramifications, and the juggling act that endures is, unfortunately, a common challenge.)

10. How has having divorced parents affected your adult romantic relationships?

Having grown up with divorced parents I have realized that I have to work twice as hard at my romantic relationship to make it work. I have decided long ago that I do NOT want to get a divorce so I work very hard.

11. What did you learn about marriage from your parents?

I learned that marriage is very, very hard work. I learned that nothing comes easy. I learned that it is very difficult to stay in a relationship for such a long period of time and that you have to work very hard at marriage.

12. What did you learn about marriage from your grandparents?

I always wondered why my grandparents were not divorced. They loved each other very much but constantly yelled at each other. Every discussion when I was little was an argument. I secretly wished that they would get a divorce so they would stop yelling. They never did. They loved each other very much.

13. Did either of your parents re-marry? (If no, please skip to question 14)
    Yes.

13a. If yes, which parent? (If both parents re-married, please answer
     questions 13a, 13b and 13c with information about your mother first,
     and then your father)
     My dad re-married.

13b. Is your re-married parent still married?
     Yes. He has been married now for thirty-three years.

13c. How would you describe your parent's second marriage?
     They seem very happy. I think they work hard at it.

14. Are you currently married? (If no, please skip to question 15)
    Yes.

14a. If yes, at what age did you marry?
     I married at twenty-eight. My husband was twenty-five.

14b. Would you describe your marriage as happy or unhappy? Why?
     **We are happy but we have to work hard. I'd say the hardest part
     of marriage is communication. If we don't communicate on a
     regular basis then we argue and then we have to sit down and
     communicate and we always work things out. We are best
     friends and I think you need to be in order to be/stay married.**

*(This subject writes honestly about the work she invests in her marriage.
Her perspective articulates the mature approach to a life partnership
that many adults with divorced parents seem to take once they commit.
It is as if what they witnessed growing up makes them more determined
to have a happy, stable marriage. This subject seems fully invested and
appears to take pleasure in being married to her best friend.)*

15. If you are not married, are you currently in a relationship? (If no, please skip to question 16)

15a. If you are currently in a relationship, would you describe this relationship as happy or unhappy? Why?

15b. Do you view your current relationship as serious and long-term? Or do you view it as temporary? Why?

16. Have you ever divorced? (If no, please skip to question 17)
No.

16a. If yes, how old were you when you married?

16b. How old were you when you divorced?

16c. What is your perspective about why you married and why you later divorced?

17. How would you describe your dating history?
I dated a few guys for fairly long periods of time. From seeing my parents divorce I never really wanted to get into a relationship and have it fail. I only wanted to commit if I was truly into it. Even early on.

18. If you are not currently in a relationship, do you think that you avoid commitment?

18a. If you avoid commitment, please describe the ways in which you avoid commitment.

18b. Do you reject available partners?

18c. Do you choose unsuitable partners? Are they abusive or unavailable?

19. If you are not currently single, was there ever a period when you feared or avoided commitment?
I would not say that I feared or avoided commitment but I definitely did not commit unless I was certain I wanted to be in the relationship. I would say I was more cautious if anything.

19a If yes, please describe the ways in which you avoided commitment.

19b Did you reject available partners?
No. I just never wanted to fail. I only signed up to be with a partner if I knew it might really have a chance at success.

19c. Did you choose unsuitable partners? Were they abusive or unavailable?
I had a boyfriend in high school that was a terrible partner. He was always cheating on me and always lying to me. At that time, I never thought I could do any better. I have since become much more intelligent and realized that you don't have to live like that. My interpretation now is that people choose to live like that. I knew that was happening and I chose not to do anything about it. I was young and stupid. Now I am older and wiser.

This response is especially relevant and worth noting. Her words about choice and the advantages of being "older and wiser" when making a life-long commitment reflect the very essence of this book. Like so many others raised in a divorced household, she has obviously grown from her difficult experiences and—at some point—she made a deliberate decision to select more suitable partners.

The last subject of interest, Paul, lends the perspective of the twenty-something generation whose parents have split.

1. First name: **Paul**

2. Age: **24**

3. Ethnicity: **Caucasian**

4. Your age when your parents separated: **2**

5. Your age when your parents divorced: **2**

6. Place of birth: **San Francisco**

7. What is your understanding of why your parents divorced?
   They were never a very good match for each other. My mom thought she could help or save my father who was troubled in many ways—psychologically troubled. Asperger's is prevalent on his side and he displays many characteristics of someone with Asperger's. At any rate, he was not a very loving husband and I'm sure they fought a lot. I imagine they separated when it got too rancid. I also think there were some extramarital things happening.

8. How did your parents' divorce affect you as a child?
   I had an extremely difficult time. My father moved to Washington DC with his girlfriend and got full custody of my older brother and joint custody of me. As a result, I alternated two months in San Francisco with my mom and two months in DC with my father. I attended four preschools—two on each coast—and was kind of a nervous wreck by the time my mom got full custody of me as a five-year-old, when I started

kindergarten. I was a very panicky child, and had a perpetual fear that I was going to be abandoned. I would burst into tears if my mom was at all late to pick me up from school or wherever, because I was sure that she would never come. My school work was the same: I always felt, when I received an assignment, that I would never finish and so would work myself into a panic and cry. For me, being so young when my parents divorced, it was the conditions of the divorce that made it so hard on me. I don't remember a time when my parents were together.

9. How does your parents' divorce affect you in adulthood?

I think most of my current psychological makeup is a direct result of my early experiences dealing with the effects of my parents' divorce. Most of my psychological fears in life can be traced to those early experiences. I do think, however, that my parents HAD to get divorced. I am very grateful to have been raised by my mother, who is an extremely loving parent. She did, however, re-marry when I was three and then get divorced again when I was fourteen. And I have much less distance from her and my stepfather's divorce, so I'm not sure how that affected me. I know that I went from being a very good student to being a pretty mediocre student right after their divorce. I did feel relief when they separated though, it felt like there was some fresh air in my life. I did and still do have a good relationship with my stepfather, so it isn't that he was a bad stepfather, I think it was that the pressure of a relationship that isn't working can be really stifling (even if I didn't know at the time that their relationship wasn't working).

(Notice this subject's ability to point out that even though various experiences affect him as an adult, none is as relevant to his psychological makeup as his parents' divorce. In spite of having

experienced the extreme scenario of attending four different pre-schools on two different coasts by the time he was only five, this articulate subject is able to identify an upside. He understands the reasons for his parents' separation and knows that the divorce was necessary. He makes lemonade from lemons and values his mother's approach to parenting. In spite of exposure to not one but TWO divorces, this subject describes a continuing and positive relationship with his stepfather. This relationship may be a good example of the kinds of relations to consider when completing Step Four and Calculating your Dividend.)

10. How has having divorced parents affected your adult romantic relationships?

    I should begin this response with a confession: I have been dating on and off (but mostly on) the same person for five and a half years, and we have an extremely loving and respectful relationship. We both have divorced parents and both would tell you that "we don't believe in marriage", but we are also very committed to each other. I think that growing up with many sour relationships has instilled in me a desire to have open, honest and true relationships. I hope at all times to be choosing to be with my partner and I don't try to ask or demand my partner to commit to loving me any longer than she wants to.

11. What did you learn about marriage from your parents?

    I think I learned that I don't really understand marriage. I see that it can be necessary to be legally bound to someone, but I'm very frightened of asking someone to love me forever, and I'm frightened of telling someone that I will love them forever.

12. What did you learn about marriage from your grandparents?

    I didn't really know them.

13. Did either of your parents re-marry? (If no, please skip to question 14)
     Yes.

13a. If yes, which parent? (If both parents re-married, please answer questions
     13a, 13b and 13c with information about your mother first, and then
     your father)
     My mom re-married.

13b. Is your re-married parent still married?
     No.

13c. How would you describe your parent's second marriage?
     **It was not a very good marriage. My mom felt trapped by my
     stepfather and I think ended up resenting him. My brother
     has fairly severe learning disabilities, coupled with Asperger's
     and my stepfather and he did not get along. And this created
     many problems.**

14. Are you currently married? (If no, please skip to question 15)
     No.

14a. If yes, at what age did you marry?

14b. Would you describe your marriage as happy or unhappy? Why?

15. If you are not married, are you currently in a relationship? (If no, please
     skip to question 16)
     Yes.

15a. If you are currently in a relationship, would you describe this relationship
     as happy or unhappy? Why?
     **Happy, but it is challenging. As I said before, we are very
     loving and caring towards each other, but I fear that I am a lot**

like my mom. I put my needs second way too much and I start to feel resentment towards my partner and that really scares me.

15b. Do you view your current relationship as serious and long-term? Or do you view it as temporary? Why?
Serious and long-term. We've been together for five years and have grown up together in many ways. I think we have an unstated commitment to being with each other. Though, I know that we want what's best for each other, and if that means breaking up, then that's what we would do.

(This subject has great awareness of how his past affects him and he seems determined to avoid repeating his parents' mistakes. His thoughtful evaluation of his past, his present, and his romantic relationship is representative of the many survey subjects, past clients and current clients whose honesty and insights inspired this book.)

16. Have you ever divorced? (If no, please skip to question 17)
No.

16a. If yes, how old were you when you married?

16b. How old were you when you divorced?

16c. What is your perspective about why you married and why you later divorced?

17. How would you describe your dating history?
I dated a tiny, tiny, tiny bit in high school, and then met my current girlfriend the first year of college and we have been dating since. I don't have much "dating" history.

18. If you are not currently in a relationship, do you think that you avoid commitment?
No.

18a. If you avoid commitment, please describe the ways in which you avoid commitment.

18b. Do you reject available partners?
Yes.

18c. Do you choose unsuitable partners? Are they abusive or unavailable?
I abuse myself through my partner sometimes.

19. If you are not currently single, was there ever a period when you feared or avoided commitment?
No.

19a. If yes, please describe the ways in which you avoided commitment.

19b. Did you reject available partners?

19c. Did you choose unsuitable partners? Were they abusive or unavailable?

Our last subject is not married, but working hard at building a rewarding relationship though still impacted by his parents' failed relationships.

chapter eleven

■

THE FIVE STEP GUIDE
AND ITS CONTINUED
RELEVANCE

■

Once you successfully complete the Five Step Guide, you have finished your initial journey. However, it is important to realize that these steps will have continuing relevance. Even after you achieve a healthy relationship, your history of growing up with divorced parents will continue to be significant as you and your partner undertake your own life as a couple. Completing the Five Step Guide and eventually building a happy relationship or–of equal importance–a happy life without a relationship, does not mean that you will no longer be affected by your parents' divorce. Overcoming trauma does not make the trauma disappear. In my opinion, the most meaningful aspect of both Wallerstein's and Marquardt's books on divorce is that they dispel the myth that a divorce has a beginning, a middle and an end. There is no end to divorce. The legacy is a lasting one. We who are the adult children of divorce are all vulnerable to reverting to old patterns, especially during stressful times, and must be vigilant. The steps in this book should be re-visited as needed in order to continue to understand how to genuinely overcome the influences of your parents' divorce and to achieve a long-term, mutually happy and satisfying relationship.

Like many other adults with divorced parents, I have found a happy and rewarding marriage. And like many other adults with divorced parents, I did so following a series of struggles while dating. But, even though I am happily married, my parents' divorce still plays a role in my adult life experience. The scars from my parents' divorce have taken resilient forms that remain challenging, even today. For instance, I still stress out too much about where Russ and I will be for various holidays and how to balance the needs of our three sets of parents. As myself and others who are adult children of divorce face such challenges, we need to remind ourselves that the divorce is a consequence of our parents' mistakes, not our own. We need to remind ourselves to stop trying to fix mistakes that are not ours to fix. We need to remind ourselves and our children that we will never have to divide up our time, our families and our commitments and realize that this is healthy.

Meg, a thirty-nine-year-old happily married survey subject whose parents separated when she was one and whose complete survey is included in this book, explains how having divorced parents affects her as a wife and parent:

> As an adult you have to deal with many things when you have divorced parents. You have separate holiday celebrations, separate evenings out, separate meeting the in-laws, separate time with grandchildren. Generally, you have to spend more time with your family because your parents are divorced. You have to see your dad, your mom and your in-laws.

Similarly, Jane, one of my happily married clients with divorced parents, once remarked that trips to her hometown with her children are especially difficult as both she and her husband are from the same hometown and both have divorced parents. All of the grandparents want to see their grandchildren, and the rushing back and forth causes Jane to re-visit the stress of her parents' divorce. As she explains:

> We love seeing our families. We really do. But we struggle with all of the different households and shuffling the babies all over the place. It's just like when I was growing up except now we are juggling four

households instead of two! The obvious upside is that we do it together and have the potential to help each other through it. But I have noticed that holidays are when I am most likely to become hostile and treat my husband just the way my mom used to treat my dad. It took a lot of work to grow out of that behavior. I need to remind myself that my extreme, out of nowhere, hostility was part of how the divorce affected me in adulthood, but it doesn't have to be that way.

Jane continues to re-visit Step Two and re-Face the Mirror by remembering how her parents' divorce affected her as a child, and as an adult. When she is stressed, she knows she is vulnerable to lashing out at Jared in unproductive ways. By remembering to Face the Mirror when she feels herself re-visiting the strain of negotiating her parents' separate households, Jane has positioned herself to continue to grow and to strengthen her marriage.

In my case, before marrying Russ, I had a tendency to become too dependent on whomever I happened to be dating at the time. Today, I am proud of having learned to be more independent. The interesting challenge, now, is that I sometimes must weigh in whether I take that independence too far.

I have had to learn to make a continuing effort to have a balanced relationship. To let Russ in, but not look to him to define (or re-define) who I am. I didn't grow up with happily married parents, but I did get to see my parents find happy marriages with partners who were more suitable for them. Obviously, my parents' respective marriages make forging my own healthy marriage easier. Still, the effects of my parents' divorce linger in strange and difficult ways. I often try to shake the sense that what I internally define as "divorce karma" will infect Russ' wholesome perspective and weigh us down. Russ' parents met in kindergarten, and they have always had a stable, solid relationship. It's understandably hard for him to relate to the way I grew up. It's not rational, but I look at him, and reflect on his stable family history, and worry that something leftover from my parents' divorce will infect our lives and our future.

One example, which reflects both the lingering effects of divorce and the Five Step Guide's potential to change things, is what I experienced during my first pregnancy. When I became pregnant, just weeks before our first anniversary, my superstitious fear of "divorce karma" was at its worst. I became convinced that my coming from a divorced family would weigh us down indefinitely. It was only by re-visiting Step Four and re-Calculating my Dividend that I was able to overcome the irrational feelings and destructive thoughts that began to sneak up and get in my way.

When I discovered I was pregnant, I couldn't wait for Russ to know. It was early on a Saturday morning that April, and he was just waking up. I wanted to break the news in a special way, so I set out to find this bowl he used to use as a child. The bowl's center displayed an illustration of a little boy and the caption, "Rusty", his childhood nickname. The bowl was buried deep in our kitchen cabinet, but I remembered noticing it when we first moved in together. I found the step stool, reached back to the furthest coves of the cluttered cabinet, and eventually excavated "Rusty" from the bottom of a pile of unused bowls. With anticipation, I placed "Rusty" with two other cereal bowls on the dining room table and waited for Russ to come downstairs. He knew my period was a few days late. We hoped together that I was pregnant and I was planning to take a test first thing in the morning. I was so excited that, in the spirit of the days of the early morning Saturday cartoons of my childhood, I woke up at 5am. Much earlier than usual, and way too early for Russ. As he slept, I followed the instructions and watched my "fact plus" pregnancy test make this perfect little plus sign telling me my dream had come true — I was positively pregnant!

Russ came downstairs and immediately asked if I had taken the test. I didn't answer and just waited for him to see the table. I'll never forget the look on his face, as if I'd read his mind and given him the most extravagant gift he'd been eyeing secretly for months. Some quiet treasure he thought no one knew he wanted. He smiled softly, and I could feel his excitement, his innocence and his love. An ideal moment that outshined even our wedding day, joined together in a rare and perfect flash of time. A clear cut and magical instant that I'll remember and treasure, always.

Our parents couldn't have been more thrilled. For all six of them, this little baby LaMotte would be the first grandchild, and plans for embracing this beloved baby formulated with the speed of high rollers on a shopping spree. Our first sonogram showed the baby's little heartbeat, and I responded by asking Russ if it was possible to be "too happy". In spite of chronic morning sickness and my swelling figure that easily greased on twelve pounds in twelve weeks, I was floating. On top of the world, and high on life. When we heard the baby's heartbeat through the doppler, I may as well have been listening to the sound equivalent of heaven on earth. Richer than music, it blew me away.

Every dream I'd ever wished for was coming true and I didn't know how to live up to so many blessings. So I just kept asking Russ if it was possible to be "too happy". I couldn't get used to it. How could we be given so much all at once? On some level, I was waiting for the floor to drop out from below and take it all away. Although I worked hard to get to the psychological place where I could exist with confidence in a relationship filled with unprecedented love and respect, the momentum with which our joy was unfolding generated flickers of my underlying fear. I worried that my dreaded "divorce karma" would catch up with us sooner or later, infecting Russ' life, along with my own. Russ assured me it was impossible to be "too happy" and that no amount of joy was over the top. No, we were not tempting the fates or jinxing ourselves, he assured me with the organic confidence of his Midwestern roots.

When I miscarried at thirteen weeks, I didn't know what hit me. It was the Friday morning of Memorial Day Weekend and I began spotting. My doctors scheduled another sonogram and they couldn't find a heartbeat. The baby's heart just stopped. For a time, mine did too. The doctors didn't know why and explained matter-of-factly that these things just happen.

"True, it's more unusual to miscarry after hearing the heartbeat," the doctor recited, "but it certainly happens. We don't know why, but these things just happen." These things just happen? What the hell is that? Breaking a nail just happens. Denting a car just happens. How degrading to hear the doctor put something with such great personal importance into such cavalier and minimizing terms.

"Is there anything that we can do to prevent it from happening again?" Russ asked with humbled optimism.

"There's nothing you can do, and we can't guarantee that it won't happen again. We don't even look into a medical explanation unless you miscarry three times. That's how normal it is to miscarry. The good news is that you can conceive, and since you got

pregnant as easily as you did, the future looks good."

The future may have looked good, but the present felt intolerable. I hurt everywhere. The whole experience felt like a tease. Confirming, just as I suspected, that I wasn't cut out for all that happiness. How could I ever enjoy being pregnant again knowing that, at any minute, the baby's little heart could just stop? All my life I'd dreamed of being pregnant. My parents' divorce made it harder to dream with assurance about marriage, but I'd always fantasized about being pregnant and becoming a mom. In spite of the challenges of my parents' divorce, I'd been parented with endless love and support and felt unquestioning confidence that I could be a good parent. When my dreams started to come true it felt even more magical than I had imagined. And now it was ruined. Gone. We could never go into it with the same innocence and pride. I'd been so proud of that little heartbeat. When the doctor smiled during my eighth week of pregnancy and told me he was impressed to pick up the sound of a heartbeat so soon, I smiled back at him and told him that my baby had the best little heartbeat in the world. He laughed and said it also helped that I was thin, thus reducing the physical barrier between myself and the baby. He could think it was my thinness if he liked, but to me, it was the majestic power of my baby's beautiful little heart.

I woke up in the middle of the night and cried to Russ.

"You see what I mean, you CAN be too happy."

"This has nothing to do with being too happy. You heard what they said, these things just happen."

"These things just happen to me, not to you. And now I feel terrible." I feared that the concept of "divorce karma" would make no sense to Russ whatsoever. Still, since he was stuck married to me and my divorce aura, he deserved to know. "You come from this stable family where everything fits and I'm wrecking it. People get married and stay married and things just work out. Now I'm ruining it for you. And you can bet I'll be one of those people who has to miscarry three times before a doctor will acknowledge that I'm defective."

"Elisabeth, that's not going to happen. And if it does, we'll deal with it." I shook my head in opposition. "Come on, if anyone can deal with it, we can. And, by the way, my grandparents had eight miscarriages before having my mom. Think about it, eight. And they dealt with it. It probably made them closer." Startled, I looked at him and imagined his grandparents. Married for over sixty years before his grandmother's death. They always held hands and were madly in love. Eight miscarriages. Eight. How did they do it? A *photograph of them hangs in our study. They are walking into the woods of Marquette Island, Michigan. He in a sunhat, she in a faded yellow sweater, arm in arm, and step in step. Russ' words and determination chipped away at my "divorce karma" theory as I fell even more in love. Still, I had trouble letting go. I telephoned my mother and cried long distance.*

"How could this happen? What did I do wrong?" I was following all of the safety measures, no caffeine, no alcohol, no sushi, no soft cheese, no hot baths, and all those nasty pre-natal vitamins. I thought I was doing everything right. And I let everybody down. I wanted the baby for everyone, not just for me. To give our parents grandchildren. And, most of all, to give Russ a baby and make the two of us into three.

"It just happened Elisabeth. There's no answer, but you have all the time in the world."

"How can I ever enjoy being pregnant again when any second it could all just end?"

"Well, you won't enjoy it in the same way." She paused. "But, I don't know, on some other level you might appreciate it even more."

"But you want grandchildren, and you were so excited."

"And I'll be so excited the next time, and for as long as it takes. I just know that — one way or another — you'll have children. And the important thing right now is you and Russ." We cried together in a way we hadn't since my father left, both of us scared and defeated, searching for meaning. "I know you will. I completely know it. This was nature's way of saying something just wasn't right."

"But we had a heartbeat. They told me once you had a heartbeat, you're not supposed to have the same risk."

"Elisabeth," she stopped for a slow moment before continuing.

"Yes," I interrupted her pause.

"I was thinking something." I held the phone with a tight grip, longing for relief. She took a deep breath and another careful pause. "Maybe Grandma was lonely. Maybe she was lonely and now you've given her a little angel to love. A little angel with a heartbeat, and so she won't be lonely anymore. Okay." She was reading my mind, helping me find some meaning and figure out how to move on.

"Okay." Was as much as I could manage to say as I imagined our little angel together with my grandma Charlotte.

"So," she waited again with the challenge of getting words out through so much

heartfelt emotion. *"So you just think of this as your way of giving Grandma a little angel with a heartbeat, a little baby angel to love so that she'll never be lonely again, okay. You just think of it like that, like you've finally helped your grandma rest in peace. She was so lonely all her life, and she stayed lonely until now. She just needed a little angel and you gave her that."*

"Okay." I whispered quietly, my voice stumbling as I spoke. This perspective somehow made sense to me, and gave me a way to find peace.

"Life just throws you these curve balls and you have to go on. You never know when it's going to happen, but life just has these awful disappointments. It just throws you these things. And it's how you handle them that says the most about who you are. So you don't let this get in your way, Little Beth, I won't let you. You just imagine Grandma's little angel and this beautiful thing you did. And you keep going and use this to make you stronger."

As I listened, I thought about the pain and anguish of my parents' divorce and realized that it will always be with me. It made growing up harder. It makes adulthood harder. It made dating harder. It makes everything harder. I realized that I was carrying over so many of my old feelings about my parents' divorce and applying them, irrationally, to my current disappointment. Of course this is a normal psychological phenomenon—any traumatic event can cause a person to knowingly or unknowingly re-visit another traumatic event from the past—and it made sense that the misfortune of losing the pregnancy would remind me of the misfortune of my parents' divorce. Yes, coming from a divorced household makes a lot of things harder, but it also helped me to open my eyes and work hard to not repeat my parents' mistakes. Their divorce inspires me to appreciate my marriage to Russ with a devotion and joy I didn't know I could have. A precious gift I try to treasure every day. So perhaps this miscarriage could mirror the divorce. Another heartbreaking, ruthless disappointment, but one that could make us stronger and teach us to appreciate parenthood even more. By re-calculating the dividend of my parents' divorce and remembering all of the ways that, in spite of the pain and hurt, I would not be who I am without it, I was able to stop irrationally assuming that my past would always weigh us down.

I had previously planted some sunflower seeds in late March, when I was barely pregnant. Gardening was a new endeavor and I had buried about thirty seeds under the guidance of my green-thumbed friend Sue. Many of them survived to the re-potting *stage, but most of them died soon after I placed them outdoors. Six, however, survived my less than green thumb and grew into towering and intense sunflowers that bloomed all summer long. Watering them along with all of my other flowers on the patio used to feel like a total chore — a tiring obligation I pulled myself through because we enjoyed the flowers when we ate dinner outside as we tended to do most summer evenings. For fifteen or so annoying minutes of each day I'd hose them down, squinting in the heat, swiping mosquitoes and feeling thoroughly bored. Not bored of the flowers themselves, but profoundly disconnected to their aliveness, and indifferent to their need for my care. I smiled at summer storms while Mother Nature took over and spared me the inconvenience.*

Watering started to feel different. I started to enjoy it. The plants became much less decorative, and much more real. I grew attached to them, and caring for them gave me pleasure and peace. I saw more beauty in them, and it seemed like more of a miracle that they lived and grew these thick stalks where they were once flimsy and weak. A miracle that we enjoyed these bright yellow flowers with deep bronze prickly faces, smiling at us each night the weather permitted us to eat on our patio. A miracle that every day their stems grew thicker and sturdier from the bottom, as they formed more flowers from the top. And they continued to grow even taller, like hopeful beanstalks racing towards the sky. Life in all of its forms felt more like a gift, and less of a given. An awesome, delicate offering to be treasured when I watered my garden, lost myself in my work, stepped outside on a beautiful day, or looked into Russ' eyes and saw his unguarded kindness and love.

Being pregnant was the happiest, most hopeful time in my life up to that point — that little innocent heartbeat my most beautiful sight and sound. And nothing could change that. I began to accept that if I were blessed with another pregnancy, I would embrace it again, probably with much more caution and anxiety, but with even more awe. And more determination to jump into each happiness with abandon and experience it. And discover its beauty. Even ladybugs began to look different. They tended to gravitate to this one windowsill in our study, and these little ladybugs suddenly looked complex and gentle and breathtaking. Even ladybugs looked breathtaking, simple and beautiful.

Having a miscarriage was obviously traumatic, and it is during times of stress when we are all most vulnerable to reverting to our most unappealing, unproductive patterns. I was so disappointed and began to put way too much stock in my irrational "divorce karma" theory. My internal response to the miscarriage represents how important it is to re-visit the Five Step Guide. In my case, it was essential to reflect on Step Four, as re-calculating the dividends of my parents' divorce and taking a broader, more positive look at all that was so very wonderful in my life helped me get through this challenging time. We were newlyweds facing a loss, but we faced it together and it made us closer. Remembering the messages conveyed in this book helped me realize that the miscarriage, as awful as it was, could generate the dividend of helping me appreciate the joys, privileges and responsibilities of parenthood to the fullest extent. And that is just what happened. Soon after our second wedding anniversary, we were blessed with our daughter, Charlotte Rose. Her sister, Amelia, was born eighteen months later. They are both our constant joy. Charlotte Rose looks just like my mother, with walnut cheekbones and chestnut ringlets and her grandmother's graceful wide-set eyes.

Amelia is adorable, electric and bubbly and has clearly inherited her grandma Kathy's vivacious sense of humor and Irish wit. She is a natural athlete, or so Russ and I believe, and perpetually active. Her first full sentence was "I bumped my head." An appropriate statement as head bumping is an all too common occurrence in her wild, wild world. We are constantly shuffling to keep up with her, and her continual motion and good humor helps me remember not to take myself too seriously.

Russ says that Charlotte Rose has inherited my mother's and my gene of psychological perception. Admittedly, she is shockingly emotionally curious. When she was only four, she questioned me while the two of us were having dinner with her "Papa Stan."

"Mommy, is Papa Stan your daddy?"

"No," I answered with some hesitation, hoping no one's feelings would be hurt or confused as we treaded gently on the new territory of what divorce would mean to the next generation.

"Papa Walter is your daddy, right?"

"That's right, and Papa Stan is my step-daddy." I smiled with exaggerated cheer, easily reflecting the nervous self-consciousness I was trying to hide. Charlotte Rose wrinkled her faintly freckled nose as she questioned on, directing her next inquiry toward Stan.

"Then who are you the daddy of?"

"Uncle Doug and Aunt Lizz." Stan's upbeat voice replied with surgical matter-of-factness as we wondered, together, where the conversation would now lead. As it happened, Charlotte Rose was satisfied with this answer for the time being.

Two days later, while I thought I was conducting a thoroughly absorbing reading of Dr. Suess' *The Lorax,* Charlotte Rose cut me off mid-sentence.

"If Bubbie is your mommy, and Papa Walter is your daddy, why don't your mommy and your daddy live in the same house?"

"Well," I paused, finding myself surprised by my lack of preparedness for this question, and by the profound sadness in my gut as I tried to answer. "Bubbie and Papa Walter did live in the same place when I was a little girl. They were married and they had me and your Aunt Kathyanne. Then some sad things happened and they stopped living together. But that will never happen with your mommy and daddy and Bubbie is very happy with Papa Stan and Papa Walter is very happy with Grandma Susan."

And so it was out there. My oldest daughter now knew that my parents had divorced. I had finally said it. Not gracefully, and probably not word for word perfect as other experts might advise, but I did the best I could. I didn't even use the word "'divorce" but I know I conveyed the concept. Charlotte Rose sat silently in an extended pause and then responded, "Oh, okay."

"Any more questions?"

"No, thanks." And it was back where we started, with Seuss' great activist Lorax who speaks so for the trees.

Russ and I continue to juggle what it means to have three sets of grandparents. We will always balance things differently because of my parents' divorce. We also continue to navigate the reality of what having divorced grandparents means to our girls. I was reminded of this challenge while in the process of completing this book, when we joined my mother and Stan in New York City for a marvelous celebration of Amelia's fifth birthday. Charlotte Rose convinced Amelia to choose the American Girl Doll "Julie" as her gift, and I began reading the doll's corresponding book *Meet Julie - 1974* to the girls during our trip.

If you are not familiar with American Girl Dolls, they are the products of a successful company that sells high-end dolls, many of whom hail from various time periods throughout American history. Books detailing the doll's childhood experience accompany each historical doll. These books attempt to teach the young reader about a particular period in American history.

We have chosen to expose the girls to these dolls because, as a therapist, I wholeheartedly approve of this company's approach to teaching girls about American history and women's roles. Interestingly, each story about each doll focuses on elements of history that were most salient—and most difficult. Unlike so much about today's approach to child-rearing, the stories in these books do not attempt to sugar-coat the girls' experiences. Children's parents die fighting in World Wars, and the harsh realities of slavery, death, poverty and war are presented to children in age-appropriate but not overly sanitized detail. Russ and I want to protect our children, but we also want to show them that life is not always easy, and that it is important to appreciate our many blessings.

Imagine my surprise to find that the doll that Charlotte Rose urged her somewhat naive but very willing sister to select was born in 1968, like myself, and that the book's opening chapter, "Moving Day" was all about young Julie's struggle to adjust to the move necessitated by her parents' separation. Julie struggles throughout the book with the difficult adjustment of her parents' break-up, which includes her move and enrollment in a new school. She leaves behind a home and best friend she adores. Julie's older, teenage sister rebels and refuses to go along with the visitation schedule. This book acts as a marvelous vehicle to detail the pain and stress of divorce from the perspective of children of the seventies, as the following conversation reveals:

"What about Dad? You can't decide not to go, just like that." Julie snapped her fingers. "We're still a family, you know, and Dad's a part of it too." The orange juice cans [acting as curlers] bounced and swung as Tracy shook her head. "Give it up, Julie. We're never going to be a regular family again. This isn't the Brady Bunch. Besides, I'm in high school now. I'm old enough to decide for myself what I do on the weekends."

Tracy rebels, while Julie internalizes her sadness, resents her mother's new-found career as a shopowner and struggles to make friends. In the end, Julie adjusts quite well to her new reality and channels her energy into becoming an inspirational activist who succeeds in an uphill battle to convince her new school to become more cognizant of women's rights and to allow her to play on the all-boy basketball team. While the book does not document the most brutal aspects of divorce that children can be exposed to such as those explored in this book—doing so would obviously be too anxiety-provoking for children — it does not sugar-coat Julie's difficult journey.

This book, with its protagonist who was the same age as I was when her parents separated (at the very same time in our country's history), has been a helpful springboard for discussion of my parents' divorce. It soothes the girls to know that their parents will not divorce. And it soothes me to be able to give them that security. I am hopefully determined that Charlotte Rose and Amelia have happy, stable, secure childhoods and can someday look back fondly at their past. I know I will make mistakes, but I am grateful that they will not grow up in a divorced household.

You may be wondering if it is strange or difficult to write, with assuredness, that we will never divorce. The answer is YES! After all, relationships do not come with lifetime guarantees. I know with all my heart that Russ and I will continue to make it work and so I live according to that knowledge. I also know that there are no absolute guarantees. This is one of the many reasons that the Five Step Guide emphasizes the vital importance of learning to be genuinely happy.

The journey we have taken in this book is meant to explore how to be on your own before you entertain making a long-term commitment.

It is a cherished gift to be Charlotte Rose and Amelia's mother, and raising them is a joy that continues to grow and to catch me off guard. Similarly, what surprises me most about being married to Russ is how easily I am surprised. How frequently I am taken aback by the utter exquisiteness of something simple that he says or does. The way Russ calls me from the office each weeknight to tell me what time he'll be home, whether it's 6:45 or 7:15 or whenever. The rushed pace of his voice communicates cheerful enthusiasm about getting home to our total chaos of a household. And the happiness on his face when he walks in the door takes my breath away day after day.

The longer we are married, the closer to him I feel. Sometimes, when he surprises me with some understated quiet observation or some unexpected gesture I catch myself surprised to feel so close to someone and so fully committed. If I had to guess, I would say that is the biggest difference with regard to how we experience our marriage. I'm surprised by what we have, and I think Russ expects it and always assumed he would have it. This sense of surprise can be viewed as a scar, a lingering effect of divorce's aftermath. A scar that leaves me astonished to experience all that I have. A scar I wouldn't trade or give up, as it has become a part of me, and its defining presence reminds me of our good fortune and makes me cherish all we have.

conclusion

■

REMEMBER—
YOU ARE
IN TRAINING!

■

The journey we have taken in this book is meant to explore how the divorces of your parents when you were children have impacted your lives. The scars are lasting. As my story, and the others in this book reveal, one's deepest scars will take permanent and unpredictable forms. The stories of my clients and of the survey subjects also reveal that children of divorce tend to enter adulthood armed with some important, powerful information. They often do not buy into the happily-ever-after princess hype that popular culture throws at children from the day they hear their very first fairy tale. Because of their history and by taking the necessary steps, they can find a meaningful, long-lasting relationship in their own lives. They frequently struggle with dating, relationships and commitment. And yet so many adults with divorced parents seem determined to grow from the mistakes they observed growing up and to chart a different course.

I want to leave you with the words of Eleanor, one of the happily married survey subjects who explains her brave journey through depression and the ways in which she avoided commitment:

It was hard to be in a relationship when I felt depressed because I had not learned how to trust that someone could help me get through it. I feel that because my household was not intact, neither parent could help me sufficiently work through my sadness and emotions. Perhaps if my parents were in a healthy marriage and could have worked as a team, they could have been there for me. I would have more often experienced people helping me through tough times.

In spite of her parents' divorce and the pain it caused, this subject has been married for five years. She describes her marriage as "happy" and explains, "We relate well [and] communicate well." Like many other adults with divorced parents, this subject appears to have created what she missed out on growing up: an intact household where open, honest communication is possible.

Congratulate yourself as you undertake the journey of the five steps outlined in this book. It isn't easy to reflect on the past and the present and to explore the relationship between the two. Take time to reflect on how far you have come. You can now view your parents' relationship from a more psychologically mature perspective. You have a better understanding of your grandparents and their relationships, and how they affected your parents and their subsequent choices. You have a clearer sense of how your parents' divorce affected you as a child and how it continues to affect you as an adult. You have sorted out what parts of your relationship work for you, and what patterns are getting in your way. You have determined whether you choose suitable or unsuitable partners, you have a stronger sense of how emotionally present you are in your relationships, and you have evaluated whether or not you choose emotionally present partners. You have calculated the upside of the relationships flowing from your parents' separation, and you have evaluated any possible dividend of your parents' divorce.

As you complete these steps, you may be working hard to Shop the Relationship Supermarket. If so, your practice and hard work can help you move forward to choose happy, healthy relationships with suitable partners. Remember that you are in training and that it is essential to be happy on your own. Remember that doing things differently can feel awkward at first. If you are more familiar with dating candy bars and renting your relationships, then this is what will feel most comfortable. But you are in training now, and you can slowly push yourself to get used to a different approach to dating. You can—and should—push yourself to get used to dating apples and buying with these more suitable partners. Pushing yourself to do things differently will most likely feel uncomfortable at first. Uneasiness, anxiety or distress as you change long-standing dysfunctional patterns is to be expected. Remember, any person in rigorous training will experience discomfort. Take good care of yourself, shop in the fruits and vegetables aisles, stay away from the candy department and remember that you are your own best coach.

Also, please keep in mind that we are all vulnerable to reverting to old, dysfunctional patterns, especially during stressful times. Even after you achieve a happy relationship with a suitable partner, be aware that your parents' divorce will continue to play a role. Especially during difficult times, remember to retrace the steps in this book when necessary and reflect on the relationship patterns that do not work for you in your adult life. Unfortunately, the ramifications of your parents' divorce are ongoing. Fortunately, these ramifications do not need to continue to weigh you down.

I think that Barbara, one of the oldest (and wisest!) survey subjects says it best. This sixty-nine-year-old whose parents separated when she was five and divorced when she was six describes her own marriage as "very happy; we've been married nearly forty years." Barbara married at twenty-nine and imparts some important wisdom about divorce:

> I think the relevant thing here is that all my family—mother, brother, grandparents—have been divorced. I don't think that inevitably leads to the same for anyone in the family. I have been happily married for forty years. My mother did repeatedly tell me not to get married too young (as she did) but rather to see the world, [and] get an education...I obviously heeded this advice and I think it has made a big difference for me.

Adults with divorced parents usually learn, early on, that marriage in and of itself is not the end all, be all, recipe for happiness. Yes, there is a tragic loss of innocence that comes with this frightening knowledge. But many, many survivors of their parents' divorce learn that there is also a valuable dividend. I hope that you, in reading this book, have gained knowledge of your own dividend and now will use all you've learned to find and nurture the healthy, happy relationship you seek.

Hopefully this book has become a friend to you and can be an ongoing guide as you move forward to build happy and healthy relationships. It has been a privilege to take this journey with you. I wish you all of the happiness you so deserve.

Notes

Notes